KNACK
MAKE IT EASY

LOW-SALT
COOKING

KNACK

LOW-SALT COOKING

A Step-by-Step Guide to Savory, Healthy Meals

Linda Johnson Larsen

Nutritional Analysis by Jean Kostak, MS, RD, CDE

Photographs by Jackie Alpers

Guilford, Connecticut
An imprint of Globe Pequot Press

Editor-in-Chief: Maureen Graney
Editor: Katie Benoit
Cover Design: Paul Beatrice, Bret Kerr
Text Design: Paul Beatrice
Layout: Kevin Mak
Cover and interior photos by Jackie Alpers

Library of Congress Cataloging-in-Publication Data
Larsen, Linda Johnson.
  Knack low-salt cooking : a step-by-step guide to savory, healthy meals / Linda Johnson Larsen ; nutritional analysis by Jean Kostak ; photographs by Jackie Alpers.
    p. cm.
  Includes index.
  ISBN 978-1-59921-784-0
  1. Salt-free diet. I. Kostak, Jean. II. Title. III. Title: Low-salt cooking.
  RM237.8.L37 2010
  641.5'6323—dc22
                    2009025975

Printed in China

10 9 8 7 6 5 4 3 2 1

To my nieces Grace and Maddie, and my nephew Michael, who are wonderful, beautiful, smart, brave, and strong. I love you!

Author's Acknowledgments

Thanks to my dear husband Doug who was a great support during the research and writing of this book. Thanks also to photographer Jackie Alpers for bringing the recipes to life in such a beautiful way. And thank you to Jean Kostak, who did the nutritional analysis and made sure my facts were straight. My agent, Barb Doyen, was so helpful and necessary to this process; thank you! To my editors, Keith and Katie, for all their help. And to my family for their love and support. Thank you all!

Photographer's Acknowledgments

I'd like to express my profound gratitude to my wonderful and amazingly talented editors at Globe Pequot Press, Katie Benoit and Keith Wallman; my equally wonderful and talented husband Jason Willis for all of his love and support; my mother Lois Ungar and brother Jonathan Alpers for teaching me how to cook and for developing my love of food; and the author, Linda Larsen for teaching me the joy of slow cooking, and for showing me (a proclaimed salt lover) that low-salt recipes can be delicious.

CONTENTS

INTRODUCTION

Most of us are encouraged to eat a diet lower in salt. But what does that mean? Salt is a ubiquitous chemical compound that appears in almost every plant and animal on the planet. It's impossible to completely avoid it, and some salt intake is necessary for a healthy body.

Much of the salt, or sodium, that we consume over the course of our day is hidden in prepared and processed foods. Therefore, reading labels becomes crucial to following a low-salt diet. You'll learn what the different legal terms for "low salt," "salt free," and "reduced salt" really mean.

You need to consume sodium, but you can usually get the amount you need from a balanced diet of whole foods. The human body needs anywhere from 500 to 1,000 mg of sodium per day to regulate muscles and proper functioning of every cell in the body. This is easily obtained by eating a diet rich in fresh foods, since sodium is present in almost every food. A glass of milk, for instance, has 130 mg of sodium.

Your body uses sodium to regulate the water concentration in your cells and to help the nerves and muscles function.

Salt is the most common seasoning in every cuisine in the world. It has the unique ability to bring out flavors. In fact when people are forced to switch from a "regular" American diet to a low-salt diet, the most common complaint is lack of flavor. While it's true that salt enhances flavor, too much of it can actually mask the flavor of foods. Part of a low-salt lifestyle is learning how to taste the true flavor of foods again.

Salt is also a key part of many recipes. It helps regulate the growth of yeast in breads and strengthens gluten formation, it brings out the sweetness of desserts, preserves food, and enhances the flavor of meat.

So how do we make up for this restriction? Fortunately there are other foods, such as lemon juice, herbs, spices, and other flavoring ingredients, that add luster to our foods.

Once you've broken your addiction to salt, you'll appreciate good-quality well-made food and better health. Here's the key: You're going to start adding flavor to your food—not salt. And you'll learn to appreciate the natural flavors of fresh foods.

Salt is essential to life; it is present in almost every edible substance on Earth, and we consume a lot of it. So, what's the problem?

Too much salt can literally make you sick. It can be a contributing factor in the development of many diseases, including heart disease and cancer. Too much sodium can cause hypertension, which is a risk factor for heart disease and stroke. Excess sodium consumption is also a surprising risk factor for diseases like stomach cancer and obesity.

Reducing your sodium intake, even if not directed by a doctor, just makes good sense. Recent studies have shown that even people who do not have high blood pressure can benefit from a reduced-sodium diet.

Unless your doctor tells you that you have to make drastic changes, try to implement them gradually. Start by eating fresh foods and removing the salt shaker from the table. Learn to read labels, and don't add salt to your recipes. In a matter of weeks, your taste buds will be reawakened and

you'll find that foods that used to taste good are now much too salty.

Much of the sodium we consume during the course of a day is found in processed foods. Everything from canned beans to fresh meat can have added sodium. Chicken, pork, and turkey can be surprise sources of sodium. Some of these meats are injected with brine, which enhances flavor and adds moisture. Always read labels. If the label says "contains a solution of water and salt," look for another brand that does not have that phrase.

Talk to your doctor about the foods you can eat and what to avoid. If possible, see a nutritionist, who can be a big help

in planning your diet. Ask for a ceiling on the amount of sodium you should consume in a single serving. For example, you may be limited to 300 mg of sodium per serving or 500 mg of sodium per meal. This type of math does require a calculator. You can use a simple calculator and keep a running total in a small notebook.

Sodium preserves food by reducing the water that bacteria need to grow. It also helps form hydrochloric acid in your stomach, which digests food and is a line of defense against food poisoning.

One of the best ways to reduce sodium intake is to consume foods that are very low on the food chain. Natural, fresh, or frozen fruits and vegetables, whole grains, legumes, nuts, and low-fat meats should form the basis of your diet.

Remove the salt shaker from the table and your kitchen. You don't need to add salt to any recipe you make. If you use any processed foods at all, including mixes or canned vegetables, you will consume more than enough sodium.

Dilute high-sodium foods using low- or no-sodium ingredients. If you use low-sodium chicken broth for a soup, add some water along with the vegetables and meats. These ingredients will add flavor to the water, and the sodium content of the overall recipe will be reduced. If you have found a low-sodium brand of salsa that you enjoy, add chopped fresh onion, green bell peppers, jalapeño peppers, and tomatoes to the mixture to reduce the sodium content even more.

There are two basic limits set by doctors for people following a low-sodium diet. One is called the 2-gram diet, where intake is limited to 2,000 milligrams, or 2 grams, a day. The other is a 1-gram diet, where intake is limited to 1,000 milligrams, or 1 gram, a day.

There are other sources of sodium you need to watch out for. Water seems safe, but even that ubiquitous substance can have hidden dangers. Softened water can be very high in sodium. Have your tap water tested. If you live in an area with hard water, plumb your kitchen sink so the cold water line doesn't go through the water softener. And watch out for flavored bottled waters and drink mixes added to water; always read the label!

Medications can have significant levels of sodium. Ask your doctor and your pharmacist about the sodium content in any medications you are prescribed. This is especially important if you are on a very low-sodium diet.

Eating out can be another minefield, but one that you can navigate by being informed and asking questions. Many

restaurants now label their low-sodium and healthy entrees with a heart symbol. Other places will prepare your food to order, especially if you call ahead and tell them about your dietary restrictions.

To avoid extra sodium when eating out ask for dressings on the side, look for grilled or baked plain entrees such as chicken or fish, skip croutons and bread sticks, and avoid any foods that are marinated.

Still, your best bet is to eat foods prepared at home, with no or very little salt added during preparation and a reliance on fresh, unprocessed foods. That's where this book comes in. Most of these recipes contain less than 250 milligrams of sodium per serving; many have much less.

High-sodium foods such as cheeses are used sparingly—for flavor—and herbs and spices are combined in ways to accent the flavor of foods.

So don't despair. You can eat a healthy low-sodium diet and not feel at all deprived. In fact you'll be eating better than anyone else on your block!

SALT & YOUR HEALTH
Most Americans consume too much sodium

Salt is ubiquitous in life. It is found in almost all cells of living things. It is necessary for life. But we can get into trouble if we consume too much of it.

Salt is made up of sodium and chloride; that's it. It acts as a flavor enhancer and preserver and has been used for centuries. Salt actually enhances flavor in your mouth. It makes meat taste richer and adds a depth of flavor to even sweet dishes.

Sodium is used in your body as ions, also known as electrolytes. The proper proportion of electrolytes helps your cells function and aids in the firing of neurons in your muscles and brain.

Too much sodium, however, can raise your risk factors for some diseases, including high blood pressure. Sodium can also cause hardening in your arteries and the muscle of your

Salt

- Salt has been used as a flavoring as long as mankind has been cooking. It can be difficult to reduce salt intake.

- Most of us are addicted to the taste of salt, and foods prepared without salt or less salt can taste flat.

- Your taste buds will gradually become accustomed to less salt, and you will begin to notice other flavors.

- Salt substitutes can be used, but try to increase your use of herbs, spices, peppers, and citrus juices instead.

High-Sodium Food

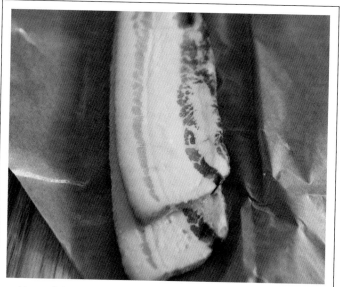

- Most of the sodium in our diets, up to 80 percent, comes from processed foods.

- Meats like bacon and cured and smoked ham, poultry, and beef are made with lots of sodium so should be avoided.

- Other processed foods like canned soups, beans, and canned vegetables can be very high in sodium.

- Look for lower sodium varieties of your favorite processed foods. If they aren't low enough, you can create your own versions.

heart, which can cause congestive heart failure and increases the likelihood of blood clots and heart disease.

The upper limit for salt consumption in one day is about 2,400 milligrams (mg), or the amount in one teaspoon of salt. Most Americans consume 5,000 to 7,000 mg of sodium each day.

Much of the sodium we consume is found in processed foods. Cooking with fresh foods and limiting the addition of salt and salty products are the best ways to limit sodium intake.

YELLOW LIGHT

There are some people with low blood pressure who should not restrict but consume a healthy amount of sodium (2,400 mg). Before you change your diet in any substantial way, check with your doctor for advice and to get a clean bill of health. Then you can start adjusting your diet.

Blood Pressure Cuff

- Excess sodium consumption can lead to high blood pressure by increasing the blood volume in your body.

- The sodium draws water into the blood from your tissues, which puts pressure on arteries, veins, and your heart.

- People with high blood pressure are advised to cut back on their sodium intake.

- They may also be put on blood pressure medicines and advised to regularly check their blood pressure.

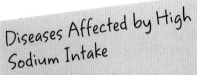

Diseases Affected by High Sodium Intake

- Hypertension
- Cardiovascular disease
- Heart attack
- Ménière's disease
- Stroke
- Kidney disease
- Gastritis and ulcers
- Peripheral artery disease (PAD)
- Obesity
- Osteoporosis
- Asthma
- Stomach cancer

WHAT IS LOW SALT?

Salt is present in most foods; the trick is to know how much

Opinions vary on what "low salt" actually is. Since the recommended daily level of sodium intake varies from 1,200 to 2,400 mg (1.2 to 2.4 grams), the definition is fluid.

When you pay attention to food labels, you can easily reduce the amount of salt you consume. Some words automatically mean high salt: *pickled, cured, teriyaki,* and *smoked* are among the terms to look for.

If you revise your diet to include much more fresh fruits, vegetables, and whole grains, you will automatically consume less sodium. Don't place the salt shaker on the table when you eat, and add very little, if any, salt to food while you cook. Also avoid adding high-sodium foods to your recipes; substitute fresh herbs, pepper, garlic, citrus, and onion.

Some foods are obviously high in sodium, like bacon, beef

Sodium Levels in Milligrams

- 1 teaspoon salt = 2,325 mg
- ½ teaspoon salt = 1,162
- ¼ teaspoon salt = 580
- 1 teaspoon baking soda = 1,000
- 1 teaspoon baking powder = 500
- 1 teaspoon Accent = 600
- Bouillon cube = 960
- 1 tablespoon soy sauce = 1,029
- 1 teaspoon lite salt = 1,100

Salt in Fresh Produce

- Fresh foods, like fresh fruit and vegetables, have very little sodium. One half cup of most raw vegetables contains about 10 mg of sodium.

- Unsalted nuts are also quite low in sodium. One quarter cup of unsalted nuts contains about 5 mg of sodium.

- Look through the recipes you typically make during the week.

- If you add one teaspoon salt to a recipe that serves four people, you're adding almost 600 mg of sodium per serving.

jerky, soy sauce, meat tenderizers, canned vegetables, and Worcestershire sauce.

Other foods you wouldn't expect to be high in salt include salad dressings, prepared mustard, ketchup, and other condiments. Bread, bakery foods, and most bottled sauces are high in sodium.

Aim for about 1,500 mg of sodium per day, after you consult with your doctor or nutritionist. You may go over some days and under others; you want an overall balance.

Salt on Food

- If you really love the taste of salt, sprinkle a tiny bit directly on your food just before you eat it.

- The salt will react directly with your taste buds, satisfying your craving with less sodium.

- Excess sodium intake may even lead to obesity. Too much sodium can create excess thirst.

- If you choose to quench that thirst with sugary drinks, wine, or beer, you'll consume too many calories.

Fresh Meats

- Meats, as long as they are not cured, smoked, brined, or injected with a brine, are naturally low in sodium.

- A three-ounce serving of most unprocessed meats contains around 40 to 60 mg of sodium.

- Season your meat with onion, garlic, peppers, herbs, spices, and citrus juices, and you can enjoy them in a balanced diet.

- Browning meats well also increases flavor without adding sodium. This caramelization adds complex flavor with heat, sugars, and proteins.

WHAT DO WE CONSUME?

Standard consumption of salt is a staggering number

It's a fact that almost 80 percent of the sodium we consume comes from processed foods. Salt has been used to preserve and flavor food since humans started cooking. It's inexpensive and effective, so manufacturers use a lot of it.

Restaurants are also notorious for adding salt to their foods. I once spent a day in a restaurant kitchen and was appalled at how the chefs would upend containers of salt and just keep pouring into the pot. The sodium content of fast-food burgers is around 700 mg. Frozen pizzas can have 1,200 mg of sodium. And canned soups can contain 600 mg of sodium per serving.

So what can you do? Avoid processed foods, choose low-sodium varieties when you can, and look for the "heart healthy" symbol on restaurant menus when eating out. You

Canned Products

- The canning process requires that low-acid foods, like canned beans or other vegetables, have lots of salt.

- You can find low-sodium varieties of these products, but they are still a significant source of sodium.

- Always rinse canned vegetables and beans before you use them.

- You can even simmer them in water for a few minutes, then rinse again to remove about 30 percent of the sodium content.

Common Foods and Sodium Content

- 3 ounces bacon = 620 mg
- 1/2 cup canned beans = 300 mg
- 2 tablespoons salad dressing = 300 mg
- 1/2 cup canned corn = 192 mg
- 3 ounces ham = 830 mg
- 3 ounces shrimp = 119 mg
- 1 large egg = 63 mg
- 1 ounce blue cheese = 400 mg
- 1 ounce Colby cheese = 170 mg
- 1/2 cup cottage cheese = 450 mg
- 1 slice French bread = 170 mg
- 1 slice wheat bread = 150 mg
- 2 tablespoons sour cream = 15 mg
- 1 cup skim milk = 150 mg

can also request that your meal be made with as little salt as possible.

Many Americans consume 7,500 mg, or 7.5 grams, of sodium per day. Our taste buds are used to a certain salt level. Since salt enhances flavors, food lower in sodium can at first taste bland. But like everything else, your taste buds can adjust.

Once you start cutting back on sodium, you will notice the taste of other foods. Learn to enjoy the simple tastes of pure food.

························· GREEN ● LIGHT ···············

Start reducing the sodium in your diet by removing the salt shaker from the table and cooking without adding salt. Reducing or omitting processed foods is also an important step. It takes time for your taste buds to adjust, but when they do, you'll enjoy the taste of your food even more.

How to Read a Label

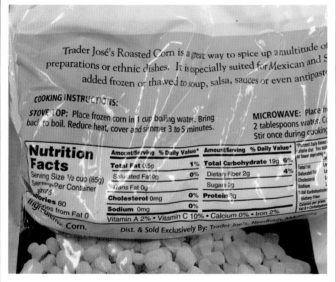

- Reading labels takes some practice, but once you know what to look for, it becomes second nature.

- The sodium content is listed in the first group of nutrients, right under the fat content.

- First the milligrams per serving is listed, then the Percent Daily Value is listed, based on a 2,000-calorie-per-day diet.

- Pay attention to serving sizes. You may be surprised at how small a serving size truly is.

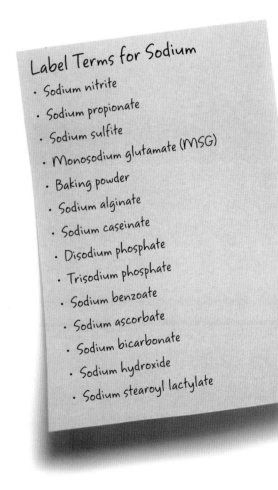

Label Terms for Sodium

- Sodium nitrite
- Sodium propionate
- Sodium sulfite
- Monosodium glutamate (MSG)
- Baking powder
- Sodium alginate
- Sodium caseinate
- Disodium phosphate
- Trisodium phosphate
- Sodium benzoate
- Sodium ascorbate
- Sodium bicarbonate
- Sodium hydroxide
- Sodium stearoyl lactylate

SALT'S FUNCTION IN FOOD

Sodium chloride has a long history and also has many functions in food

Salt has been used in our food since the beginning of time. It was once very costly, a highly desirable item that was literally the cause of many wars before the twentieth century. Roman soldiers were once paid with salt.

Salt is harvested from the sea and rocks. Sea salt is more expensive and can be found in many high, expensive grades

and colors. It is made with solar evaporation or pan production from brines. Rock salt is literally minced from the earth, from dried up sedimentary lakes and seas. These underground mines were once worked by slave labor.

Salt serves many functions in food. It naturally enhances taste, making meat taste richer and desserts sweeter and

Salt's Function in Recipes

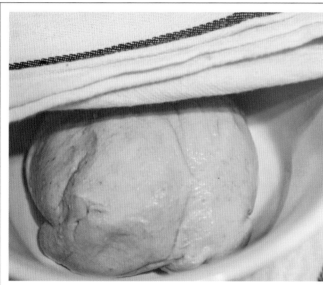

- Salt performs many functions in recipes. Perhaps its most important use is in bread.

- Salt acts as a natural control on yeast development, so the yeast doesn't over-multiply and lead to a collapse of the structure.

- Salt-free yeast bread recipes usually have a reduced yeast amount for this reason.

- Salt also provides flavor to bread. But if you use slow-rise or long-rising recipes, the flavor of the wheat and yeast will develop more instead.

Salt Enhances Flavor

- Salt enhances flavor and it also helps reduce the taste of acid or bitter ingredients.

- Not only does salt come in many colors, but you can find it in many flavors, too.

- Garlic salt, celery salt, onion salt, and smoked salt can be used to help reduce sodium intake.

- These flavored salts have about half the sodium content of regular table salt. But that's still 1,000 mg per teaspoon.

bringing out the flavor of savory vegetables.

Salt was commonly used as a food preservative before modern times. It inhibits bacterial growth by limiting the amount of "free water" in the cells that bacteria need to grow. Foods that were salted as a method of preservation include meats and fish.

Most of the salt you buy today has been iodized. This means that iodine has been added to prevent thyroid problems that are common in populations where iodine in the soil is low.

Salt is also used as a functional ingredient in bread.

Salt with Meat

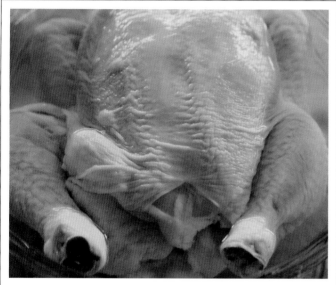

- Brines must be made with salt and sugar. The salt in the brine affects the fibers in the meat.

- The fibers will uncoil, which lets the meat absorb water and some seasonings from the brine.

- This extra water makes the meat more moist, as cooking tightens the fibers and squeezes water out.

- As long as you don't overcook meat, you don't need to brine. Also avoid meats labeled "extra tender," as they may have been injected with a salt solution.

Salt in Cooking

- If you sprinkle a bit of salt on vegetables cooking in fat in a skillet, they won't burn.

- The salt helps release water from the vegetables, meaning they will "sweat" instead of fry.

- That water also softens the vegetables as they cook, creating a pleasing texture in soups and casseroles.

- Salt can also help draw out bitter liquids in foods like cucumbers and eggplant if sprinkled on the food before cooking.

LOW-SODIUM FOODS
Many foods are naturally low in sodium and so good for you

The best way to reduce sodium in your diet is to eat more foods that are naturally low in sodium.

Fruits, vegetables, nuts, and whole grains form the basis of a healthy diet. And these foods are naturally very low in sodium.

One of the most satisfying results of reducing the sodium content in your diet is that you will literally teach your taste buds to recognize more subtle flavors. Adding herbs, spices, garlic, onion, and condiments to foods will help compensate for less salt, but it's still a good idea to eat plain foods.

You'll notice that carrots have a wonderfully sweet taste with a slight tartness from their centers. Bell peppers are sweet, a little bit bitter, and smoky when roasted. Fruits are sweet and tart, and unsalted nuts taste rich and buttery. Whole grains

Low-Sodium Foods
- 3 ounces turkey = 75 mg
- 3 ounces roast beef = 60 mg
- 1 cup 1 percent milk = 120 mg
- 3 ounces ground beef = 65 mg
- 2-ounce candy bar = 130 mg
- 3 ounces chicken breast = 58 mg
- 3 ounces beef chuck = 65 mg
- 3 ounces trout = 130 mg
- 3 ounces pork loin = 50 mg
- 1 ounce dried apricots = 3 mg
- 3 ounces chicken thigh = 79 mg
- 1 cup plain yogurt = 110 mg

Surprising Higher Sodium Foods

- Even though they don't taste salty, some products are actually quite high in sodium.

- Breads, for instance, contain about 150 to 300 mg of sodium per slice. When you make a sandwich, that's 300 to 600 mg of sodium!

- Cake and bread mixes can also be very high in sodium. One piece of corn bread from a mix can have as much as 500 mg of sodium.

- Carefully read labels and consider making cakes, rolls, and breads from scratch.

taste rich and nutty, with a complex depth of flavor.

Much of the taste of a food is in its aroma. Because salt doesn't have an aroma, concentrate more on the smell of foods. Take some time to smell the food before you put it in your mouth. Breathe in when the food is in your mouth and try to focus on the aroma instead of solely on taste.

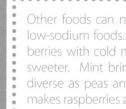

ZOOM

Other foods can naturally enhance the flavor of low-sodium foods. For instance, if you eat strawberries with cold milk, the strawberries will taste sweeter. Mint brings out the flavor of foods as diverse as peas and watermelon, and lime juice makes raspberries and grapes taste sweeter.

Vegetables and Fruits

- Fresh and frozen fruits and vegetables are naturally very low in sodium.

- Avoid canned vegetables, because they are high in sodium. Look for low-sodium varieties of canned veggies.

- If you rinse off canned foods, you can remove some of the sodium.

- Fresh vegetables and fruits are your best choice. They taste delicious; learn to love their subtle flavors.

Nuts and Grains

- Nuts and grains are good sources of protein and healthy monounsaturated fats. They are naturally low in sodium.

- If you're used to eating salted nuts, it may take time to get used to the unsalted variety.

- But you'll notice the taste of the actual nut; rich, meaty, and, well, nutty. You can season your nuts with herbs and spices.

- Grains are healthy and satisfying. You can add herbs and spices to them instead of salt to enhance their flavor.

A DELICATE BALANCE

These three salts have advantages and disadvantages

Your body has to maintain a balance between sodium and potassium. If you have too much sodium in relation to potassium, health problems can develop.

Potassium helps your body remove excess sodium, so consuming more potassium-rich foods, like bananas and potatoes, is good for you.

Using a potassium chloride salt substitute is more proble-matic. The most popular brand, NoSalt, does have a warning label that reads in part, "Persons having diabetes, heart disease . . . should consult a physician before using a salt alternative or substitute."

Potassium chloride can make your body retain water, which is dangerous if you have diabetes, kidney, or heart disease. The best path to take is to learn to enjoy foods with less sodium.

Salt Substitute

- The main brands of salt substitute include NoSalt, NuSalt, and AlsoSalt. They all contain different ingredients.

- Potassium is used in all of these substitutes, but other ingredients are used, like amino acids, natural flavor, and cream of tartar.

- Other ingredients prevent clumping and remove moisture so the mixture flows freely.

- If your doctor approves the use of these products, use the one that tastes best to you. And still use them sparingly.

Seasoned Salt
- Garlic salt
- Onion salt
- Celery salt
- Seasoned salt
- Chipotle salt
- Chili lime salt
- Roasted garlic salt
- Bacon salt
- Citrus salt
- Ginger salt
- Rosemary salt
- Curry salt
- Lemon salt
- Szechuan pepper salt

Sea salt is not lower in sodium than the regular processed salt you buy in the blue box. It is 97 percent sodium chloride, with 3 percent other minerals from seawater. But it does have more flavor, which means you can use less.

Sea salt also has more texture than regular salt, so when lightly sprinkled on top of food, you can use much less. Most chefs do use sea salt, usually the unrefined moist sea salt known as gray salt.

Seasoned salts contain less sodium because they have other ingredients, such as spices and dried garlic and onion powder.

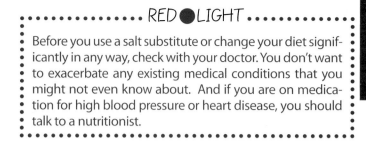

········· RED ● LIGHT ·········

Before you use a salt substitute or change your diet significantly in any way, check with your doctor. You don't want to exacerbate any existing medical conditions that you might not even know about. And if you are on medication for high blood pressure or heart disease, you should talk to a nutritionist.

Gray Sea Salt

- Sea salt is considered higher quality than table salt, which is usually made from rock salt.

- Fleur de sel is literally raked from the surface of the sea in shallow water areas of the Mediterranean.

- This mixture is then washed with more sea water and dried again. The salt is very rich tasting and worth seeking out.

- There are many types of salts from different parts of the world. Since these salts are unrefined, they have more flavor and character.

Fancy Salts

- Salt comes in almost all the colors of the rainbow. Hawaiian sea salt is red because of the volcanic clay found in the area from which it's harvested.

- Black salt, which is more gray than black, is used in Indian cooking. It's also called sanchal and kala namak.

- Himalayan pink salt has lots of minerals like calcium, copper, and iron that color it.

- And smoked salt has literally been smoked to add a rich flavor and deepen the color.

SODIUM FREE

For a food to be labeled "sodium free" it has to meet certain standards

To read and interpret labels on processed and prepared foods, you have to understand the terms.

The U.S. Government has established several criteria for sodium content that have strict definitions. The most important terms and their meanings are listed in this chapter.

Technically, "sodium free" foods have less than 5 mg per serving. The foods that meet this standard are usually fresh produce, nuts, and whole grains. It is possible to find processed foods that are labeled sodium free, but they aren't common.

The front of a box or can of processed food begins to tell the story. If it has any phrases like "sodium free" or "without

Reading the Label

- Servings Per Container: Pay attention to this number. Many people eat two to three servings in one sitting.

- Sodium: This is the amount of sodium per serving in milligrams. If you eat more than one serving, you'll consume two to three times the amount of sodium.

- % Daily Value: This is the percentage of your total recommended sodium intake one serving of this food provides.

- % Daily Values: This is how much sodium you should consume in one day.

Grains

- Whole grains should be an important part of your diet. In fact, in the USDA food pyramid whole grains are a big part of a healthy diet.

- When you buy products made of grains, look for the phrase "whole grain" on the label or product.

- Cooking your own whole grains, like oatmeal, wheat berries, or brown rice, is preferable to using a mix.

- These foods are also very high in fiber, which can help reduce cholesterol, and high in B vitamins.

sodium," look at the nutrition label. The amount of sodium must be 5 mg or less per serving. Be sure you check the number of servings per container; many people don't follow that and just eat the entire thing.

When you're trying to get used to the taste of a low-sodium diet, it's a good idea to concentrate on the flavors of these foods. Apples don't need sodium because they have a natural sweet and tart taste. Avocados taste sweet and nutty, and even vegetables like broccoli, with their bitter taste, can be appreciated in their natural state.

Fruits and Vegetables

- Natural, unprocessed, or frozen fruits and vegetables are naturally sodium free.

- These foods also have lots of fiber and nutrients. Five to eleven servings a day are essential to good health.

- But watch out for canned vegetables and for foods that contain fruits and vegetables but are then processed.

- Refrigerate fruits and vegetables promptly when you get them home from the store and use within a few days.

LIGHT

If you haven't been eating many fresh, unprocessed fruits and vegetables, be careful to increase the amount gradually. If you suddenly go from eating one to two servings a day to eleven, your digestive system may be affected. If you experience gas or bloating, cut back on fresh produce and increase your intake gradually.

Phrases That Mean "Sodium Free"

- Sodium free
- Salt free
- No sodium
- Without sodium
- Trivial source of sodium
- Negligible source of sodium
- Zero sodium
- Dietarily insignificant source of sodium

VERY LOW & LOW IN SODIUM
Two more standards for food labeling, with their quantities

Legally, low-sodium foods must contain 150 mg or less of sodium per serving. To be a very low-sodium food, it must contain 35 mg of sodium or less per serving.

"Very low" in sodium isn't a strict definition, but it means that these foods can be included often in your diet without exceeding the daily dietary limit.

Make sure when you find a processed food labeled this way that you read the number of servings per container. Very often a serving size is much smaller than what Americans normally eat.

If you see a health claim on a label that states the product can help lower your blood pressure, that food must be low in sodium.

While unprocessed meats meet the claim of "low in sodium,"

Very Low in Sodium Foods

- 1 apple = 1 mg
- 1 avocado = 4 mg
- 1 banana = 1 mg
- 1/2 cup cooked barley = 3 mg
- 1/2 cup broccoli = 10 mg
- 1 cup shredded wheat = 3 mg
- 1/2 cup cherries = 2 mg
- 1 cup endive = 14 mg
- 1 cup melon = 12 mg
- 1/2 cup nuts = 3 mg
- 1 tomato = 3 mg
- 1/2 cup strawberries = 1 mg
- 1/2 cup oatmeal = 3 mg
- 1 pear = 2 mg
- 1/2 cup fresh corn = 1 mg
- 1/4 cup dried kidney beans = 2 mg

Low in Sodium

- Eating foods lower in sodium means eating lower on the food chain.

- Natural foods, which are unadorned and unprocessed, are healthier for you in every single way.

- They fill you up with fewer calories, have lots of vitamins, minerals, and fiber, and are low in fat and sodium.

- And these foods taste better. Once your taste buds get used to less salt (and sugar), you'll notice the fresh flavors of foods.

only natural fruits and vegetables, along with nuts and grains, meet the definition of "very low in sodium" or "sodium free."

Once you know the foods that are naturally low or very low in sodium, it will become easier to plan menus and make recipes. You can alter recipes by substituting frozen vegetables for canned or by cooking your own dried beans and substituting them for canned.

Enjoy discovering the taste of fresh foods without their flavor being buried beneath salt.

YELLOW LIGHT

Some nutrients don't have a daily value listed on the label. Trans fats, protein, and sugars do not have a percentage on any food label. Protein deficiency isn't a problem in this country, so it isn't included. Sugars should be limited, and trans fats should be omitted from your diet.

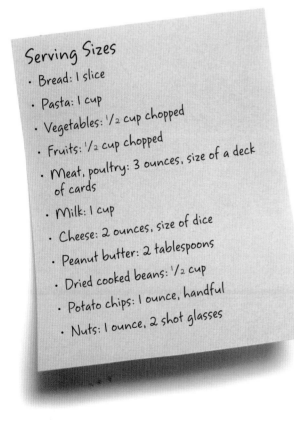

Serving Sizes

- Bread: 1 slice
- Pasta: 1 cup
- Vegetables: 1/2 cup chopped
- Fruits: 1/2 cup chopped
- Meat, poultry: 3 ounces, size of a deck of cards
- Milk: 1 cup
- Cheese: 2 ounces, size of dice
- Peanut butter: 2 tablespoons
- Dried cooked beans: 1/2 cup
- Potato chips: 1 ounce, handful
- Nuts: 1 ounce, 2 shot glasses

Dried Fruits and Vegetables

- Dried fruit will be naturally low in sodium, because fresh fruit has very little sodium.

- Some dried vegetables, on the other hand, will be higher in sodium. Sun dried tomatoes can have 280 mg of sodium per ¼ cup.

- Dried mushrooms are low in sodium. Check labels or check sodium content tables online for anything you consume.

- It's a good idea to keep a notebook for tallying the sodium content of food you eat. Eventually choosing foods will become second nature.

15

LIGHT IN SODIUM
These more ambiguous words still have a clear legal meaning

"Light in sodium" means that the sodium has been reduced by at least 50 percent from the reference food. The reference food is the typical food made by standard processing methods.

If a food is usually prepared with 500 mg of sodium in each serving, a product labeled "light in sodium" would have 250 mg of sodium per serving. The term is usually applied to

foods that have more than 3 g of fat per serving, or more than 40 calories per serving.

This term applies to processed foods, from canned beans to bakery breads to complete frozen dinners. The term will be printed on the front of the product, since the manufacturer knows this is a selling point.

Making a list of the foods that are light in sodium can help

Light in Sodium Label

- The claim "light in sodium" is usually on the very front of the label, right at the top.

- The manufacturer usually explains what this means, stating "50 percent less sodium than regular soup".

- The manufacturer may use other ingredients to help preserve the food. Don't be afraid of the ingredients list.

- Preservatives and flavor enhancers are safe to eat in moderation. These ingredients have been thoroughly tested by the FDA.

Light in Sodium Foods
- Vegetable juice
- Canned soups
- Canned fruits
- Frozen lasagna
- Mayonnaise
- Crackers
- Canned vegetables
- Frozen entrees
- Pasta sauce

you become accustomed to looking for them in the grocery store.

Some companies specialize in foods light in sodium. The food manufacturer *Amy's Kitchen* has a line of organic foods that are light in sodium. Browse through the health food aisle of your supermarket, or visit a food co-op or health food store to learn about more brands that concentrate on this type of food.

These foods will taste slightly different: They are a bit sweeter than the foods you're used to.

YELLOW ● LIGHT

Even though a food is labeled light in sodium that doesn't mean you can consume a lot of it. Focus on fresh foods that have little or no sodium and use these types of foods as accent flavors. You can probably consume two or three servings of these types of foods in a day.

Low-Sodium Foods

- We are not born with a taste for salt; it develops over the years.

- Since the taste for salt is an acquired taste, it can be unlearned with some time and patience.

- Get used to tasting the flavors of unsalted foods and those naturally light in sodium.

- Concentrate on aroma, texture, color, and temperature when building your plate. And be sure that the food looks beautiful, too.

Manufacturers of Low-Sodium Products
- Amy's Kitchen
- R. W. Knudsen
- Alpine Lace
- Better'n
- Bremner
- Pacific Natural Foods
- Imagine Organic
- Ener-G
- Herbox
- Lorraine Cheese
- B&G
- Nabisco
- Lindsay

REDUCED SODIUM
Less sodium doesn't mean low sodium

"Reduced sodium" on a label means that the food contains 25 percent less sodium than the reference food. The reference food is one made without any special restrictions, like canned pinto beans or canned tomato soup.

If the label already claims "low sodium," it can't have the "reduced sodium" label as well. Using both terms would stress that the food is lower in sodium, and a 25 percent reduction, while significant, isn't enough to make a difference if you consume lots of processed foods.

If the reference food, like canned beans, is already very high in sodium, this standard may not be good for you. If you are following a 1 g diet, even one or two servings of a reduced-sodium food can put you close to your daily limit.

Again, this designation applies to processed foods. The

Foods That Have Reduced-Sodium Versions

- Canned soups
- Canned vegetables
- Rice mixes
- Pasta sauce
- Cereals
- Canned legumes
- Dairy products
- Baked goods
- Beverage mixes
- Condiments

Facts about Reduced Sodium

- Contains 25 percent less sodium than its reference food.
- May use potassium chloride as a salt substitute.
- Foods may taste sweeter.
- Cereals may have added sugar for flavor.
- Spices and herbs are added to compensate for the reduced sodium.

types of foods that are typically reduced sodium are frozen foods, especially entrees like lasagna or frozen meals, canned foods like soups and vegetables, and mixes, from cake mixes to rice blends.

Some foods can be high in sodium and not taste salty, which is where a lot of people get into trouble. A milkshake, for instance, which doesn't taste salty at all, can have up to 300 mg of sodium per cup.

Reduced-Sodium Peanut Butter

- It will take a bit of time to get used to reduced-sodium processed foods, but you can do it.

- It's important to check the labels on every processed food you buy, every single time.

- Manufacturers can change ingredients without notice, and if you're used to reaching for a certain brand, you can get into trouble.

- This is also where your notebook comes in handy. Keeping track of sodium content and your intake is also a track record of the foods you buy.

Reduced-Sodium Rice Mixes

- You can find reduced sodium mixes at many health food stores and online.

- Look at sites like Livinglow sodium.com to order foods online if you have trouble finding them in your area.

- Read the labels of mixes you like and try to duplicate them at home using your favorite herbs and spices.

- Many of these mixes can be made from scratch to help avoid other additives along with sodium.

UNSALTED OR NO SALT ADDED
Each of these terms has a specific meaning

These terms just mean that no additional salt was added to the food during processing. If there is naturally occurring sodium in the food, the informational panel must state, "This is not a sodium-free food."

The label will tell the story. It's important to compare labels on foods even when the health claims sound promising. Check the amount of sodium in milligrams per serving. Since some foods, especially dairy products, naturally have sodium present, you have to be careful.

Even in people who have normal blood pressure, reducing sodium can have a life-enhancing effect. Cutting sodium intake in half by reading labels and changing what you eat can reduce blood pressure by 10 mmHg over a few years, reducing the risk of heart disease and stroke.

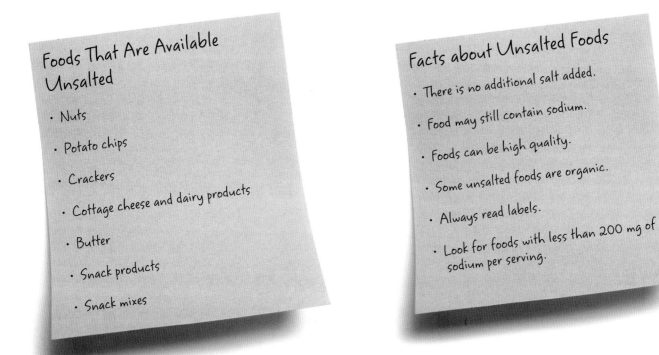

Foods That Are Available Unsalted

- Nuts
- Potato chips
- Crackers
- Cottage cheese and dairy products
- Butter
- Snack products
- Snack mixes

Facts about Unsalted Foods

- There is no additional salt added.
- Food may still contain sodium.
- Foods can be high quality.
- Some unsalted foods are organic.
- Always read labels.
- Look for foods with less than 200 mg of sodium per serving.

Vegetables do contain sodium. Tomatoes and celery both have sodium, but these foods are so high in fiber and vitamins that they are considered healthy foods. And eating celery has been proven to reduce blood pressure.

If you're used to snacking a lot, unsalted snack foods can be quite delicious. Baked potato chips and corn chips are delicious without salt, and unsalted nuts taste intensely of the nut itself.

Add up the total amount of sodium you consume during the day so you can be sure your diet is truly low in sodium.

Unsalted Butter

- Salt was originally added to butter to help preserve it. The amount added per cup can range from ¾ to about 1½ teaspoons.

- Unsalted butter is more expensive, but it's worth it to add butter's flavor to food.

- Some recipes are only made with unsalted butter, like sauces or baked goods.

- Be sure to look for expiration dates on unsalted butter and other dairy products and follow them to the letter.

Unsalted Breads

- Some unsalted foods can be quite wonderful, especially unsalted potato chips, nuts, and crackers.

- You can sprinkle these foods with spices like curry powder, cumin, or dried herbs to add more flavor.

- Serve these foods with a homemade dip or spread for a satisfying snack or light lunch.

- Breads made with no salt may taste slightly different, so look for sourdough breads or breads with other ingredients, like roasted garlic, added.

IS IT REALLY "HEALTHY"?

A "healthy" label doesn't always mean low sodium

Watch out for the "healthy" moniker on labels. The FDA allows food processors to use this claim on foods that contain at least 10 percent of the daily intake of vitamin A, vitamin C, protein, iron, calcium, and fiber.

There are limits on sodium content for these products. If a single serving of a meat product, like canned soups with meat, exceeds 480 mg of sodium, the food can't be labeled "healthy." Nonmeat products must not have more than 360 mg of sodium per serving.

That amount of sodium per serving really isn't considered healthy by doctors and nutritionists. But the government had to put a limit somewhere, and food manufacturers lobbied to be able to use as much sodium as possible. After all, salt is an inexpensive preservative and flavor enhancer.

"Healthy" Label

- "Healthy" doesn't mean low in sodium.

- Sodium content must be less than 480 mg per serving.

- The FDA must approve these health claims.

- Since manufacturers change the content of food, nutrient amounts can change. Always read the label, even on foods you have bought before.

"Healthy" Attributes

- "Healthy" foods must contain 10 percent of nutrients per serving

- Raw produce can be labeled "healthy."

- Canned fruits and vegetables can carry the "healthy" designation.

- Frozen fruits and vegetables can as well.

- Labeling of fresh produce, poultry, meat, and fish is voluntary.

If a food has another health claim on the label, like "heart healthy," and has more than 480 mg of sodium per serving, the label must say "See nutrition facts for sodium content" to alert you to this fact.

The bottom line: You can't just load up your grocery cart with foods labeled "healthy" and assume you have all healthy foods. You still have to read the labels and comprehend the sodium content of the foods.

Homemade Soup

- Canned soups are notoriously high in sodium. Even reduced sodium soups that are labeled "healthy" contain a lot.

- Some brands, like Campbell's Healthy Choice, meet the standard of 480 mg per serving.

- But read the label. A can of that soup actually feeds two people, which equals about a cup of soup.

- Homemade soups, when made without sodium, can be eaten freely.

Fresh Produce

- The FDA is continually updating and revising these rules, so you still have to read labels on all processed foods.

- Some fresh foods now have labels, but they are mainly used to point out health benefits.

- Eating a lot of salads can help you include more fruits and vegetables in your diet. But salad dressings are high in sodium.

- Homemade dressings are easy to make and accent the flavor of these foods so you'll eat more of them.

CITRUS JUICES & ZEST

Lemon, orange, and lime juices and zest promote flavor

Citrus juices and zest are wonderful ingredients to use to add flavor to your food. In fact they are probably the favorite flavor of those who must consume a low-sodium diet.

Lemon juice can actually make food taste a bit salty. Lime juice and zest perk up a marinade for ribs. The sweetness of orange juice adds flavor to chicken, fish, and pork dishes, and grapefruit juice sparks up a vinaigrette for your green salad.

Since many condiments such as ketchup, mustard, and chutneys can be high in sodium, substituting lemon juice or other citrus ingredients adds lots of flavor without compromising taste.

Think about using lemon, lime, grapefruit, and orange juices and zest in unusual ways. Stir some orange zest into your morning oatmeal. Add lime juice and zest to a fruit salad

KNACK LOW-SALT COOKING

Juicing Citrus Fruit

- Old-fashioned hand juicers can be found in any grocery or hardware store.

- You'll find handheld juicers, good for small fruits, and larger juicers, both mechanical and electric.

- To get the most juice out of these fruits, first roll them

on the counter to break down the cells. Or you can pierce, then microwave the fruits for ten seconds on high.

- You will need to strain juices before you use them. Seeds have an unpleasant taste and texture.

Grate the Zest

- Thoroughly wash the skins before you remove the zest. Use food-safe soaps or solutions used for washing produce.

- There are zesting tools available, or you can use a grater. Or peel the fruit and process it in a food processor.

- Microplane graters work very well at zesting citrus fruits. They remove only the skin.

- Avoid getting any of the white skin, or pith, under the colored skin in your zest; it has a bitter taste.

or a fruit parfait. Marinate fish for a few minutes in a mixture of grapefruit juice, honey, and jalapeño pepper.

Citrus juices and citrus zest both bring different flavors to your food. Juices are both sweet and tart and can have a sharp acidic aftertaste. Zest contains essential oils that make up the aroma of citrus fruits, so they add concentrated flavor without a sharp taste.

Slicing Citrus Fruit

- A good sharp knife and a cutting board are all the equipment you need to slice citrus fruits.

- Slice using a sawing motion. Don't push down too hard on the fruit as you slice or you'll lose juice.

- To cut supremes (wedges of fruit without pith), first peel the fruit. Remove the zest first if you are using it in the recipe.

- Then cut between the fibers, releasing each segment with a twist of your knife.

Dried Zest and Extracts

- Dried citrus zests are found in the baking aisle of the supermarket, right next to the flavored extracts.

- These products can add lots of flavor to your food with no sodium. You may want to rehydrate them before use.

- Extracts like lemon extract can add lots of fresh citrus flavor to baked goods.

- Use them sparingly, as they are very strong. Look for pure extracts. Buy the best quality you can find, as they will last a long time.

HERBS
Fresh and dried herbs are healthy flavor boosters

Rely on herbs, both fresh and dried, to season your food without sodium. In fact using more herbs, especially fresh herbs, can add more vitamins to your diet.

Herbs, since they are leaves of a plant, add phytonutrients and antioxidants to your diet as well. These compounds help prevent the risk of cancer and heart disease and protect your body against inflammation and oxidation, two causes of disease.

For instance, fresh basil is a good source of vitamin A. If you grow basil in your backyard or on a sunny windowsill, you can make your own fresh pesto, a spicy Italian condiment that can be very low in sodium.

Scientists are discovering that the essential oils found in herbs can improve your immune system and help prevent other diseases, like diabetes and asthma.

Herbs on Windowsill

- Since fresh herbs can be expensive, you can grow herbs on a sunny windowsill, using kits you purchase from hardware stores.

- Or just assemble some small pots, fill them with a good sandy potting mix, and add herb seeds.

- As long as you continue to harvest the herbs by cutting them, the plants will keep producing.

- They are not only delicious added to almost any food, they add a fresh decorative touch to your kitchen.

Herbs for Vegetables
- Basil
- Oregano
- Parsley
- Dill
- Cilantro
- Thyme
- Lemon balm
- Borage

Using herbs is easy. When you harvest them or get them home from the supermarket, rinse them off, shake off the excess water, then wrap in a paper towel and place in a plastic bag. They will stay fresh for days. Just pull off the leaves, or slice them off the stems using a chopping motion. Tear, chop, or mince and add to food.

Herbs' taste and aroma also elevate the simplest grilled fish or chicken to a gourmet dish.

Herbs for Meat and Chicken

- Basil
- Oregano
- Marjoram
- Sage
- Savory
- Mint
- Rosemary
- Thyme
- Bay leaf
- Tarragon
- Chervil

Using Dried Herbs

- Dried herbs are an easy and inexpensive substitute for fresh. One tablespoon of fresh herbs is equal to one teaspoon dried.

- To get the most flavor out of dried herbs, be sure they are still potent. The herbs only last about six months.

- Smell them before you use them. If the aroma isn't intense, discard that jar and purchase another.

- Increase the flavor of dried herbs by rubbing them between your fingers to release essential oils before you add them to food.

ADDING FLAVOR

27

SPICES & SEEDS
Spices and seeds, from cinnamon to fennel, add great flavor

Spices are a fabulous way to add lots of delicious flavor to your recipes. You can grate or grind whole spices yourself or buy them already ground in small packages.

Spices are the dried root, bark, leaf, seed, or fruit of a plant. They are usually ground into a powder before being added to a recipe. Be sure to smell the ground spices before using them. They should smell very strong. If the aroma is weak,

discard them and buy a new bottle.

Spices can be purchased in tiny bottles, which are great for experimentation. They do lose their flavor after a few months, so buy the smallest quantities you can, unless you use a lot of that particular spice.

Seeds can be added to recipes whole or ground. Toasting seeds helps bring out their aromatic oils and enhances

Spices
- Nutmeg
- Cloves
- Cinnamon
- Vanilla
- Curry powder
- Turmeric
- Saffron
- Paprika
- Cloves
- Anise
- Mace
- Cardamom
- Allspice
- Star anise
- Cumin
- Dry mustard
- Pepper

Whole and Ground Spices

- Nutmeg, cinnamon, cloves, cardamom, vanilla beans, and star anise are the most common whole spices.

- These can be grated using a small microplane rasp. Store the rasp with the whole spices in a glass jar.

- Keep the whole spices in a cool, dark, dry place, not near the stove, for the longest life.

- These whole spices will keep their flavor and intensity for up to one year as long as they are properly stored.

the flavor so you can use less. Buy seeds in small quantities. Because they are high in oils, they can become rancid. Always taste one seed before using a lot.

You can grind seeds and spices in a spice grinder or coffee grinder or with a mortar and pestle.

Add spices judiciously to your recipes, especially if you're trying one for the first time. You can always add more, but too much cinnamon or chili powder can ruin a recipe.

••••••••••••••• RED ● LIGHT •••••••••••••••

Chili powder is a blend of several spices, not a single spice. Be sure to read the labels on this product. Some contain salt. Make your own chili powder by mixing 1 tablespoon each ground and dried chiles and cumin, 2 teaspoons each paprika and garlic powder, and ½ teaspoon each red and black pepper.

Seeds
- Annatto
- Caraway
- Anise
- Cumin
- Dill
- Fennel
- Nigella
- Pumpkin
- Sunflower
- Poppy
- Sesame
- Vanilla pod

Toasted Sesame Seeds

- You can use seeds whole or ground. In some recipes— especially breads—dill, caraway, and fennel seeds are used.

- For more flavor toast the seeds in a small dry saucepan over low heat until fragrant.

- Sesame seeds, cumin seeds, and fennel seeds will "pop" as they roast; that's just fine.

- Do not let the seeds burn. Cool the toasted seeds completely before storing them. For best results toast the seeds as you need them.

ADDING FLAVOR

29

CONDIMENTS
Condiments vary in the amount of sodium they contain

Condiments are a versatile way to add lots of flavor to foods. But commercially prepared mustards, ketchups, and chutneys can be loaded with salt.

You can find low-salt varieties of these products, but they can be few and far between. If you make your own, you can season them as you like and make the condiment more or less intense in flavor.

Some condiments are naturally low in sodium, including vinegar, Tabasco sauce, low- or no-salt seasoning blends, and flavoring extracts.

Stir some homemade mustard into a sandwich spread, or use low-sodium ketchup to top your perfectly grilled burger. Chutney adds great flavor to a recipe for chicken curry, while Tabasco sauce is great for sprinkling on any meat or vegetable.

Mustard

- Mustard is a combination of mustard seeds, some seasonings, and white wine or vinegar.

- To make your own, combine 2 tablespoons each yellow and brown mustard seeds with ¼ cup white wine vinegar or white wine.

- Add 1 minced garlic clove and ¼ teaspoon white pepper; mix and refrigerate overnight.

- Then blend the mixture in a food processor; store in the fridge at least 3 days, stirring once a day, before using.

Flavored Vinegar

- Flavored vinegars add wonderful flavor to food without adding fat or calories.

- Vinegar is a safe environment for herbs and spices, so no need to worry about botulism.

- Place herbs in a clean bottle with a cork top. Heat good

quality vinegar to steaming, then add. Let stand 2 weeks, then use.

- Try using garlic, chives, tarragon, or rosemary for your flavored vinegar, or a combination of these ingredients. Store in a cool, dark place for up to 3 months.

If you make condiments at home, be sure to label them with the preparation date; they will keep up to two weeks. Store these homemade goodies in the refrigerator for the longest shelf life.

Many people who restrict sodium in their diets become fans of spicy or peppery foods. In fact invest in a variety of gourmet peppers and pepper mills. They can replace the salt shaker on your table. Peppercorns come in many varieties, from pink to green to Szechuan, and add depth of flavor to many foods.

ADDING FLAVOR

Chutney

- Chutney is a cooked sauce used in Indian cooking; it is sweet, tart, and thick.

- To make your own chutney, combine 1 cup sugar, ½ cup vinegar, and 2 peeled and diced mangos in a saucepan.

- Add ½ cup finely chopped onion, 2 minced garlic cloves, and 1 tablespoon grated ginger root.

- Simmer 1 hour, stirring frequently. Add ½ cup dried currants, ¼ teaspoon cayenne pepper, and 1 tablespoon Dijon mustard.

Salsa

- Salsa adds wonderful flavor and nutrition to Tex-Mex and Mexican foods. It's also a great topping for grilled chicken, pork, or fish.

- To make it, chop 4 to 5 tomatoes. You can use red or yellow tomatoes or look for heirloom types at the farmers' market.

- Add 1 minced jalapeño or serrano pepper, 1 minced red onion, 2 cloves minced garlic.

- Add 2 tablespoons lime juice and ⅓ cup chopped cilantro; mix well. Store in the fridge up to four days.

HOMEMADE HERB BLENDS
You can blend your own herb combinations for excellent flavor

One of the best things about fresh and dried herbs is making your own blends. Herb blends add lots of flavor to foods, with no sodium.

Think about your favorite herbs and about combining them for different foods. If you really get into this, buy some small glass jars and create your own blends for different recipes.

When you cook with dried herbs and herb blends, start out using just a little bit. It's easy to add more, but you can't take it out if you've used too much.

When you mix herbs, don't combine several very strong flavors. Dried herbs are more concentrated than fresh, so you should use less.

For instance, thyme is a mild herb with a minty lemon scent, while rosemary is very sharp, strong, and piney. Basil is warm

Classic Herb Blend

- 2 tablespoons dried basil leaves
- 1 tablespoon dried marjoram leaves
- 2 tablespoons dried thyme leaves
- 1 teaspoon minced dried rosemary leaves
- 1 teaspoon dried sage leaves

Classic Herb Blend

- If you have dried the herbs yourself, be sure they are completely dry before combining.

- If there is any moisture in the herbs, they will develop mold, which is a safety hazard.

- Dried rosemary, like the spine in bay leaves, is very sharp and prickly. Mince the leaves finely before using.

- Store your herb blend, well labeled, in a cool, dry place. Use within 3 to 4 months.

and slightly spicy, and oregano is strong and pungent. Combine thyme with oregano, or basil with rosemary.

Don't store dried herbs or spices near the stove. The heat will release their aromatic oils, and they will lose flavor faster. Store them in a dark, cool place in tightly sealed containers.

Have fun experimenting with your herb blends and be sure to keep a record of your successes. Keep a shaker or two of herb blends on your table in place of the salt shaker.

Bouquet Garni

- Bouquet garni is a combination of rosemary, thyme, sage, bay leaves, and peppercorns tied in a cheesecloth bundle. Use it in soups and stews.

- Fines herbes is a mixture of thyme, tarragon, chervil, and parsley. Use this blend in egg dishes and sauces.

- Herbs de Provence is made from basil, marjoram, thyme, summer savory, bay leaves, fennel, white pepper, and lavender.

- Italian seasoning is a combination of dried basil, thyme, oregano, and bay leaves. Use in pasta sauces, marinara sauce, and pizza.

Dry Herbs

- To dry fresh herbs, first rinse them well and gently blot dry on paper towels.

- Gather the herbs by the stems into small bunches and tie together using white cotton kitchen string.

- Hang the bundles upside down, at least 6 to 8 inches apart so the herbs can dry without touching.

- When they crumble easily to the touch, they're done. Store in a cool, dark place in airtight containers up to 3 months.

ADDING FLAVOR

33

CHILES

Chiles, from mild to red hot, are great substitutes for salt

As Tex-Mex and Mexican food has become more popular in this country, the use of chiles, both dried and fresh, has soared.

If you enjoy hot and spicy food, adding chiles and pepper to your cooking and at the table is probably the best way to compensate for using less salt.

But chiles aren't just about heat. They have complex flavors, especially when roasted. Fresh chiles have a sweet undertone, and roasted chiles taste smoky and rich. Dried chiles taste smoky too, with a slightly spicy flavor.

Chiles are "rated" according to the Scoville scale, developed by Wilbur Scoville in 1912. He measured how much sugar it takes to dilute the heat of peppers; that heat comes from capsaicin, an oil in the pepper's seeds, membranes, and flesh.

Chiles and Scoville Units
- Sweet bell peppers: 0
- Pepperoncini: 200
- Coronado: 800
- Poblano: 1,500
- Ancho: 1,500
- Pasilla: 1,800
- Mirasol: 3,000
- Jalapeño: 4,000
- Chipotle: 6,000
- Serrano: 10,000
- Tabasco: 40,000
- Cayenne: 50,000
- Piquin: 55,000
- Thai: 70,000
- Bird's eye: 150,000
- Habanero: 180,000
- Scotch bonnet: 200,000
- Naga Jolokia: 1,000,000
- Pure capsaicin: 15,000,000

Dried Chiles

- When you buy dried chiles, look for a deep color and firm texture.

- The chiles should be firm but not brittle or hard. If they are slightly pliable, that's just fine.

- You can grind dried chiles to make your own chili powder or paste (be careful to protect your eyes!).

- Or you can soak them in hot water for ten to fifteen minutes. Remove the stem and mince or chop the chiles before use.

The mildest peppers are sweet bell peppers, with no capsaicin. As the peppers get hotter, the Scoville number increases, going up to 15 million. That means the chiles have to be diluted with 300,000 units of sugar before the capsaicin can't be detected.

The heat is detected by pain receptors in the tongue, which are located slightly under the surface. That's why it takes a few seconds for a chile's heat to register when you take a bite of hot and spicy food.

Fresh Chiles

- Fresh chiles should be firm and brightly colored, with no soft spots or wet spots.

- They will keep in the refrigerator for five to six days if in a crisper or plastic bags.

- The seeds and membranes hold most of the heat, so if you want a milder taste, remove and discard those parts of the chile.

- Even though chiles are rated for hotness, the heat can vary from pepper to pepper depending on the growing conditions and the variety.

Roasted Chiles

- Roast chiles on the grill, under the broiler, or over a gas flame.

- Chiles can be roasted whole or cut in half. On the broiler, it's easier to roast if they are cut in half. You can also purchase roasted chiles in adobo sauce.

- Rinse the chiles and pat dry, then place on the grill or broiler pan, or skewer on a long skewer for cooking on a gas flame.

- Place the chiles in a paper bag, then peel off the skin. Don't rinse; you'll rinse away all the flavor!

ROASTED GARLIC DIP

Roasted garlic is a healthy and delicious ingredient to flavor low-salt recipes

Garlic is an excellent food that can be used to replace the salt flavor in many foods. When roasted, garlic becomes sweet and nutty, with a full and satisfying flavor.

You can make lots of roasted garlic at one time. Just remove the cloves from the skins after they are soft and golden. Place in freezer bags, label, seal, and freeze up to 3 months. To use,

add to soups or skillet meals, or thaw in the refrigerator a few hours first.

In this recipe, if you use canned beans instead of the home-made beans, you'll add about 900 mg of sodium.

Serve this dip with salt-free crackers, carrot and celery sticks, and Garlic Toasts. *Yield: Serves 8*

Ingredients

2 large heads garlic

2 tablespoons olive oil

1 onion, chopped

1 tablespoon unsalted butter

3 tablespoons lemon juice

1 cup Slow Cooker Beans, made with cannellini beans

$1/2$ cup sour cream

1 tablespoon minced fresh rosemary leaves

$1/8$ teaspoon pepper

Calories 96, **Fat** (g) 8, **Carbohydrates** (g) 6, **Protein** (g) 1, **Sodium** (mg) 11, **Fiber** (g) 0, **Saturated Fat** (g) 3, **Cholesterol** (mg) 10

Roasted Garlic Dip

- Cut garlic heads in half crosswise, through the equator. Place, cut side up, on baking sheet; drizzle with olive oil.

- Roast garlic at 375°F for 50 to 60 minutes, until browned. Remove cloves from skin.

- Cook onion in butter until very tender, about 6 to 7 minutes.

- In food processor place garlic cloves, lemon juice, beans, onion, and remaining ingredients; process until smooth. Chill.

Roasted Garlic Spread: Make recipe as directed, except omit the Slow Cooker Beans. Add an 8-ounce package softened cream cheese in place of the sour cream. Add 1 teaspoon dried thyme leaves. Serve spread with toasted French bread.

Garlic Toasts: Slice French or Italian bread ½-inch thick. Place bread on broiler pan; broil 3 to 4 minutes, turning once, until golden brown and very crisp. Peel two cloves garlic and cut in half. When toasts come out of the oven, immediately rub with garlic. Serve immediately.

Roast the Garlic

Blend Ingredients

- You can use roasted garlic for many recipes. Add to a soup, use as a spread on bread, or knead into yeast breads.

- You can roast a whole garlic bulb instead of cutting it in half. Just cut off the top ½ inch of the bulb and remove the excess papery skin.

- When the cloves are done, the head will feel soft when gently squeezed with your fingers.

- Roast the garlic ahead of time and refrigerate until you're ready to make the dip.

- Be sure that all the papery skin is removed from the garlic flesh, or it will create an unpleasant texture.

- You can process this dip until smooth or leave some small pieces of garlic and beans for some texture.

- Serve the dip immediately or cover and chill for a few hours to blend the flavors.

- Add herbs to this dip for more flavor. Thyme, marjoram, basil, and oregano are all good choices.

APPETIZERS

CARAMELIZED ONION SPREAD

When caramelized, onions become very sweet and tender

Caramelization is a complex process involving sugars, protein, and heat. The sugars and protein break down in the heat and recombine to form hundreds of different compounds.

Those compounds form a complex caramel flavor and deep brown color. The flavor becomes sweet, smoky, and rich with a deep aroma. Caramelization takes time, so be patient. The onions will lose their sharp taste and become very soft and deep golden brown. The onions are combined with yogurt and cream cheese to make a spread that's delicious with toasted bread or crackers.

Serve this low-carb spread at the beginning of a dinner that includes roast beef, mashed potatoes, a gelatin salad, and roasted green beans. *Yield: Serves 8–10*

Ingredients

- 1 tablespoon olive oil
- 2 tablespoons unsalted butter
- 3 onions, chopped
- 3 cloves garlic, minced
- 1/4 teaspoon white pepper
- 1 teaspoon dried marjoram leaves
- 1 (8-ounce) package low-fat cream cheese, softened
- 1/2 cup thick Greek yogurt
- 1 tablespoon fresh thyme leaves

Calories 69, **% Calories from Fat** 66%, **Fat** (g) 5, **Carbohydrates** (g) 5, **Protein** (g) 1, **Sodium** (mg) 9, **Fiber** (g) 1, **Saturated Fat** (g) 2, **Cholesterol** (mg) 10

Caramelized Onion Spread

- Combine olive oil and butter in large saucepan. Melt over medium heat. Add onions; cook and stir 6 minutes.

- Reduce heat to low and simmer onions 30 to 40 minutes, stirring frequently, until very deep golden brown.

- Add garlic, pepper, and marjoram to onions during last 5 minutes.

- Beat cream cheese, yogurt, and thyme in a bowl; stir in half the onion mixture. Place in serving bowl; top with remaining onion mixture. Chill 2 to 4 hours before serving.

Caramelized Onion Dip: Make recipe as directed, except omit the cream cheese. Blend the caramelized onion and garlic mixture with the thick Greek yogurt and ½ cup sour cream. Beat mixture, adding some skim milk as needed until desired consistency is reached.

Slow Cooker Caramelized Onions: Combine all ingredients except cream cheese, yogurt, and fresh thyme leaves in a 2-quart slow cooker. Make sure the slow cooker is filled one-half to two-thirds full. Cover and cook on low 7 to 8 hours, until the onions are deep golden brown, stirring once. Continue with recipe as directed.

Caramelize Onions

- Watch the onions carefully as they are caramelizing; stir very frequently.

- If there is any hint of burning, you'll have to start over, because the burned flavor will permeate the dish.

- The onions will first turn light brown and reduce in volume. The liquid will evaporate slowly.

- As the onions become a deeper color, you can stop the cooking at any time. Just don't let them burn.

Add Yogurt

- If you can't find the thick Greek yogurt, don't substitute regular plain yogurt; it will be too thin.

- You need to drain the plain yogurt first. Place the yogurt in a coffee filter, in a bowl, in the fridge 8 to 12 hours. Discard the whey.

- You can use all yogurt or all cream cheese if you'd like, in place of the combination of the two.

- This mixture can be turned into a dip if you thin it with some cream or whole milk.

GINGERBREAD SNACK MIX

Homemade snack mixes are great as an appetizer or as a gift

Purchased snack mixes are very high in fat and sodium. It's fun to make your own, and you get to control the sodium content.

You will use processed foods to make this snack mix. You can look for low-sodium varieties of these products, but not all of them are available with that nutritional variation. To really control the sodium, use all air-popped popcorn and omit the cereal. You can add no-salt-added tiny crackers or pretzels.

Snack mixes make great after-school snacks for the kids, or they can be tucked into lunchboxes as a substitute for sugary desserts. Or you can package them in nice containers to give as gifts during the holiday season. *Yield: Serves 8–10*

KNACK LOW-SALT COOKING

Ingredients

¹/₂ cup unsalted butter

1 tablespoon grated ginger root

1 cup brown sugar

¹/₂ cup sugar

¹/₄ cup honey

¹/₄ cup molasses

1 teaspoon ground ginger

¹/₄ cup finely minced candied ginger

1 teaspoon cinnamon

¹/₄ teaspoon nutmeg

¹/₂ teaspoon baking soda

5 cups popped popcorn

2 cups round oat honey cereal

2 cups corn Chex cereal

1 cup small unsalted pretzel rods

Calories 462, **% Calories from Fat** 45%, **Fat** (g) 23, **Carbohydrates** (g) 64, **Protein** (g) 4, **Sodium** (mg) 233, **Fiber** (g) 3, **Saturated Fat** (g) 10, **Cholesterol** (mg) 37

Gingerbread Snack Mix

- Preheat oven to 225°F. In 3-quart saucepan, cook butter and ginger root 3 minutes.

- Add brown sugar, sugar, honey, molasses, and ginger; heat, stirring frequently, until mixture boils. Boil 5 minutes.

- Remove from heat; stir in candied ginger, cinnamon, and nutmeg. Then add baking soda; mixture will foam up.

- While sauce is cooking, combine remaining ingredients in roasting pan. Drizzle sugar mixture over; toss to coat. Bake 1 hour, stirring every 15 minutes, until glazed.

Brown Sugar Snack Mix: Make recipe as directed, except omit ginger root, candied ginger, ground ginger, and molasses. Increase honey to ⅓ cup and increase brown sugar to 1¼ cups and add 2 teaspoons vanilla. Boil coating mixture, add baking soda, pour over dry ingredients, and bake as directed.

Curried Sweet Snack Mix: Make recipe as directed, except omit candied ginger and molasses. Increase honey to ½ cup. Omit ground ginger and add 1 tablespoon curry powder. Add 2 teaspoons vanilla. Prepare recipe as directed, adding 1 cup unsalted peanuts before baking.

Add Baking Soda

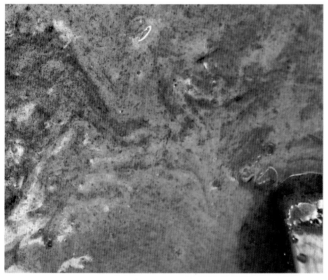

Stir Mixture

- The baking soda does add sodium, but it serves a critical purpose in the recipe.

- It will react with the acids in the brown sugar and will make the syrup mixture fizz and foam, almost doubling in size.

- This helps the syrup evenly coat the ingredients and creates a light crisp coating as it bakes.

- Use a large saucepan and be careful when you add the baking soda. Stir with a long-handled spoon.

- Quickly drizzle the foamy syrup over the combined crisp ingredients and stir to coat.

- Spread the mixture out evenly so it will bake evenly and become crisp and golden.

- When you stir the mixture

as it is baking, be careful to include the mixture at the edges so it doesn't burn. Stir thoroughly and spread the mixture into an even layer again.

- Store mixture in airtight container at room temperature only after it has completely cooled.

APPETIZERS

41

THREE TOMATO BRUSCHETTA
Tomatoes mixed with onions and garlic make a flavorful snack

Bruschetta is an Italian word that means "to roast over coals." It is made with bread that has been seasoned with olive oil and garlic, toasted or grilled, then topped with a mixture of anything from fresh tomatoes to salmon and cream cheese.

This versatile appetizer can be made ahead of time. Grill the bread until crisp, and make the tomato mixture and refrigerate it. Combine the two when you're ready to serve, then serve cold or broil until hot. The bread can be toasted, baked, pan fried, or grilled. For an authentic Italian flavor, instead of brushing it with the oil from the tomatoes, toast the bread dry and rub it with a cut fresh garlic clove. *Yield: Serves 16*

Ingredients

1 onion, chopped

4 cloves garlic, minced

1 tablespoon olive oil

4 plum tomatoes, chopped

2 yellow tomatoes, chopped

$1/4$ cup minced sun-dried tomatoes in oil

$1/4$ cup chopped green onion

2 tablespoons balsamic vinegar

$1/2$ cup fresh basil leaves, chopped

$1/8$ teaspoon pepper

16 slices homemade low sodium French bread

3 tablespoons oil from sun-dried tomatoes

Calories 50, **% Calories from Fat** 31%, **Fat** (g) 3, **Carbohydrates** (g) 4, **Protein** (g) 1, **Sodium** (mg) 35, **Fiber** (g) 3, **Saturated Fat** (g) 2, **Cholesterol** (mg) 11

Three Tomato Bruschetta

- In small saucepan cook onion and garlic in olive oil, stirring frequently, until just starting to brown, 10 to 12 minutes.

- Remove from heat and add to large bowl with tomatoes, green onion, vinegar, basil, and pepper.

- Place bread on broiler pan. Broil on first side until golden, then turn. Brush with oil from sun-dried tomatoes.

- Broil again until golden, then top with tomato mixture. At this point you can serve the Bruschetta, or broil again until tomatoes are hot.

Mushroom Bruschetta: Make recipe as directed, except omit tomatoes. Add 1 cup sliced button mushrooms, 1 cup sliced cremini mushrooms, and 1 cup sliced portobello mushrooms to the onion mixture. Cook until moisture has evaporated and mushrooms are deep golden brown. Brush bread with 3 tablespoons olive oil; proceed with recipe.

Garlic Bruschetta: Make recipe as directed, except omit all tomatoes. Increase garlic to 8 cloves. Cook onions and garlic as directed. When toast has been broiled on first side, rub each piece with a fresh cut garlic clove. Brush with 3 tablespoons olive oil and proceed with recipe.

Combine Tomatoes and Onion

Top Bread with Tomato Mixture

- If you can't find yellow tomatoes, try to use another tomato that's different from the plum tomatoes.

- You can find heirloom tomatoes at a farmers' market, or look for grape tomatoes or yellow pear tomatoes.

- Ripe tomatoes are sweet and flavorful and don't need salt to bring out their flavor.

- Don't substitute canned tomatoes for the fresh; they are high in sodium. If you can't find good tomatoes, use chopped grape or cherry tomatoes.

- Serve the Bruschetta as soon as they are made so you get the texture contrast of crisp bread with tender topping.

- You can offer the bread and topping separately, and let your guests assemble their own Bruschetta.

- While the sun-dried tomatoes may taste salty, they only have 300 mg per cup.

- You can omit the dried tomatoes, but you'll only save 72 mg of sodium, about 4.5 mg per serving.

APPETIZERS

CRISP EGG ROLLS

Lots of vegetables fill in for soy sauce in this easy recipe

Most egg rolls that you get in Asian restaurants or from the frozen section in the grocery store are packed with sodium. One tablespoon of soy sauce contains 1,100 mg of sodium. And low-sodium varieties aren't much better; about 550 mg per tablespoon.

You can make egg rolls with no soy sauce at all; just use other flavorful ingredients like dried mushrooms, five spice powder, onion, garlic, sherry or rice wine, and ginger root.

Be sure to serve the egg rolls piping hot to start a Chinese or Japanese meal. Let them stand for a few seconds on a paper towel after frying, then cut them in half and serve, with or without a dipping sauce. *Yield: Serves 12*

Ingredients

¹/₂ cup dried wood ear mushroom

1 cup hot water

³/₄ pound ground pork

1 onion, chopped

4 cloves garlic, minced

2 tablespoons grated ginger root

¹/₂ teaspoon five spice powder

2 cups shredded green cabbage

1 cup shredded carrots

2 tablespoons dry sherry or rice wine

¹/₄ teaspoon pepper

1 (16-ounce) package egg roll wrappers

1 egg white, beaten

2 tablespoons peanut oil

Calories 208, **% Calories from Fat** 33%, **Fat** (g) 8, **Carbohydrates** (g) 25, **Protein** (g) 8, **Sodium** (mg) 243, **Fiber** (g) 1, **Saturated Fat** (g) 2, **Cholesterol** (mg) 20

Crisp Egg Rolls

- Combine mushrooms and hot water; let stand 15 minutes. Drain, remove stems, and chop mushrooms.

- Combine with pork, onion, garlic, ginger root, and five spice powder in large saucepan; stir-fry until pork is browned.

- Drain mixture; add cabbage, carrots, sherry, and pepper; cook 4 to 5 minutes longer.

- Divide among egg roll wrappers. Brush edges with egg white, roll up, folding in ends. Brush with oil and bake at 400°F 12 to 18 minutes, until crisp and browned.

Dipping Sauce: For hot mustard dipping sauce, combine 6 teaspoons dry mustard powder with 3 teaspoons cold water, 3 teaspoons white vinegar and ½ teaspoon melted butter. For hot chili oil, heat ½ teaspoon crushed red pepper flakes in ⅓ cup peanut oil 3 minutes. Cool 15 minutes and serve.

··· GREEN ● LIGHT ···

You can make these egg rolls ahead of time. Cool and cover tightly; refrigerate up to 24 hours. To reheat, place in a single layer on a rack on a cookie sheet and bake at 350°F 15 to 20 minutes until crisp and hot.

Stir-Fry Filling

- The filling should be fairly dry so the egg roll wrappers don't get wet and break apart.

- You can find egg roll wrappers in the deli, dairy, or produce aisles of your supermarket, or they may be in the frozen foods or produce sections.

- Cook the filling until the liquid evaporates and all the vegetables are tender.

- The ingredients in the filling won't cook in the time it takes the wrappers to become crisp, so they must be fully cooked first.

Assemble Egg Rolls

- The egg white is used to help the egg rolls hold together while they are cooking.

- You can also use a mixture of water mixed with cornstarch to seal the edges of the egg rolls.

- Don't overfill the egg rolls or they may explode during cooking. Use about ¼ to ⅓ cup filling for each.

- You can make the egg rolls ahead of time; cover with a damp paper towel and refrigerate. Bake just before serving.

APPETIZERS

MUSHROOM TARTLETS
Tender mushrooms are baked into little quiches using phyllo shells

Little tartlets are the perfect appetizer for a buffet or a large crowd. They need no utensils to eat; just pop them into your mouth.

You can fill mini–phyllo tartlet shells with everything from chocolate mousse to a quiche mixture to diced cheese and fruit. Use your imagination and have fun playing with the little shells.

The tartlet shells are naturally low in sodium, so have fun filling them with delicious low-sodium mixtures. You can just thaw and fill them, or thaw and bake them if you'd like a hot appetizer.

Arrange these on a platter with some curly parsley or sprigs of fresh thyme for a pretty garnish. *Yield: Serves 12*

Ingredients

- 1 tablespoon olive oil
- 1 onion, finely chopped
- 2 cloves garlic, minced
- 1 cup sliced cremini mushrooms
- 2 eggs, beaten
- 1/3 cup light cream or milk
- 1 teaspoon dried thyme leaves
- 1 teaspoon dried marjoram leaves
- 1 tablespoon Dijon mustard
- 1/2 cup shredded Havarti cheese
- 45 frozen mini-phyllo tart shells
- 1/4 cup grated Parmesan cheese

Calories 140, % Calories from Fat 44%, Fat (g) 7, Carbohydrates. (g) 14, Protein (g) 5, Sodium (mg) 205, Fiber (g) 1, Saturated Fat (g) 3, Cholesterol (mg) 46

Mushroom Tartlets

- In saucepan, heat olive oil on medium heat. Add onion, garlic, and mushrooms.

- Cook, stirring frequently, until mushrooms darken and all liquid has evaporated; remove to medium bowl. Cool 10 minutes.

- Add eggs, cream, thyme, marjoram, mustard, and Havarti. Place phyllo shells on baking sheet.

- Preheat oven to 375°F. Fill shells with mushroom mixture; sprinkle with Parmesan. Bake 15 to 18 minutes, until puffed and set. Let cool 10 minutes, then serve.

Homemade Tartlet Dough: In bowl, mix 1¼ cups flour with 6 tablespoons cold unsalted butter until fine. Mix 1 egg yolk with 2 tablespoons milk; add to mixture until dough forms. Press into bottom and up sides of 12 (2-inch) mini-tartlet or -muffin cups. Prick with fork; bake at 375°F 10 to 11 minutes.

Vegetable Tartlets: Make recipe as directed, except reduce mushrooms to ½ cup sliced. Reduce onion to ½ onion, finely chopped. Add ⅓ cup each minced red bell pepper and grated carrot; cook until tender. Proceed with recipe and bake as directed.

Make Filling

Fill Tart Shells

- It's important that the vegetables are very tender before you add the egg and cream.

- The mushrooms, especially, are full of water. They must be cooked until the liquid evaporates.

- If the mushrooms aren't cooked until dark, they will release liquid in the tart shells and the shells will become soggy.

- So keep an eye on the filling mixture. When the liquid has evaporated, the mushrooms will be deep brown.

- Frozen mini–tart shells are a great shortcut for appetizers and desserts.

- They are made of phyllo dough layered with butter and baked into a small cup shape.

- You find them in the frozen foods aisle of the supermarket. They defrost in about 5 minutes at room temperature.

- Don't overfill the little cups; add food just so the filling is slightly below the top edge.

APPETIZERS

APPLE OATMEAL

Oatmeal cooked with two forms of apple makes a delicious healthy breakfast

Breakfast is the most important meal of the day. Your body needs fuel in the morning, or you'll find yourself lagging. Studies have shown that people who eat breakfast better control their diets and weigh less than those who skip.

But the traditional breakfast, like bacon and eggs, can be very high in sodium. Prepared breakfast foods have lots of salt. Making your own breakfast not only guarantees good nutrition, but also the best taste.

Oatmeal is wonderfully accented in this recipe with the fresh, sweet, and tart taste of apples and apple juice. Oatmeal is so good for you because it's a whole grain, high in fiber and B vitamins. *Yield: Serves 6*

Ingredients

2 cups quick-cooking oats

1 Granny Smith apple, peeled and chopped

2 cups apple juice

1 cup water

1/4 teaspoon salt

1 teaspoon cinnamon

1/8 teaspoon cardamom

1/8 teaspoon nutmeg

1 cup milk

2 teaspoons vanilla

1/2 cup dried cherries

1 cup toasted chopped walnuts

1/3 cup brown sugar

1/4 cup honey

Calories 374, **% Calories from Fat** 38%, **Fat** (g) 16, **Carbohydrates** (g) 53, **Protein** (g) 9, **Sodium** (mg) 120, **Fiber** (g) 5, **Saturated Fat** (g) 2, **Cholesterol** (mg) 4

Apple Oatmeal

- Place oats in large dry skillet. Toast over medium heat, stirring frequently, until oats are fragrant.

- In large saucepan, combine apple, apple juice, water, salt, cinnamon, cardamom, and nutmeg; bring to a boil. Add toasted oats.

- Bring back to a boil; boil 1 minute, stirring frequently. Add milk; heat until steaming.

- Remove from heat and add vanilla, cherries, walnuts, and brown sugar; stir, cover, and let stand 4 minutes. Stir and serve drizzled with honey.

Raisin Oatmeal: Make recipe as directed, except add ½ cup dark seedless raisins and ½ cup golden seedless raisins in place of the apple. Omit nutmeg and dried cherries. Reduce apple juice to 1 cup, and increase water to 2 cups.

Crisp Fried Oatmeal Squares: Pour cooked oatmeal mixture into a greased 13- x 9-inch pan. Refrigerate until firm, at least 6 hours. When ready to eat, melt 3 tablespoons butter in large skillet. Cut oatmeal mixture into 4-inch squares. Fry, turning once, until crisp, about 8 to 12 minutes.

Toast Oats

- Toasting the oats really enhances the flavor of this dish without adding salt.

- Oats, like all whole grains, have aromatic fats. Toasting brings out the flavor of these fats and enhances the nutty taste of the grain.

- Be careful to not burn the oatmeal while it's toasting. Stir frequently and watch it carefully.

- You can toast the oatmeal ahead of time; store it in an airtight container up to 4 days.

Simmer Oatmeal

- Quick cooking oats cook, well, quickly. If you want a sturdier oatmeal, use regular oats.

- And for even more texture, steel-cut oats are very hearty. They are made of oat grains cut into slices.

- Follow package directions for cooking regular or steel-cut oats; cook until just tender.

- Serve oatmeal hot drizzled with cold honey or maple syrup, or splurge with a drizzle of light cream.

BREAKFAST

EGGS BENEDICT
Scrambled eggs are the easiest way to make this classic recipe

Eggs Benedict is a classic and rich dish that's perfect for a company brunch or holiday breakfast. It's typically made with poached or lightly fried eggs, which brings food safety into question.

Unless you use pasteurized eggs, they should be cooked well-done, which is not the texture you want in this recipe. Scrambled eggs solve this problem; the eggs are moist and tender and are still thoroughly cooked.

Salmon, with its low-sodium content, takes the place of Canadian bacon, which is very high in sodium. The rich meat is also good for you and tastes delicious, so you won't miss the bacon.

Serve with a fruit salad and some hot coffee. *Yield: Serves 6–8*

Ingredients

2 (8-ounce) salmon fillets

1 tablespoon lemon juice

8 eggs

1/4 cup light cream

1 teaspoon dried thyme

1/8 teaspoon white pepper

1 tablespoon Dijon mustard

2 tablespoons unsalted butter

1/2 cup sour cream

2 tablespoons milk

1 tablespoon lemon juice

4 English muffins

2 tablespoons unsalted butter

Calories 349, **% Calories from Fat** 52%, **Fat** (g) 20, **Carbohydrates** (g) 15, **Protein** (g) 26, **Sodium** (mg) 284, **Fiber** (g) 1, **Saturated Fat** (g) 10, **Cholesterol** (mg) 285

Eggs Benedict

- Preheat broiler. Place salmon on broiler pan; drizzle with 1 tablespoon lemon juice. Broil 5 to 6 minutes, until cooked through; remove and flake.

- Beat eggs with cream, thyme, pepper, and mustard. In large saucepan, melt 2 tablespoons butter.

- Add eggs; cook, stirring occasionally, until set. Fold in salmon. Meanwhile, combine sour cream, milk, and 1 tablespoon lemon juice; whisk.

- Split muffins, toast, and spread with butter. Top with eggs, then sour cream mixture. Broil 5 to 6 minutes.

Plain Eggs Benedict: Make recipe as directed, except omit salmon and 1 tablespoon lemon juice. Increase eggs to ten, and light cream to ⅓ cup. Continue with recipe as directed. Top scrambled eggs with sour cream mixture and broil until browned and bubbly.

English Muffins: Combine 1 (0.25-ounce) package dry yeast with 1 cup warm water. Add 1 cup milk, ¼ cup melted butter, ½ teaspoon salt, and 1 tablespoon sugar. Beat in 5-6 cups flour until soft dough. Knead; let rise. Roll to ½-inch thick; cut 3-inch rounds. Let rise. Cook on ungreased griddle 18 to 22 minutes until browned.

Broil Salmon

Cook Eggs

- The rack with the salmon should be about 6 inches below the heat source; adjust it before you turn on the broiler.

- If the salmon fillets are about ½ inch thick, they should cook through in 5 minutes.

- If they are thicker, turn them over gently and cook on the second side just until they flake when tested with a fork.

- You can cook the salmon ahead of time; cover and refrigerate up to 2 days.

- Don't combine the eggs with the cream and seasonings until you're ready to cook them or they could become watery.

- Turn the eggs as they cook and run a spatula along the bottom of the pan so the uncooked mixture flows under the cooked.

- You can also toast the English muffins ahead of time to save time. They'll reheat when you broil the whole dish.

- Don't assemble the whole recipe until you're ready to broil the food and serve.

51

BANANA CHOCOLATE CHIP MUFFINS
Homemade muffins fresh from the oven are a morning treat

The bakery is the source for some wonderful foods, but these products are usually quite high in sodium. Make your own muffins and bread and control what you eat.

Muffins are easy to make as long as you follow a few rules. Follow the directions carefully. Measure the flour correctly by lightly scooping it into a measuring cup and level off the top with a knife. Never scoop the measuring cup directly into the flour or you can add up to 25 percent too much, which will make your muffins dry. And don't overmix the batter.

Serve these muffins with some orange juice, coffee, and grapefruit topped with a drizzle of honey. *Yield: Makes 12 muffins*

Ingredients

- ¹/₃ cup unsalted butter, softened
- ³/₄ cup brown sugar
- 1 egg
- 3 ripe bananas, mashed
- 1 teaspoon cinnamon
- ¹/₄ teaspoon nutmeg
- 1 teaspoon vanilla
- 1¹/₄ cups flour
- ¹/₂ cup whole wheat flour
- 1 teaspoon baking powder
- ¹/₂ teaspoon baking soda
- 1¹/₂ cups chocolate chips

Calories 308, **% Calories from Fat** 35%, **Fat** (g) 12, **Carbohydrates** (g) 46, **Protein** (g) 5, **Sodium** (mg) 112, **Fiber** (g) 3, **Saturated Fat** (g) 6, **Cholesterol** (mg) 36

Banana Chocolate Chip Muffins

- Preheat oven to 375°F. Spray 12 muffin cups with nonstick baking spray containing flour.

- In large bowl, combine butter and brown sugar; beat well. Add egg, banana, cinnamon, nutmeg, and vanilla.

- Add flour, baking powder, and baking soda; beat until combined. Stir in chocolate chips.

- Fill prepared muffin cups three-quarters full. Bake 18 to 22 minutes, until muffins are golden brown and firm. Remove from pans immediately; cool on wire racks.

Banana Nut Muffins: Make recipe as directed, except add 1½ cups chopped, toasted pecans or walnuts in place of the chocolate chips. Increase nutmeg to ½ teaspoon and add ¼ cup granulated sugar with the brown sugar.

Banana Streusel Muffins: Make recipe as directed, except combine 3 tablespoons each flour, brown sugar, and melted butter with ½ teaspoon cinnamon; mix until crumbly. Omit chocolate chips. Top muffin batter with crumbly mixture; bake as directed.

Combine Butter and Sugar

- These muffins aren't made like typical muffins, where wet ingredients are just combined with dry and mixed just until combined.

- This recipe is more like a cake batter. But you still have to be careful to not overbeat the mixture.

- Mix the butter and sugar, preferably with an electric beater, until smooth and fluffy.

- Add the egg and spices and mix until blended. Then add dry ingredients and mix just until blended.

Drop Batter into Cups

- For muffins that are all the same size, use a measuring cup or an ice cream scoop to place the batter into the cups.

- A 1½- to 2-inch ice cream scoop is just about the right size, or use a ¼ cup measure.

- Make sure that your oven temperature is accurate, and place the oven rack in the middle of the oven.

- Bake the muffins until they spring back when you touch them with a finger. Cool on wire racks; serve warm.

BREAKFAST

FLUFFY PANCAKES
Serve these light and tender pancakes with maple syrup

Pancakes are easy to make. Once again, you need a light hand and accurate measuring ability, along with fresh ingredients.

Wet ingredients should be measured with measuring cups made for liquids. These are usually glass and have a pouring spout. Add liquid until the measuring line you want Is reached. And be sure to read the amount at eye level.

When flipping pancakes, the trick is all in the wrist. Gently ease a spatula under the pancakes, then quickly flip them using your wrist.

Serve these pancakes with warmed maple syrup or honey, or sprinkle them with powdered sugar. Fruit compote is also a great topping that adds nutrition and fiber. A selection of jams adds great color and flavor. *Yield: Serves 6–8*

Ingredients

2 cups sifted flour

1 teaspoon baking powder

1 teaspoon baking soda

3 tablespoons sugar

2 eggs, beaten

$1^1/_2$ cups buttermilk

$^1/_4$ cup unsalted butter, melted

1 teaspoon vanilla

$^1/_8$ teaspoon nutmeg

Calories 215, **% Calories from Fat** 29%, **Fat** (g) 7, **Carbohydrates** (g) 31, **Protein** (g) 6, **Sodium** (mg) 100, **Fiber** (g) 1, **Saturated Fat** (g) 4, **Cholesterol** (mg) 19

Fluffy Pancakes

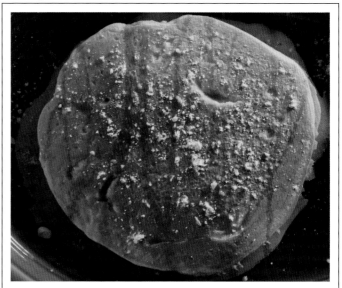

- Measure flour and place in sifter with baking powder and baking soda.

- Sift into a large bowl. Add sugar. In another bowl, combine eggs, buttermilk, butter, vanilla, and nutmeg; beat.

- Add wet ingredients to dry ingredients and mix with whisk just until combined. Let stand 5 minutes.

- Lightly oil griddle over medium heat. Pour batter onto griddle, using ¼ cup for each. Cook until bubbles form and start to break; turn and cook 2 to 3 minutes.

Make Ahead Pancakes: Make recipe as directed, except substitute 1 teaspoon active dry yeast for the baking powder and baking soda. Cover batter and store in the fridge for three days, using as needed. Make pancakes as directed.

Brown Sugar Pancakes: Make recipe as directed, except substitute ¼ cup brown sugar for 3 tablespoons granulated sugar. Increase nutmeg to ¼ teaspoon. Cook pancakes as directed, and serve with warmed maple syrup.

Sift Flour

- Sifting flour helps ensure lump-free pancakes, and also ensures that you measure accurately.

- You can use a sifter or a sieve. Place the flour in the sieve and shake into another bowl. Sift flour before measuring, not after.

- The wet ingredients should be mixed well before adding them to the flour mixture.

- Stir just until combined; there will be some lumps in the batter that will cook out on the grill.

Flip Pancakes

- Lightly grease the griddle before you make the first pancakes. Pour batter quickly.

- The batter will automatically form into a round shape. Let the pancakes cook until bubbles form on the surface.

- When the edges look dry and the bubbles start to break, turn the pancakes quickly and gently.

- Cook on the second side until light brown. The second side will never be as dark as the first side; that's okay.

BREAKFAST

BROWN SUGAR WAFFLES
Brown sugar caramelizes as the waffles bake, making them crisp

Waffles, whether for an everyday breakfast or a special occasion, are a great choice to start your day.

The batter for baking powder pancakes can be used to make waffles, too. For a change, yeast pancakes are lighter and crisper, and they are not difficult to make.

This batter has to be beaten longer than pancake or muffin batter because of the yeast. The gluten in the flour has to develop to form strong webs that will trap and hold the carbon dioxide generated by the yeast over time. Beating for just a few minutes will develop the gluten to the perfect consistency.

Serve these waffles hot from the waffle iron with melted unsalted butter, warmed maple syrup, and lots of jellies and jams. *Yield: Serves 6*

Ingredients

1 (0.25-ounce) package dry yeast

$^1/_3$ cup warm water

$1^1/_2$ cups milk

2 eggs, beaten

$^1/_2$ cup brown sugar

1 teaspoon cinnamon

$^1/_8$ teaspoon cardamom

2 teaspoons vanilla

$^1/_4$ cup unsalted butter, melted

2 cups flour

$^1/_4$ cup whole wheat flour

Calories 282, **% Calories from Fat** 28%, **Fat** (g) 9, **Carbohydrates** (g) 43, **Protein** (g) 7, **Sodium** (mg) 43, **Fiber** (g) 2, **Saturated Fat** (g) 5, **Cholesterol** (mg) 73

Brown Sugar Waffles

- In large bowl, combine yeast and water; let stand 10 minutes, until foamy. Add milk and eggs; beat well.

- Add brown sugar, cinnamon, cardamom, vanilla, and butter; mix. Stir in flour and beat 2 minutes.

- Cover and let rise 1 hour, or cover and refrigerate overnight. When ready to bake, stir down batter.

- Heat waffle iron and grease with oil. Make waffle according to manufacturer's directions. Serve hot.

Blueberry Waffles: Make recipe as directed, except reduce cinnamon to ½ teaspoon. Toss 2 cups frozen or fresh blueberries with the whole wheat flour and add to the batter after it is mixed. Cook waffles as directed and serve immediately.

Mix Batter

- Be sure that you follow the expiration dates on your packets of yeast.

- Proofing the yeast is an important first step to make sure it's viable. When the mixture is foamy, proceed with the recipe.

- The nice thing about yeast batter is that you can make it ahead and store it in the refrigerator.

- Then in the morning, just heat up the waffle iron and start baking; serve each one the second it's done.

Bake Waffles

- Follow the manufacturer's directions for heating the waffle iron. Some are greased before heating, some after.

- Always use unsalted butter or oil to grease the waffle iron. Salted butter will add sodium and make the batter stick.

- The first waffle is usually a test waffle. It almost always sticks, even when you've greased the waffle iron.

- Just discard it and keep going. Add batter, close the iron, and bake until the steaming stops.

BREAKFAST

SPICY POTATO STRATA
A casserole for breakfast will feed a crowd with ease

KNACK LOW-SALT COOKING

Stratas are made with layered bread or potatoes, covered in an egg custard and seasonings and baked until puffed and golden brown.

Stratas are great for serving a crowd and can also be made ahead, so they're good for entertaining. Stratas made with bread usually have to be refrigerated; this recipe can be baked immediately.

Be sure the potatoes are sliced thinly and evenly so they cook in the same amount of time and are the same texture in the strata.

You can make this recipe as mild or as spicy as you'd like by adding more jalapeño and chipotle chiles, or omitting them. The chili powder will add enough spice if you like it mild. *Yield: Serves 6*

Ingredients

2 tablespoons olive oil

1 onion, chopped

4 cloves garlic, minced

1 jalapeño pepper, minced

1 chipotle pepper in adobo, minced

6 potatoes, thinly sliced

1 cup shredded Pepper Jack cheese

5 eggs, beaten

1½ cups milk

1 tablespoon chili powder

⅛ teaspoon cayenne pepper

1 tablespoon adobo sauce

2 tablespoons grated Cotija cheese

1 cup homemade low-sodium salsa

Calories 338, **% Calories from Fat** 44%, **Fat** (g) 12, **Carbohydrates** (g) 45, **Protein** (g) 13, **Sodium** (mg) 221, **Fiber** (g) 5, **Saturated Fat** (g) 5, **Cholesterol** (mg) 24

Spicy Potato Strata

- In medium pan heat olive oil over medium heat. Add onion, garlic, and jalapeño; cook 4 minutes. Add chipotle pepper; remove from heat.

- In greased 13- by 9-inch baking dish, layer potatoes with onion mixture and Pepper Jack cheese.

- In medium bowl combine eggs, milk, chili powder, pepper, and adobo sauce; mix well. Pour over potatoes.

- Sprinkle with Cotija cheese. Cover; bake at 350°F 1 hour; uncover; bake 15 minutes, until strata is puffed. Serve with salsa.

Tex-Mex Bread Strata: Make recipe as directed, except substitute 12 slices whole wheat bread, cubed, for the thinly sliced potatoes. Layer ingredients as directed, then pour egg mixture over. Cover and refrigerate 8 to 24 hours. Bake at 275°F 45 to 55 minutes, until puffed and golden brown.

All American Strata: Make recipe as directed, except omit jalapeño and chipotle pepper. Omit Pepper Jack cheese, chili powder, cayenne pepper, Cotija cheese, and salsa. Add 1 green bell and 1 red bell pepper, chopped, to onion mixture. Use extra sharp cheddar cheese. Serve with low-fat sour cream.

Layer Potatoes in Dish

Pour Egg Mixture into Dish

- You can peel the potatoes or not, according to your taste. Unpeeled potatoes add more nutrition and fiber to the recipe.

- Don't prepare the potatoes ahead of time or they will turn brown.

- Beat the egg mixture well so the chili powder and adobo sauce are well mixed. You don't want to bite into a pocket of adobo sauce.

- Spread the onion mixture and the cheese evenly over the potatoes as you work.

- The egg mixture can be seasoned with more peppers or spices if you'd like. Cumin and dried oregano are good choices.

- Be sure the salsa you serve with the strata is also low sodium; read the label.

- You can make your own by mixing chopped tomatoes with green onion, jalapeños, lemon juice, fresh cilantro, and pepper.

- Serve the strata hot and the salsa cold. This temperature contrast enhances the flavors of the dish.

BREAKFAST

OATMEAL SCONES

Scones should be served hot with unsalted butter and honey

Scones are a cross between a biscuit and a muffin. They can be sweet or savory. This quick bread originated in Scotland. It was usually served with tea in the afternoon.

There's a controversy about what a real scone is. The originals were baked on griddles like pancakes. American versions of scones are more like biscuits, usually sweet, served warm with butter (unsalted, of course).

As with all quick breads, it's important to work the mixture as little as possible, as the flour is added so the gluten doesn't develop.

Scones are best served as soon as they are baked. They can cool on a rack for a few minutes, but eat them quickly. One or two is perfect for a quick breakfast. *Yield: Makes 16 scones*

Ingredients

1 1/2 cups flour

1/2 cup whole wheat flour

1 1/2 cups quick-cooking oatmeal

1/3 cup brown sugar

2 teaspoons baking powder

1/2 teaspoon baking soda

1/2 cup unsalted butter

1/4 cup milk

1/4 cup orange juice

1 teaspoon grated orange peel

2 eggs, beaten

1 1/2 teaspoons vanilla

1/2 cup chopped toasted pecans

1 cup powdered sugar

2 tablespoons orange juice

1/2 teaspoon vanilla

Calories 225, **% Calories from Fat** 39%, **Fat** (g) 10, **Carbohydrates** (g) 31, **Protein** (g) 5, **Sodium** (mg) 98, **Fiber** (g) 2, **Saturated Fat** (g) 4, **Cholesterol** (mg) 39

Oatmeal Scones

- Preheat oven to 375°F. In large bowl, combine flour, oatmeal, brown sugar, baking powder, and baking soda.

- Cut in butter until particles are fine. In medium bowl, combine milk, orange juice, orange peel, eggs, and vanilla.

- Stir milk mixture into dry ingredients. Add pecans. Shape into two 1/2-inch thick circles on baking sheet; cut each into 8 wedges.

- Bake 18 to 23 minutes, until golden brown. Combine powdered sugar, orange juice, and vanilla; drizzle over scones.

• • • • RECIPE VARIATION • • • •

Drop Scones: Make recipe as directed, except increase milk to ½ cup. You may need to add more to make a soft, droppable dough. Drop by tablespoons onto parchment paper–lined cookie sheets, making about 20 scones. Bake at 400°F 15 to 18 minutes, until golden brown; cool on wire rack.

Chocolate Chip Scones: Make recipe as directed, except use ½ cup milk instead of ¼ cup milk and ¼ cup orange juice. Add 1 cup semisweet or dark chocolate chips to the dough when mixed. Bake as directed. For glaze, combine 2 tablespoons cocoa, 1 cup powdered sugar, 2 tablespoons milk, and vanilla.

Cut in Butter

- Mix the dry ingredients, then cut in the butter. That means to manipulate the butter with a pastry blender or two knives.

- Keep working the mixture until the butter disappears and the particles are fine.

- When you pick up a bit of the mixture, the pieces will hold together if you press them in your fingers.

- Then add the liquid and mix until a dough starts to form. You may not need all the liquid, or you may need more.

Shape Scones

- If you want your scones to have softer sides, just cut the circle into wedges and leave them in place.

- For scones with crunchy edges, separate the wedges slightly, right on the baking sheet.

- You can omit the sweet glaze and brush the scones with beaten egg instead. This will create a shiny crust.

- Make scones ahead of time and reheat them in the oven at 350°F 8 to 10 minutes, until hot and tender.

61

BANANA BREAD

Tender banana bread is studded with walnuts and dried cherries

Banana bread is the perfect snack to grab on your way out the door. If you have some in the house, your kids will have a delicious and healthy treat that is ready in seconds.

The best banana bread is made with very ripe bananas. The banana skins should be mostly dark, and the bananas themselves very soft. This adds the most flavor to the bread and also adds moisture.

Most bread and muffins you buy from the bakery and quick bread mixes are packed with sodium. Making your own breads is easy and satisfying.

To help increase flavor in sweet quick breads, increase the amount of vanilla you add. One teaspoon of vanilla per loaf adds great flavor. *Yield: Serves 16*

KNACK LOW-SALT COOKING

Ingredients

1/2 cup unsalted butter, softened

1 cup brown sugar

2 eggs, beaten

3 ripe bananas, mashed

1/2 cup sour cream

2 teaspoons vanilla

2 cups flour

1 teaspoon baking soda

1 teaspoon cinnamon

1/8 teaspoon nutmeg

1/8 teaspoon cardamom

1 cup chopped walnuts

1 cup dried cherries

1/2 cup brown sugar

1/2 cup flour

3 tablespoons butter

1/3 cup chopped pecans

Calories 340, **% Calories from Fat** 44%, **Fat** (g) 17, **Carbohydrates** (g) 45, **Protein** (g) 5, **Sodium** (mg) 116, **Fiber** (g) 2, **Saturated Fat** (g) 7, **Cholesterol** (mg) 51

Banana Bread

- Preheat oven to 325°F. Spray two 9- x 5-inch pans with nonstick baking spray.

- In a bowl combine butter and 1 cup brown sugar; beat well. Add eggs, bananas, sour cream, and vanilla; beat well.

- Add flour, baking soda, cinnamon, nutmeg, and cardamom and mix. Stir in walnuts and cherries.

- Pour into prepared pans. In a small bowl, combine remaining ingredients; mix until crumbly and sprinkle over batter. Bake 70 to 80 minutes, until bread tests done; remove from pans.

· · · · · **RECIPE VARIATION** · · · ·

Spicy Banana Bread: Make recipe as directed, except add 1 teaspoon curry powder and ¼ teaspoon ground cloves to the batter. Increase nutmeg to ½ teaspoon. Make batter as directed and pour into pan. Add ½ teaspoon cinnamon and ½ teaspoon curry powder to the crumbly topping; bake.

Mix Butter and Ingredients

- Make sure the butter and sugar are well mixed before you add the other ingredients.

- The banana won't mix evenly into the wet ingredients if it's added along with the sugar and eggs.

- Beat the batter until fairly smooth. It's okay if some small pieces of banana are still visible.

- You can omit the walnuts or use pecans or cashews. Or try adding dried currants or cranberries in place of the dried cherries.

Sprinkle Topping on Batter

- Mix the topping just until crumbly. If you overmix, it will be tough and fall off the bread.

- Press the topping lightly into the batter as you sprinkle it on. Some will sink into the bread as it bakes.

- This will create a slight swirl of streusel in the bread. In fact you can layer the topping with the batter for a streusel bread.

- The bread is done when a toothpick stuck into the center comes out clean. Cool five minutes, then remove from pans and cool on racks.

CRANBERRY NUT BREAD

Fresh and dried cranberries add flavor and color to this easy bread

Cranberries are available fresh around the holiday season. You can find them other times of the year, but the winter months are when they are harvested and fresh.

Cranberries freeze well, so you can buy a bunch, put them into freezer bags, and freeze up to six months. Don't thaw the cranberries before using them in baking; just chop them frozen and stir into the batter.

Let the bread cool on a wire rack for at least one hour before wrapping it in plastic wrap. Store at room temperature for up to three days.

This beautiful bread is perfect for a holiday breakfast, particularly Christmas morning. The tart cranberries contrast really well with the sweet and tender bread; you won't miss the salt! *Yield: Serves 10*

Ingredients

2 cups flour

1 cup brown sugar

1 teaspoon baking powder

$^1/_2$ teaspoon baking soda

$^1/_3$ cup butter

1 egg

$^1/_2$ cup orange juice

$^1/_4$ cup sour cream

1 tablespoon grated orange peel

1 teaspoon vanilla

1 teaspoon cinnamon

$^1/_4$ teaspoon nutmeg

$^1/_8$ teaspoon cardamom

1 cup fresh cranberries

$^1/_2$ cup dried cranberries

1 cup chopped walnuts

Calories 348, **% Calories from Fat** 41%, **Fat** (g) 16, **Carbohydrates** (g) 48, **Protein** (g) 5, **Sodium** (mg) 163, **Fiber** (g) 2, **Saturated Fat** (g) 6, **Cholesterol** (mg) 40

Cranberry Nut Bread

- Preheat oven to 350°F. Spray 9- x 5-inch loaf pan with nonstick baking spray containing flour.

- In a large bowl, combine flour, brown sugar, baking powder, and baking soda. Cut in butter until particles are fine.

- In another bowl, combine egg, orange juice, sour cream, orange peel, vanilla, cinnamon, nutmeg, and cardamom; add to flour mixture and stir.

- Add both kinds of cranberries and walnuts. Pour into pan. Bake 65 to 75 minutes, until done; cool on wire rack.

•••• RECIPE VARIATION ••••

Lower Fat Cranberry Nut Bread: Make recipe as directed, except use ⅓ cup oil in place of butter and use low-fat sour cream. Cut the walnuts down to ⅓ cup and increase the dried cranberries to ⅔ cup. Prepare bread, bake, and cool as directed.

YELLOW LIGHT

To make the best quick breads, follow a few rules. The most important is to not overmix the batter. If gluten in the flour develops too much as you stir, the quick bread will have tunnels running through the slices and the texture will be tough. Mix just until all the ingredients are combined.

Cut Butter into Flour

- This is a more unusual method for making quick bread, but it results in a very tender loaf.

- To "cut in" means to manipulate the butter with two knives or a pastry blender until it combines with the flour.

- The particles should be fine and even, and no butter should be visible in the mixture.

- The liquid ingredients are combined before adding to the flour mixture, so you don't have to stir much to blend the ingredients.

Add Batter to Pan and Bake

- Stir the batter just until everything is combined; don't overmix or the gluten in the flour will overdevelop.

- You can spray the pan with nonstick baking spray containing flour, or use unsalted butter or shortening.

- Never use salted butter to grease pans when baking. Not only does this add some sodium to the product, it makes batters stick.

- Let the bread cool in the pan for 5 minutes, then gently shake it to release and turn onto a cooling rack.

FRENCH BREAD

Sour cream and orange juice are secrets to low-salt yeast bread

Yeast breads are typically quite high in salt. Not only does the salt add to the flavor of the bread, but it helps regulate the development and growth of the yeast.

Bread made without salt either needs to have less yeast or sugar added, or it needs ingredients added that will help inhibit the yeast's growth. Acidic ingredients like orange juice, sour cream, yogurt, and vinegar are all good additions.

And they give the bread a slight sour flavor, reminiscent of sourdough bread from San Francisco.

Kneading bread is easy and can be a great stress reliever. Flour the work surface, place the dough on it, then fold it over and push with your hands. Incorporate more flour until the dough is elastic and smooth. *Yield: Serves 16*

French Bread

KNACK LOW-SALT COOKING

Ingredients

2¹/₂ cups whole wheat flour

2 to 3 cups bread flour, divided

2 (0.25-ounce) packages dry yeast

¹/₄ teaspoon salt

³/₄ cup milk

¹/₄ cup orange juice

¹/₂ cup sour cream

¹/₂ cup yogurt

2 tablespoons cider vinegar

1 egg

1 egg yolk

1 egg white, partially beaten

Calories 108, **% Calories from Fat** 13%, **Fat** (g) 2, **Carbohydrates** (g)19, **Protein** (g) 5, **Sodium** (mg) 56, **Fiber** (g) 3, **Saturated Fat** (g) 1, **Cholesterol** (mg) 28

- Combine whole wheat flour, ½ cup bread flour, yeast, and salt. In saucepan mix milk, orange juice, sour cream, yogurt, and vinegar; warm over low heat.

- Add milk mixture to flour mixture with egg and yolk. Add remaining bread flour until firm dough forms.

- Knead. Cover; let rise 1 hour. Punch down; divide in half. Roll to 14- x 6-inch rectangle; roll up, pinch ends; place on sheet.

- Let rise 45 minutes. Bake at 375°F 20 minutes. Brush with egg white; bake 15 to 20 minutes.

• • • • RECIPE VARIATION • • • •

Round Sourdough Bread: Make recipe as directed, except instead of forming into 2 long loaves, form the mixture into 2 rounds, 9 inches in diameter. Roll the dough on floured surface until it is smooth, then press down until 1-inch thick. Let rise, then cut 3 slashes in the bread. Bake as directed, adding 5 to 10 minutes.

French Bread Rolls: Divide the dough into 18 pieces after the first rise. Shape each into a 5- x 2-inch rectangle, rounding the ends. Place on baking sheet and let rise. Bake 18 to 23 minutes. While still hot, brush the tops of the rolls with unsalted butter. Cool completely on wire rack.

Mix Dough

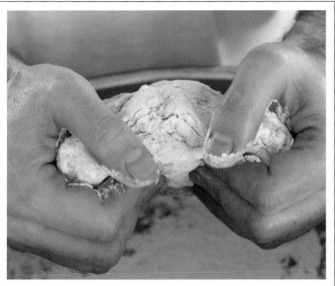

- Heat the liquid mixture until it feels very warm. Add flour until you can't stir anymore.

- Gluten, the protein in dough that forms when it mixes with water, is essential to yeast bread's texture.

- The dough is beaten, then kneaded to ensure gluten forms a fine web that holds the CO_2 from the yeast.

- Knead the dough until it doesn't stick to your hands and feels smooth and elastic. Place dough in greased bowl to rise, turning to grease top.

Form into Loaf

- Punch down the dough with your fist to release the air and redistribute the yeast in the dough.

- When you roll up the dough, roll it up tightly, but not so tightly the dough splits as you work.

- Grease a cookie sheet with two long swipes of shortening; sprinkle with cornmeal for a crunchy bottom.

- For a nice decoration, you can slice the tops of the loaves after they rise; use a single-blade razor. Slice ⅛-inch deep.

DINNER ROLLS

Homemade light and fluffy dinner rolls are delicious and better than those from any bakery

Dinner rolls complete a meal. There's nothing better than breaking open a soft, warm roll straight from the oven and spreading it with unsalted butter or some honey.

The dough for soft dinner rolls is much softer than the dough for French bread. It should be smooth and elastic after kneading, but still soft enough that you can easily tear off a ball and roll it into a smooth shape.

You can shape these rolls any way you'd like—from single buns to Parkerhouse rolls, single rolls, or knot rolls.

These rolls are also easily reheated. Cool them completely, then wrap well. Unwrap and place in a preheated 350°F oven 5 to 10 minutes to reheat. *Yield: Makes 24 rolls*

Ingredients

2 (0.25-ounce) packages active dry yeast

¹/₂ cup warm water

¹/₂ cup buttermilk

1 egg

¹/₃ cup unsalted butter, melted

¹/₄ teaspoon salt

2 tablespoons sugar

2 tablespoons oat bran

4–5 cups flour, divided

3 tablespoons unsalted butter

Calories 132, **% Calories from Fat** 31%, **Fat** (g) 5, **Carbohydrates** (g) 20, **Protein** (g) 3, **Sodium** (mg) 34, **Fiber** (g) 1, **Saturated Fat** (g) 3, **Cholesterol** (mg) 20

Dinner Rolls

- Mix yeast with warm water; let stand 10 minutes, until bubbly. Add buttermilk, egg, ⅓ cup butter, salt, sugar, and oat bran; mix. Add 1 cup flour; beat 1 minute.

- Add 3–4 cups flour to form soft dough; knead 5 minutes. Cover; let rise 1 hour.

- Divide dough into fourths, then into 24 balls. Grease 24 muffin tins. Divide each ball into 3 pieces; place side by side in tins.

- Let rise 30 minutes; bake at 350°F 20 to 25 minutes. Remove to wire racks, brush with more unsalted butter.

• • • • RECIPE VARIATION • • • •

Honey Pan Rolls: Make recipe as directed, except press the dough into a greased 13- x 9-inch pan. Cut diagonal lines through dough 1½ inches apart; repeat in the opposite direction, forming diamonds. Let rise; melt 3 tablespoons each unsalted butter and honey; drizzle over rolls. Let rise; bake at 375°F 30 to 40 minutes.

Hoagie Buns: Make recipe as directed, except divide dough into 12 balls after the first rise. Roll into oblong shapes about 2- x 5-inch and flatten with your hand. Place on greased baking sheet and let rise until doubled. Bake at 375°F 25 to 35 minutes until the buns are deep golden brown.

Knead Bread

- To knead dough, place it on a floured work surface. Begin kneading when you can no longer stir in flour by hand.

- Sprinkle the dough with flour and fold in half toward you. Push down with the heel of your hand, pushing into the dough.

- Turn the dough a quarter turn and repeat the folding and pushing action.

- Sprinkle dough with flour as you work, just enough to keep it from sticking to your hands and the work surface.

Form Rolls

- When the dough is smooth and elastic and no longer sticky, place in a greased bowl and cover to let rise.

- When the dough has literally doubled in size, turn it out onto the work surface again and punch down.

- Use a sharp knife to cut the dough into pieces. Roll the dough between your hands until each ball is smooth.

- Cover with a clean kitchen towel and let rise again until the rolls are doubled in size. Bake until golden brown.

WHOLE WHEAT BREAD

This special recipe makes a light and tender whole wheat bread

Whole wheat bread is made from whole wheat flour. That means the wheat grains have just the hull removed, but the bran and germ are still intact. This increases the fiber and B vitamin content of the flour and therefore the bread.

Bread flour is a good choice to pair with whole wheat flour. The brain and germ pieces in whole wheat flour interfere with gluten formation, so adding a high-protein bread flour will result in the finest crumb and most tender bread.

Whole wheat bread is delicious toasted and spread with honey or jam for breakfast. It also makes excellent sandwiches, especially when cooked on a panini maker. Enjoy the aroma of this wonderful bread drifting through your kitchen. *Yield: Serves 16 (slice is 1 serving)*

Ingredients

3 cups whole wheat flour

3–4 cups bread flour, divided

2 (0.25-ounce) packages active dry yeast

¹/₄ teaspoon salt

1 cup milk

¹/₃ cup orange juice

¹/₃ cup water

¹/₂ cup honey

¹/₄ cup brown sugar

2 teaspoons grated orange zest

¹/₄ cup unsalted butter, melted

2 eggs, beaten

Calories 139, **% Calories from Fat** 15%, **Fat** (g) 2, **Carbohydrates** (g) 26, **Protein** (g) 4, **Sodium** (mg) 29, **Fiber** (g) 2, **Saturated Fat** (g) 1, **Cholesterol** (mg) 18

Whole Wheat Bread

- Mix whole wheat flour, ½ cup bread flour, yeast, and salt.

- In saucepan, heat milk, orange juice, water, honey, sugar, zest, and butter until 120°F Add to flour mixture with eggs.

- Beat 2 minutes. Add 2½ to 3½ cups bread flour to form firm dough. Knead 10 minutes. Cover; let rise 1 hour. Punch down.

- Divide in half; roll to 13- x 7-inch rectangles. Roll up, pinch ends, place in greased 9- x 5-inch pans. Let rise 30 minutes. Bake at 375°F 30 to 40 minutes until done.

···· RECIPE VARIATION ····

Whole Wheat Hamburger Buns: Make recipe as directed, except after the first rising, divide the dough into 24 pieces. Roll each piece between your palms to make a smooth ball. Place on parchment-lined cookie sheets; press down with your hand; let rise. Bake at 375°F 20 to 25 minutes until golden brown. Brush with unsalted butter; cool.

Pita Bread: Cut flour, salt, and yeast amounts in half. Omit orange juice, honey, brown sugar, zest, butter, and eggs. Add 1 tablespoon vegetable oil and about 1 cup water. Knead; let rise. Divide dough into 8 pieces, roll to 7-inch circles; let rise. Bake directly on rack in 500°F oven 4 to 5 minutes until puffy and set.

Form and Knead Dough

- Orange juice is used in whole wheat breads because the sweet and tart flavor mitigates the slight bitterness of the flour.

- It also helps control the yeast development in the absence of salt.

- You can use whole wheat flour or bread flour to sprinkle over the dough as you knead it; it doesn't matter.

- When using bread flour, it's a good idea, after the first rise, to let the dough stand 10 minutes to relax a bit.

Form Loaves

- Use a ruler to measure the dough to make sure you're rolling it to the correct size.

- Start at the shorter side and roll up the dough, pressing firmly but not so firmly that the dough tears.

- As you roll, the loaf will get longer, so it will fit snugly into the loaf pan.

- Make sure the ends of the dough touch the ends of the pan. Let the dough rise until the pan is full, then bake.

GRILLED CRANBERRY CHICKEN

Chicken brushed with a cranberry glaze is colorful and flavorful

Chicken is a wonderful choice for any healthy diet. It's mild and versatile and can be combined with many other ingredients to make an infinite variety of recipes.

Buy chicken that hasn't been injected with a sodium solution. The claim "all natural" doesn't mean the chicken hasn't been processed. Injecting chicken with salt water just combines two "natural" ingredients. Compare sodium content on labels.

Grilling chicken is easy. Prepare and preheat the grill, building a charcoal fire with a hot side and a cool side by gradually increasing the charcoal depth from one side to the other. Move the chicken around on the grill as it cooks.

Serve this chicken with a fruit salad and some grilled bread. *Yield: Serves 8*

Ingredients

1 onion, chopped

3 cloves garlic, minced

1 tablespoon olive oil

2 tablespoons honey

1 teaspoon dried thyme leaves

3 tablespoons brown sugar

1 cup jellied cranberry sauce

2 tablespoons no-salt-added tomato paste

1/8 teaspoon cayenne pepper

8 bone-in, skin-on chicken breasts

2 tablespoons olive oil

1/8 teaspoon pepper

Calories 287, **% Calories from Fat** 41%, **Fat** (g)13, **Carbohydrates** (g) 24, **Protein** (g) 19, **Sodium** (mg) 71, **Fiber** (g) 1, **Saturated Fat** (g) 3, **Cholesterol** (mg) 56

Grilled Cranberry Chicken

- Cook onion and garlic in olive oil 5 to 6 minutes.

- Add honey, thyme, brown sugar, cranberry sauce, tomato paste, and cayenne pepper; cook and stir over low heat 5 minutes.

- Loosen skin from flesh on chicken; rub some cranberry mixture on flesh.

- Prepare and preheat grill. Brush chicken with olive oil and sprinkle with pepper. Place on grill, skin-side down; grill 10 minutes. Turn, cover, and grill 15 to 20 minutes longer, brushing with sauce during last 15 minutes.

Honey Mustard Chicken: Make recipe as directed, except omit cranberry sauce and tomato paste. Add ½ teaspoon dry mustard powder and 2 tablespoons Dijon mustard to the marinade. Add ½ cup chicken broth. Prepare and grill chicken as directed; don't simmer the sauce to serve on the side.

Sweet-and-Sour Grilled Chicken: Make recipe as directed, except omit cranberry sauce. Add ½ cup low-sodium ketchup to the marinade along with 2 tablespoons cider vinegar. Marinate the chicken 6 hours in the fridge before grilling. Don't simmer sauce to serve on the side.

Make Sauce

Cook Chicken and Sauce

- You can make the sauce ahead of time and store it in the refrigerator until you're ready to cook the chicken.

- The sauce can be used as a marinade. Just immerse the chicken in the mixture, cover, and refrigerate 8 to 24 hours.

- Always cook meat marinades before serving. Boil for 2 minutes to kill bacteria; then serve.

- Part of the sauce is spread on the chicken flesh itself to add more flavor to the dish.

- Keep an eye on the chicken and always use an instant-read thermometer to check the temperature; it should be 160°F.

- Leaving the skin on the chicken keeps it moist and tender while cooking.

- Just remove the skin before you eat it to omit most of the fat and calories.

- To serve the sauce with the chicken, simmer in a small saucepan for at least 2 minutes after you dip the basting brush into the sauce for the last time.

CHICKEN BREASTS ALFREDO
Chicken in a creamy, cheesy sauce is delicious and comforting

Alfredo is a creamy white sauce made with lots of cream and cheese. It is typically served with pasta, but is delicious served over some crisp and moist chicken breasts.

Lots of herbs make the chicken flavorful without adding any salt. You can reduce the sodium in this recipe even further by using low-sodium cream cheese and by making your own bread crumbs. Just crumble day-old homemade bread

and dry in a 350°F oven 8 to 10 minutes, until brown.

Serve this dish with some cooked pasta tossed with onions and garlic sautéed in a bit of olive oil. A spinach salad made with raspberry vinaigrette and some sliced strawberries is the perfect accompaniment. *Yield: Serves 6*

Ingredients

¹/₂ cup dried bread crumbs

1 teaspoon dried oregano

1 teaspoon dried basil

1 teaspoon dried thyme

¹/₄ cup flour, divided

¹/₄ teaspoon pepper

1 egg

¹/₄ cup buttermilk

6 boneless, skinless chicken breasts

1 onion, chopped

3 cloves garlic, minced

1 (8-ounce) package sliced mushrooms

2 tablespoons olive oil

1 teaspoon dried Italian seasoning

1 cup light cream or milk

1 (3-ounce) package cream cheese

2 tablespoons grated Parmesan cheese

Calories 329, **% Calories from Fat** 37%, **Fat** (g) 14, **Carbohydrates** (g)16, **Protein** (g) 34, **Sodium** (mg) 251, **Fiber** (g) 1, **Saturated Fat** (g) 7, **Cholesterol** (mg) 135

Chicken Breasts Alfredo

- Preheat oven to 350°F. On plate, combine bread crumbs, oregano, basil, thyme, 3 tablespoons flour, and pepper.

- In bowl, beat egg with buttermilk. Dip chicken into egg mixture, then into bread crumb mixture.

- Place chicken on baking pan; bake 20 to 30 minutes. Cook onion, garlic, and mushrooms in oil.

- Add Italian seasoning and 1 tablespoon flour; cook 3 minutes. Add cream or milk, cream cheese, and Parmesan; cook until thick. Serve sauce with chicken.

•••• RECIPE VARIATION ••••

Chicken Breasts Marinara: Prepare the chicken as directed; bake until crisp. Meanwhile, cook onions, garlic, and mushrooms as directed. Omit cream, cream cheese, and milk. Add 6 chopped plum tomatoes and 2 red tomatoes along with 1 cup tomato juice; simmer while the chicken is baking. Serve sauce with chicken.

ZOOM

You can make this recipe or the marinara variation using grilled chicken. Just sprinkle the chicken with some dried Italian herbs and grill over medium coals 8 to 11 minutes, until done. Prepare the sauce while the chicken is grilling and serve together with cooked rice or pasta.

Prepare Chicken

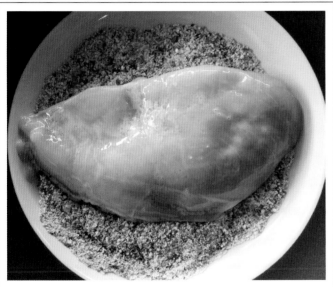

- If the chicken breasts are thicker than 1 inch, pound them so they cook evenly.

- To pound, place between sheets of plastic wrap and pound gently using a meat mallet or rolling pin.

- Use one hand to dip the chicken in the buttermilk and egg mixture and another to dip into the bread crumbs; this makes cleanup easier.

- For really crisp chicken, place the chicken on a wire rack on the baking pan to let the heat circulate.

Make Sauce

- As the cream cheese melts into the sauce, it will at first look curdled. But keep stirring and it will smooth out.

- For the smoothest sauce stir the sauce mixture with a wire whisk as it's heating.

- You can make the sauce ahead of time. Store it, covered, in the refrigerator.

- To reheat, pour into a saucepan and add some more milk; heat until steaming, stirring frequently.

SLOW COOKER CHICKEN STEW

A spicy stew cooks to perfection in your slow cooker

A slow cooker is the next best thing to having a cook in your employ. All you do is add food, turn it on, and come back hours later to perfectly cooked food that fills your home with wonderful aromas.

But there are some rules to follow. Fill the slow cooker about two-thirds full for best results. Place root vegetables at the bottom of the appliance and meats and more delicate vegetables and fruits at the top.

Don't lift the lid often, except to stir once or twice. And check for doneness at the minimum cooking time.

Serve this excellent stew with some homemade rolls from Chapter 6: Breads and a spinach salad with an oil and vinegar dressing. *Yield: Serves 8*

Ingredients

2 tablespoons olive oil

1 onion, chopped

3 cloves garlic, minced

2 jalapeño peppers, minced

1 sweet potato, peeled and cubed

6 boneless, skinless chicken thighs

2 tablespoons flour

$1/4$ teaspoon pepper

1 (16-ounce) jar low-sodium salsa

2 tomatoes, chopped

1 tablespoon chili powder

1 teaspoon cumin

1 (15-ounce) can low-sodium black beans, rinsed

2 cups frozen corn

3 cups low-sodium chicken broth

2 tablespoons lime juice

1 tablespoon cornstarch

Calories 326, **% Calories from Fat** 25%, **Fat** (g) 9, **Carbohydrates** (g) 48, **Protein** (g) 19, **Sodium** (mg) 180, **Fiber** (g) 6, **Saturated Fat** (g) 2, **Cholesterol** (mg) 37

Slow Cooker Chicken Stew

- Heat olive oil in saucepan; cook onion, garlic, and jalapeño 5 minutes. Remove to 5-quart slow cooker with sweet potato.

- Coat chicken in flour and pepper; brown in same saucepan. Add to slow cooker with salsa, tomatoes, chili powder, cumin, beans, corn, and broth.

- Cover and cook on low 7 to 8 hours, until chicken is tender.

- Shred chicken; return to slow cooker with mixture of lime juice and cornstarch. Cover and cook on high 15 to 20 minutes, until thickened.

76

Curried Chicken Stew: Make recipe as directed, except omit jalapeño peppers, salsa, and chili powder. Add 1 tablespoon curry powder to the onions and garlic as they are sautéed. Add 3 stalks celery, chopped, to the stew. Omit corn; add 2 cups frozen peas with the cornstarch mixture.

All American Chicken Stew: Make recipe as directed, except omit jalapeño peppers, salsa, chili powder, cumin, and black beans. Add 3 carrots sliced and 1 green bell pepper, chopped, to the mixture. Increase chicken broth to 4 cups. Mix cornstarch with heavy cream instead of lime juice.

CHICKEN

Brown Chicken

Add Broth

- The chicken is browned to add flavor and color to the stew. This step also helps the flour thicken the stew.

- You can substitute chicken breasts for the thighs; reduce cooking time to 6 to 7 hours.

- To remove the most sodium from the canned beans, rinse them well, then place in a saucepan and cover with water.

- Heat the beans about 10 minutes, then drain and rinse again. This will reduce sodium content by 30 percent.

- Homemade chicken broth, made with no salt, is the best choice for any low-sodium recipe.

- You can find good quality low-sodium stocks and broths—and even low-sodium bouillon cubes, but homemade still has less salt.

- You can substitute water for the broth in this recipe, because the chicken, as it cooks, will add lots of flavor.

- If the stew is already thick enough, you can omit the cornstarch. Just stir in the lime juice right before serving.

BAKED CRISP DRUMSTICKS

Yes, drumsticks can be crisp and juicy when baked in the oven

Drumsticks, those delicious chicken pieces favored by children, are a great choice for low-sodium diets. You can flavor them any way at all, and when baked with a crisp coating, they are succulent.

When you make chicken without salt, you'll notice the flavor of the meat. Chicken has a rich flavor, evocative of eggs, but heartier. Be sure you buy chicken that hasn't been injected with a marinade, sodium solution, or brine.

Serve these drumsticks with a flavorful dip made with lots of herbs and spices, or Roasted Garlic Dip. Since drumsticks come with their own handle, this is a fun recipe to serve. Add a fruit salad with a yogurt dressing and grilled bread for a great meal. *Yield: 8 drumsticks*

Ingredients

8 chicken drumsticks, skin removed

1 cup instant potato flakes

¹/₂ cup dried bread crumbs

2 tablespoons flour

1 teaspoon paprika

1 teaspoon dried oregano

¹/₄ teaspoon pepper

¹/₄ cup unsalted butter, melted

3 tablespoons Dijon mustard

Calories 171, **% Calories from Fat** 39%, **Fat** (g) 7, **Carbohydrates** (g) 16, **Protein** (g)10, **Sodium** (mg) 91, **Fiber** (g) 1, **Saturated Fat** (g) 4, **Cholesterol** (mg) 44

Baked Crisp Drumsticks

- Pat drumsticks dry. Preheat oven to 375°F. Place wire racks on rimmed baking sheet.

- On plate combine potato flakes, bread crumbs, flour, paprika, oregano, and pepper.

- In small bowl combine butter and mustard. Dip drumsticks in butter mixture, then in potato flake mixture to coat.

- Place on racks on baking sheets. Bake 55 to 65 minutes, until chicken is crisp and 165°F.

···· RECIPE VARIATION ····

Herb Dip: In medium bowl combine 1 cup thick Greek yogurt and 2 tablespoons lemon juice; whisk until smooth. Add 1 tablespoon chopped basil, 1 tablespoon fresh oregano leaves, 1 tablespoon fresh thyme leaves, and ¼ teaspoon white pepper; blend well. Cover and refrigerate up to 3 days.

Spicy Crisp Drumsticks: Make recipe as directed, except omit dried oregano. Add 1 teaspoon each chili powder, cumin, crushed dried red pepper flakes, and ground red chiles to the bread crumb mixture. Bake as directed; serve with a homemade salsa for dipping.

Coat Drumsticks

- The potato flakes add a depth of flavor to the coating. Be sure you buy plain flakes that are low in sodium.

- Also read the bread crumb package label. Plain dry bread crumbs are your best bet; flavored crumbs may have added sodium.

- Don't prepare this recipe ahead of time, or the coating will soften as the potato flakes absorb moisture.

- You can leave the skin on the drumsticks, but remove it for less fat; with this coating, it won't be missed.

Bake on Wire Racks

- You can find racks to fit in your baking pans or sheets in any grocery store.

- Buy the sturdiest racks you can find; some are quite cheap and will fall apart after several uses.

- The racks allow the heat to circulate all the way around the chicken so the coating becomes crisp.

- Let the drumsticks cool 5 minutes before serving with dip.

PASTA CHICKEN CASSEROLE

The flavors of Greece make this casserole come alive

Casseroles are a wonderful way to serve a crowd with ease. They'll feed a family with just the addition of a green salad or fruit salad and some bread or bread sticks.

Greek recipes are usually flavored with lemon, garlic, feta cheese, and olives. The last two ingredients are very salty. While olive oil contains no sodium, olives are processed with lots of salt. Olives can be added to the recipe; be advised they

will add 70 to 80 mg of sodium per tablespoon.

Feta cheese is very strong, so it can be used in recipes sparingly. If you can consume more sodium, sprinkle some feta on top of the casserole for more flavor. Each tablespoon has 100 mg of sodium. *Yield: Serves 6*

Ingredients

1 onion, chopped

3 cloves garlic, minced

1 tablespoon olive oil

3 boneless, skinless chicken breasts, cubed

2 tablespoons flour

1 teaspoon paprika

1 teaspoon dried oregano

1/4 teaspoon white pepper

3 tomatoes, chopped

2 green bell peppers, chopped

1 cup low-sodium chicken broth

2 tablespoons lemon juice

1 teaspoon grated lemon zest

1/4 cup crumbled feta cheese

1/4 cup chopped parsley

12 ounces rotini pasta

Calories 410, **% Calories from Fat** 26%, **Fat** (g) 12, **Carbohydrates** (g) 50, **Protein** (g) 25, **Sodium** (mg) 136, **Fiber** (g) 3, **Saturated Fat** (g) 4, **Cholesterol** (mg) 52

Pasta Chicken Casserole

- Bring large pot of water to a boil. Preheat oven to 350°F. Grease a 3-quart casserole dish.

- Cook onion and garlic in olive oil. Coat chicken in flour, paprika, oregano, and pepper; add to skillet. Cook and stir until chicken is done.

- Add tomatoes, green peppers, broth, juice, and zest; simmer until thickened. Add cheese and parsley; remove from heat.

- Cook pasta until al dente. Drain; add to chicken mixture. Pour into casserole. Bake 25 to 35 minutes.

·········· GREEN ● LIGHT ··········

Most casseroles can be made well ahead of time. If they contain pasta, undercook the pasta slightly, as it will soften as it sits in the casserole. Most casseroles also freeze well. Do not bake the casserole; cool after assembly, then seal, label, and freeze up to 4 months. Thaw overnight in the fridge and bake.

Add Tomatoes and Broth

- To chop tomatoes, wash first, then cut in half. Place cut side down on work surface and cut into slices.

- Then cut those slices into cubes. You can seed the tomato before cubing it.

- To seed, just gently squeeze the tomato halves over the sink to release the seeds and some of the tomato jelly.

- But the casserole is good with the seeds and jelly, and they add more vitamin C to the recipe.

Add Pasta to Casserole

- Make sure to grease the casserole dish with unsalted butter or use a nonstick cooking spray.

- Read the labels on the cooking spray! Smart Balance is one brand that has no sodium, cholesterol, or trans fats.

- Stir the mixture gently when you add the pasta so it doesn't break up.

- The casserole will be bubbly and browned around the edges when it's done. Let cool 5 to 10 minutes, then serve.

ROAST LEMON CHICKEN

This classic lemon chicken is roasted with garlic and olive oil

There's almost nothing that smells better than a chicken roasting in the oven. The rich flavor, especially when accented with lemon and garlic, will make you swoon.

And the taste is just as good! If you can, look for organic and free-range chickens. Since they were raised in sunshine and fresh air, the meat has much more flavor. Anything that adds flavor to a low-sodium diet is a good thing.

Butter is an important ingredient in roast chicken. It adds lots of flavor and helps keep the chicken moist. You can reduce the amount if you'd like, but be sure to use unsalted butter.

Serve this chicken with mashed potatoes flavored with garlic and roasted green beans. *Yield: Serves 4*

Ingredients

- 1 (3-pound) roasting chicken
- 2 lemons, sliced
- 4 cloves garlic, crushed
- 3 tablespoons unsalted butter
- 1 teaspoon paprika
- 1/2 teaspoon dry mustard
- 1/4 teaspoon garlic powder
- 1/4 teaspoon white pepper
- 3 tablespoons lemon juice

Calories 273, **% Calories from Fat** 43%, **Fat** (g) 13, **Carbohydrates** (g) 6, **Protein** (g) 33, **Sodium** (mg) 125, **Fiber** (g) 1, **Saturated Fat** (g) 7, **Cholesterol** (mg) 125

Roast Lemon Chicken

- Rinse chicken and pat dry. Preheat oven to 350°F.

- Place half of the sliced lemons in roasting pan. Top with chicken. Place remaining lemon slices in cavity of chicken along with garlic.

- In saucepan, melt butter; add paprika, mustard, garlic powder, pepper, and lemon juice. Pour half over chicken.

- Roast chicken 30 minutes, then baste with remaining butter mixture. Roast 40 to 45 minutes longer, until chicken registers 180 °F. Cover and let stand 15 minutes; slice to serve.

Plain Roasted Chicken: Make recipe as directed, except omit the garlic and lemon juice. Add several sprigs of fresh thyme, basil, and oregano to the chicken cavity. Add 1 teaspoon each dried thyme, basil, and oregano to the butter mixture used to baste the chicken. Roast as directed.

Curried Roasted Chicken: Make recipe as directed, except reduce lemon juice to 1 tablespoon. Omit dry mustard and garlic powder; add 1 tablespoon curry powder to the butter mixture. Roast chicken as directed. Serve with mango chutney, toasted coconut, and chopped unsalted peanuts.

Lemons and Garlic in Cavity

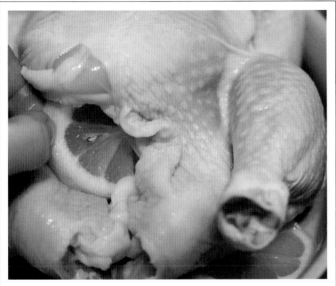

Baste Chicken

- For even more flavor and to release more juice, roll the lemons on the countertop before you slice them.

- The garlic should be crushed with the side of a chef's knife. You can leave the peel on.

- The lemons and garlic in the cavity of the chicken are just for flavor.

- They won't look pretty when the chicken is done, so don't remove them. Just carve the chicken at the table and leave these ingredients in the cavity.

- The chicken is basted while it's roasting to make the skin crisp and turn it a beautiful brown color.

- The basting also adds flavor to the chicken and keeps it from drying out.

- You can make a pan sauce with the drippings. Pour and scrape them into a pan and add 1 cup sodium-free chicken broth.

- Bring the sauce to a boil; simmer 4 to 5 minutes while the chicken rests. Serve sauce with chicken.

GRILLED HAMBURGERS

Hamburgers grilled over charcoal are juicy and delicious

Hamburgers cooked on the grill have a flavor and aroma that just can't be duplicated indoors. The outsides become crisp and smoky tasting, while the burger stays tender and juicy.

For the best grilled burgers, follow a few rules. Make sure the coals are covered with gray ash before you start, or pre-heat a gas grill at least 10 minutes. Never press down on the burgers while they are grilling; that just removes the juice!

And always cook burgers well-done, or to165°F.

A panade, made with bread crumbs and buttermilk, keeps the well-done burgers moist and juicy.

Serve these burgers on toasted buns, with homemade salt-free mustard or low-sodium ketchup. *Yield: Serves 4*

Ingredients

1 tablespoon unsalted butter

$1/2$ cup minced onion

3 tablespoons buttermilk

1 slice Whole Wheat Bread, crumbled

$1/4$ teaspoon pepper

1 tablespoon minced chives

1 teaspoon dry mustard

$1 1/2$ pounds 80 percent lean ground beef

4 whole wheat hamburger buns

2 tablespoons unsalted butter

$1/3$ cup low-sodium ketchup

4 lettuce leaves

1 tomato, sliced

Calories 638, **% Calories from Fat** 46%, **Fat** (g) 32, **Carbohydrates** (g) 50, **Protein** (g) 38, **Sodium** (mg) 157, **Fiber** (g) 157, **Saturated Fat** (g) 4, **Cholesterol** (mg) 158

Grilled Hamburgers

- In small pan melt 1 table-spoon butter. Add onion; cook until caramelized, about 12 to15 minutes.

- Place in bowl; add butter-milk, bread crumbs, pepper, chives, and mustard; mix well. Add beef; mix gently.

- Form into four patties; make an indentation in cen-ter with a spoon. Grill over medium direct coals 10 to 12 minutes, turning once, until 165°F.

- Spread buns with 2 table-spoons butter; toast on grill. Assemble burgers with buns, ketchup, lettuce, and tomato.

Grilled Stuffed Hamburgers: Make recipe as directed, except reduce buttermilk to 1 tablespoon and bread crumbs to 2 tablespoons. Shape mixture into eight thin patties. Top four patties with 2 tablespoons shredded low-sodium cheese; place remaining patties on top and seal edges. Cook, turning only once, until well-done.

Spicy Grilled Hamburgers: Make recipe as directed, except add 3 minced garlic cloves to the onion mixture. Omit chives. Add 2 minced jalapeños to the onion mixture. Add ¼ teaspoon cayenne pepper to the burger mixture. Top the grilled burgers with low-sodium salsa and some sliced avocados.

Add Beef

Shape and Cook Burgers

- It's important to handle the beef as little as possible for the juiciest burgers.

- Combine all the additions to the meat first, then add the beef and mix gently but thoroughly using your hands.

- If you overwork the mixture after the beef is added, the burgers will be tough.

- For the lowest sodium content, make your own bread crumbs from homemade bread. Cube bread and pulse in a food processor until fine. Store bread crumbs in the freezer.

- To shape the burgers, form into round patties about ¾-inch thick. Shape the edges so they are smooth and firm.

- An indentation is pressed into the center of the burgers so they will remain flat when they are done.

- If you don't make the indentation, using the back of a spoon, the burgers will puff up and not sit on the buns or hold condiments.

- Watch the burgers carefully on the grill. Move them to lower heat if they are cooking too quickly.

BEEF

85

MEATBALLS IN TOMATO SAUCE

Tender meatballs in rich tomato sauce are perfect on pasta

Meatballs are traditional in many cuisines, especially Italian. They are fun and easy to make and can be used in many ways, from sandwiches to pasta sauces.

Meatballs are the perfect convenience food. The precooked frozen meatballs you find in the supermarket are delicious and easy, but they can be very high in sodium. Make your own to control your salt intake. Meatballs freeze very well;

cook them completely and freeze, then you can use them as you would the processed type.

As with burgers, don't handle the meat much when making meatballs. Mix all the other ingredients first, then add the meat. And make sure that you make the meatballs the same size so they cook evenly. *Yield: Serves 6*

KNACK LOW-SALT COOKING

Ingredients

1 cup finely chopped onion

6 garlic cloves, minced, divided

2 tablespoons unsalted butter, divided

2 tablespoons chopped parsley

1 teaspoon dried oregano

2 tablespoons grated Romano cheese

1 (6-ounce) can no-salt-added tomato paste, divided

1/4 teaspoon pepper

1 cup soft fresh bread crumbs

1 1/4 pounds 80 percent lean ground beef

2 (14.5-ounce) cans no-salt-added diced tomatoes

3 tablespoons vodka

1/2 cup light cream

1/4 cup chopped parsley

1/2 teaspoon crushed red pepper flakes

Calories 373, **% Calories from Fat** 50%, **Fat** (g) 21, **Carbohydrates** (g) 21, **Protein** (g) 23, **Sodium** (mg) 167, **Fiber** (g) 3, **Saturated Fat** (g) 10, **Cholesterol** (mg) 89

Meatballs in Tomato Sauce

- Cook minced onion and 2 cloves garlic in half the butter until tender.

- Place in bowl with parsley, oregano, cheese, 1 tablespoon tomato paste, pepper, and bread crumbs.

- Add ground beef; form into 24 meatballs. Brown in same saucepan in remaining butter; remove and set aside.

- In same saucepan, cook 4 cloves garlic. Add remaining tomato paste, tomatoes, vodka, cream, parsley, and red pepper flakes; simmer 5 minutes. Add meatballs; simmer 40 minutes. Serve over hot cooked pasta.

ZOOM

To form meatballs quickly and evenly, use a small ice cream scoop. A 2-tablespoon scoop is just about the right size. Dip into the ground beef mixture and form a ball; smooth out the edges with your hands. This method will make very tender meatballs because they aren't overworked.

• • • • RECIPE VARIATION • • • •

Tex-Mex Meatballs: Make recipe as directed, except add 2 minced jalapeño peppers to the onion mixture. Use ½ cup crushed baked unsalted tortilla chips in place of the bread crumbs. Omit the vodka and cream; add ½ cup low-sodium salsa to the tomato mixture; simmer meatballs as directed.

Form Meatballs

- The onions and garlic must be cooked and softened before adding to the meatballs.

- They just won't soften in the meatballs, as the sauce doesn't penetrate to the center of the meat.

- Chop the onions and garlic finely for best results. They will add moisture as well as flavor to the meatballs.

- The meatballs, like any ground meat product, should be cooked to 165°F.

Simmer Sauce

- Stir the sauce very well so the tomato paste dissolves into the sauce. Be sure the sauce is combined before you add the meatballs.

- Stir the sauce often as it cooks. Because tomatoes are high in sugar, they can burn easily unless they are manipulated.

- You can substitute a low-sodium bottled pasta sauce for the homemade sauce if you'd like.

- But if you do that, be sure to read the label and compare sodium milligrams per serving.

BEEF

SWISS STEAK

Swiss steak is pure comfort food, and this version is easy

Swiss steak is made from round steak that has been tenderized, sautéed, then cooked in a rich tomato sauce.

Round steak is an inexpensive cut and is easy to find in the supermarket. Look for well-marbled meat that is firm, with little or no juices in the package.

Use a very sharp knife to cut the steak into six even pieces. If you use a meat mallet to pound the steak, the side with

points is classically used for Swiss steak. In fact you can pound the flour mixture into the steak for the classic recipe.

Swiss steak should be served with mashed potatoes to soak up all the wonderful sauce, or you can use hot cooked pasta. *Yield: Serves 6*

Ingredients

2 pounds round steak

$^1/_8$ teaspoon salt

$^1/_4$ teaspoon pepper

1 teaspoon paprika

$^1/_4$ cup flour

1 teaspoon dried thyme leaves

2 tablespoons unsalted butter

1 tablespoon olive oil

1 onion, chopped

3 cloves garlic, minced

2 stalks celery, chopped

1 (8-ounce) package mushrooms, sliced

2 (14.5-ounce) cans no-salt-added diced tomatoes, undrained

$^1/_4$ cup dry red wine

Calories 306, **% Calories from Fat** 36%, **Fat** (g) 12, **Carbohydrates** (g) 11, **Protein** (g) 34, **Sodium** (mg) 165, **Fiber** (g) 2, **Saturated Fat** (g) 5, **Cholesterol** (mg) 86

Swiss Steak

- Cut steak into 6 pieces; pound with meat mallet or rolling pin. Sprinkle with salt and pepper.

- Mix paprika, flour, and thyme; dredge meat. Melt butter and olive oil in large saucepan; brown meat 4 to 5 minutes, turning once; remove.

- Add onion, garlic, celery, and mushrooms to pan; cook and stir 5 to 6 minutes. Add tomatoes; simmer 10 minutes.

- Return steak to sauce with wine; simmer, covered, 35 to 45 minutes, until meat is very tender; serve.

Slow Cooker Swiss Steak: Make recipe as directed, except when the steak is browned, place in a 3- to 4-quart slow cooker. Make the sauce as directed; simmer 10 minutes, then pour over the meat in the slow cooker. Cover and cook on low 7 to 9 hours, until the meat is tender. To thicken the sauce, uncover and cook 30 minutes on high.

Swiss Steak with Peppers: Make recipe as directed, except omit celery and mushrooms. Add 1 green bell pepper, 1 red bell pepper, and 1 orange bell pepper, all sliced, to the sauce, for the last 10 minutes of cooking time, until the peppers and steak are tender.

Pound Steak

- Place the steak on plastic wrap before you pound it. Pound the steak gently but thoroughly.

- The goal is to make the steak about half as thick as it was originally. Be careful not to tear or rip the meat.

- You can dredge the steak in the flour mixture before or after it is pounded.

- Flouring the steak before pounding really helps flavor the meat and helps it become very tender as it cooks.

Simmer Steak in Sauce

- Push the steak into the sauce so it is covered, but make sure there is sauce under the steak to keep it tender.

- Simmer the steak in the sauce over low heat so it won't burn during the long cooking time.

- The vegetables will almost dissolve into the sauce as they cook, adding flavor and lots of nutrition.

- You can use other vegetables in the sauce, like bell peppers, corn, or more exotic mushrooms.

GRILLED STEAK

A perfectly grilled steak is one of the joys of summer, and you don't need added salt

Steaks are a splurge, but although they are high in fat, a juicy and flavorful steak can be very low in sodium.

Since this is a special occasion recipe, buy the best steak you can afford. Rib-eye steaks are a good value, because they combine good flavor with a tender and juicy texture.

Let the steaks stand at room temperature for 15 to 30 minutes before you put them on the grill. The steaks will experience less of a shock when placed on the grill and will be more tender.

These steaks are seasoned with garlic, paprika, herbs, pepper, and lemon juice for great flavor. Sear them over high heat, then cook over medium heat until desired doneness. *Yield: Serves 4*

Ingredients

4 (6- to 8-ounce) rib-eye steaks

4 cloves garlic, minced

1 teaspoon paprika

1/4 teaspoon pepper

1 tablespoon lemon juice

1 teaspoon dried marjoram

2 tablespoons unsalted butter

Calories 418, *% Calories from Fat* 59%, **Fat** (g) 27, **Carbohydrates** (g) 2, **Protein** (g) 40, **Sodium** (mg) 84, **Fiber** (g) 0.4, **Saturated Fat** (g) 12, **Cholesterol** (mg) 177

Grilled Steak

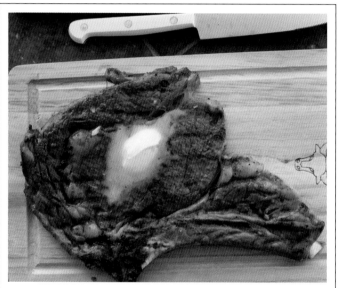

- Let steaks stand at room temperature 15 minutes. Meanwhile, combine garlic, paprika, and pepper; mash into a paste.

- Stir lemon juice and marjoram into garlic paste. Rub on steaks, both sides; let stand 15 minutes.

- Prepare and preheat grill. Place steaks on rack 6 inches from medium coals; cover grill.

- Grill without moving 5 minutes, then turn. Grill, covered, 6 to 10 minutes, until desired doneness. Remove; top with butter and cover. Let stand 5 minutes, then serve.

To build a charcoal fire, use a chimney starter. Place the coals in the starter, add newspaper to the bottom, and light the paper. Let the coals burn until covered with ash, then arrange in the grill pan. You'll need about 100 coals to cook four to six steaks.

Steak Sauce: Cook 1 onion, chopped, and 3 cloves garlic, minced, in 1 tablespoon oil until tender. Add ⅓ cup chopped apple, ¼ cup raisins, ½ teaspoon each ground celery and fennel seeds; cook 5 minutes. Add ½ cup low-sodium ketchup and 2 tablespoons low-sodium mustard; simmer 10 minutes. Blend until smooth and refrigerate up to 3 days.

Rub Marinade into Steaks

- This marinade has concentrated flavor. You can use any combination of herbs or spices to create your own.

- Rub the marinade evenly into the steaks using your hands. You can make the marinade ahead of time; refrigerate it until you want to eat.

- The steaks can be marinated in the refrigerator 2 to 3 hours instead of at room temperature.

- Make sure the grill rack is clean, and rub it lightly with oil before adding the steaks.

Turn Steaks on Grill

- Be sure the coals are ready before you add the steaks. They will be covered with gray ash, with no flames.

- Don't move the steaks until they release from the grill. When they are ready to turn, they will be easy to move.

- When you turn the steaks, leave them alone again until they release easily.

- Cook the steaks with the grill lid down. This helps hold in the heat so the meat cooks evenly.

BEEF

BEEF BRISKET

Long-cooking brisket is meltingly tender and juicy

When you want some real beef, brisket is the best choice, as it has a lot of flavor. This cut is tough, though, so has to be cooked at low temperature for a very long time.

Because this is a tougher cut, it is quite inexpensive, so is a boon to tight budgets. The cut has a lot of connective tissue, which has to melt before the meat is done.

Choose a brisket that Is firm, with good marbling and a narrow rim of white fat. When cooked in the slow cooker, the meat does not need to be browned, but for added flavor this step adds caramelization.

Serve this brisket with mashed potatoes and sautéed green beans and a fruit pie for dessert. *Yield: Serves 8*

Ingredients

1 teaspoon black pepper

$^1/_2$ teaspoon crushed red pepper flakes

1 teaspoon paprika

1 teaspoon dried oregano leaves

4 cloves garlic, minced

1 (3-pound) beef brisket, trimmed

2 onions, chopped

$^1/_2$ cup low-sodium beef broth

Calories 233, **% Calories from Fat** 39%, **Fat** (g) 10, **Carbohydrates** (g) 4, **Protein** (g) 30, **Sodium** (mg) 120, **Fiber** (g) 1, **Saturated Fat** (g) 4, **Cholesterol** (mg) 92

Beef Brisket

- In small bowl, combine pepper, pepper flakes, paprika, oregano, and garlic; mash into a paste.

- Rub all over the brisket. Place onions in 4- to 5-quart slow cooker; add beef broth.

- Place brisket on top of onions. Cover and cook on low 8 to 10 hours, until beef is very tender.

- Remove beef, cover with foil, and let stand 10 minutes. Strain the broth and place in small bowl for serving. Slice beef to serve.

Stovetop Beef Brisket: Season the brisket as directed, then brown in 2 tablespoons olive oil in a very large skillet. Chop onions and add to pan. Pour over 1 cup low-sodium beef broth and ¼ cup dry red wine and bring to a simmer. Reduce heat to low, cover tightly, and simmer 2½ hours, until beef is very tender.

Oven Beef Brisket: Rub seasonings into brisket. Heat 2 tablespoons olive oil in a large skillet and sear the meat on all sides. Place onions in the roasting pan and add the brisket. Pour beef broth over. Cover tightly with foil or the pan lid and bake at 300°F 5 to 6 hours, until the meat is very tender.

Season Brisket

- Make sure the paste is evenly distributed over the brisket so no one spot has too much.

- You can use any combination of herbs and spices to create your own seasoning blend.

- Combine ground cumin with cayenne pepper, ground red chiles, and dry mustard for a potent rub.

- Or use a combination of dried herbs and pepper for a milder rub that adds lots of flavor.

Cook Brisket

- Trim off excess fat from the brisket. There should only be about ¼ inch of fat on any one part of the meat.

- This fat will change how the meat cooks in the slow cooker, so it has to be removed.

- You can add other vegetables to the slow cooker if you'd like. Potatoes and carrots are good choices.

- Let the meat stand after it comes out of the slow cooker so the juices redistribute.

BEEF

POT ROAST

Everyone needs a good pot roast recipe; this one is low sodium, too

Pot roast really isn't pot roast unless it's cooked with lots of root vegetables. The vegetables add wonderful flavor to the meat and add fiber and vitamins, too.

Root vegetables such as parsnips, potatoes, carrots, and onions are traditionally used with pot roast. They become meltingly tender in the moist environment and long cooking time. You can cut them into chunks or slices as you prefer.

The first step, browning the meat in oil, is important to flavor development. This high heat causes the sugars and proteins in the meat to break down and recombine, forming complex flavor and beautiful color.

Serve this beautiful one-pot meal with a fresh green salad and some dry red wine, with toasted garlic bread on the side. *Yield: Serves 10*

Ingredients

1 (4-pound) tri tip beef roast

3 tablespoons flour

2 teaspoons paprika

¹/₄ teaspoon pepper

1 tablespoon unsalted butter

1 tablespoon olive oil

2 onions, chopped

2 cloves garlic

2 carrots, sliced

1 cup sliced mushrooms

¹/₂ cup low-sodium beef broth

¹/₂ cup dry red wine

1 (14.5-ounce) can no-salt-added tomatoes

1 teaspoon dried basil

¹/₂ teaspoon dried savory

1 teaspoon sugar

Calories 418, **% Calories from Fat** 49%, **Fat** (g) 23, **Carbohydrates** (g) 7, **Protein** (g) 43, **Sodium** (mg) 127, **Fiber** (g) 1, **Saturated Fat** (g) 8, **Cholesterol** (mg) 156

Pot Roast

- Rub roast with flour, paprika, and pepper. Heat butter and olive oil in Dutch oven; brown roast on all sides.

- Add onions, garlic, carrots, and mushrooms to pan with roast. Pour broth, wine, and tomatoes over all; add basil, savory, and sugar.

- Cover and bake at 300°F 3½ to 4½ hours, until meat is very tender.

- Remove meat; cover with foil to keep warm. Puree ingredients in Dutch oven with immersion blender; boil 5 to 6 minutes. Serve with beef.

The best cuts of beef for pot roast include chuck, top round, bottom round, rump, and brisket. These cuts are full of flavor and tough unless cooked in low, moist heat. Ask your butcher for the best cuts, since many stores have different names for different cuts and types of beef.

· · · · RECIPE VARIATION · · · ·

Slow Cooker Pot Roast: Make recipe as directed, except after the beef is browned, remove from pan and add onions; cook 5 minutes. Place onions, carrots, and 3 sliced potatoes in 4- to 5-quart slow cooker and top with beef. Add broth, tomatoes, and seasonings. Cover and cook on low 8 to 9 hours, until tender.

Brown Roast

- For even more flavor, cut garlic cloves into slivers. Pierce the meat with a knife and insert the slivers.

- Don't move the meat until it releases easily from the pan. When it is properly browned, it will be easy to turn.

- Brown the roast over medium heat. Don't let the roast burn; keep an eye on it and turn it as soon as it releases from the pan.

- You can sprinkle the roast with other ingredients, too; dry mustard or dried herbs would be delicious.

Puree Sauce

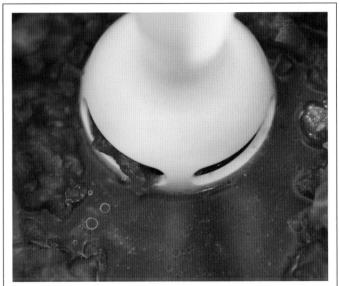

- The vegetables will be very soft and meltingly tender when the roast is cooked.

- An immersion blender is the easiest way to puree the sauce, but you can puree it, in batches, in a blender or food processor.

- If you want to add potatoes or parsnips to this recipe, arrange them around the roast.

- Remove the potatoes with tongs along with the meat before you puree the sauce.

BEEF

GRILLED CHOPS

Marinated pork chops are juicy and tender cooked on the grill

Pork chops are delicious and succulent when properly prepared. Marinating them will always add flavor and make them very tender.

The grill adds wonderful smoky flavor to pork chops. The exterior is caramelized, and the interior stays moist and juicy.

Pork does not need to be cooked to well-done. Today's pork is very safe. Cook it to medium well, which is 150°F on a food thermometer. Remember: The temperature will rise 5 to 10 degrees after the meat is pulled from the heat, so it will reach the safe temperature during standing time.

Pork chops can be marinated 24 to 36 hours, but no longer or the meat may become mushy. Serve these chops with grilled corn on the cob and a tomato salad. *Yield: Serves 6*

Ingredients

2 tablespoons Dijon mustard

3 tablespoons lemon juice

1 teaspoon grated lemon zest

1 tablespoon olive oil

3 cloves garlic, minced

¼ teaspoon pepper

1 teaspoon dried oregano

6 (6-ounce) 1-inch thick pork chops

Grilled Chops

- In large heavy-duty plastic bag, combine mustard, lemon juice, zest, olive oil, garlic, pepper, and oregano.

- Add pork chops; seal and massage to coat. Place in dish in refrigerator. Marinate 8 to 24 hours, turning twice.

- Prepare and preheat grill. Remove chops from marinade; reserve marinade.

- Grill chops 6 inches from medium coals 11 to 14 minutes, brushing once with reserved marinade and turning once, until temperature registers 150°F. Cover; let stand 5 minutes.

Calories 378, **% Calories from Fat** 54%, **Fat** (g) 23, **Carbohydrates** (g) 2, **Protein** (g) 40, **Sodium** (mg) 142, **Fiber** (g) 0.4, **Saturated Fat** (g) 8, **Cholesterol** (mg) 122

Marinate Chops

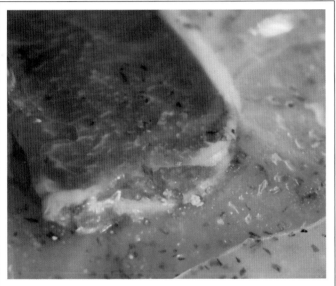

- Preparing a marinade in a heavy-duty plastic bag helps make cleanup a breeze.

- Always put the bag into a dish in the refrigerator. If the bag leaks, you won't have a mess on your hands.

- You can make a marinade out of just about any ingredients. Just be sure to include an acid like vinegar or lemon juice and some oil.

- To use a marinade as a sauce, add 1 cup chicken broth to the reserved mixture; boil for 2 minutes, then pour over the finished chops.

Grill Chops

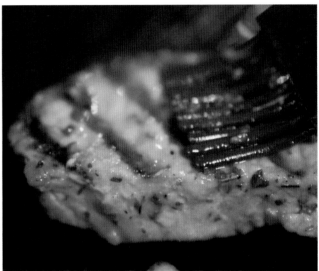

- Pork chops should always be grilled over medium heat, not high heat.

- The chops are leaner than steak, so cooking them over high heat will dry them out quickly.

- Always discard any remaining marinade when the chops are done unless you boil it to serve on the side.

- Be sure to "cook off" the marinade. This means to turn the marinade to the heat when you brush it on, just for a minute or two.

PORK

GLAZED TENDERLOIN

Pork tenderloin is marinated in a flavorful mixture, then baked

Pork tenderloin is a more expensive cut than other types of pork. But it's easy to use, lean, and tender, and there is no waste.

Because this cut is so lean, it's better if marinated first. You can find marinated pork products in the supermarket, but these are usually full of salt.

Once you hit on a marinade you really enjoy, you can freeze

the pork in the marinade. Let thaw in the refrigerator overnight, then cook as directed.

Read the label to make sure that the tenderloin you buy hasn't been injected with a brine solution.

A glaze is a bit thicker than a marinade and clings to the meat as it cooks. This forms a coating or crust on the meat that is very delicious. *Yield: Serves 8*

Ingredients

1 tablespoon olive oil

3 cloves garlic, minced

$1/2$ cup minced onion

1 star anise

1 tablespoon brown sugar

2 tablespoons rice vinegar

1 tablespoon chile paste

1 tablespoon grated ginger root

$1/2$ teaspoon ground ginger

$1/2$ teaspoon pepper

1 tablespoon low-sodium soy sauce

2 (1 $1/2$-pound) pork tenderloins

Calories 222, **% Calories from Fat** 38%, **Fat** (g) 9, **Carbohydrates** (g) 3, **Protein** (g) 30, **Sodium** (mg) 146, **Fiber** (g) 0.3, **Saturated Fat** (g) 3, **Cholesterol** (mg) 94

Glazed Tenderloin

- In large heavy-duty plastic bag, combine all ingredients except tenderloins.

- Pierce tenderloins with fork 10 times each. Add to bag with other ingredients. Seal and knead.

- Place in glass dish; marinate in refrigerator 8 to 24 hours. Preheat oven to 400°F.

- Place tenderloins and marinade in glass dish; remove star anise. Bake 35 to 45 minutes, until meat thermometer registers 150°F. Cover, let stand 5 minutes, then serve.

Spicy Pork Tenderloin: Make recipe as directed, except omit star anise, rice vinegar, ginger root, ground ginger, and soy sauce. Add 1 minced serrano pepper to the onion mixture along with 2 teaspoons chili powder and 1 teaspoon cumin. Marinate and bake chops as directed; serve with homemade tomato salsa.

Honey Glazed Tenderloin: Make recipe as directed, except omit anise, chile paste, ginger root, ground ginger, and soy sauce. Add ¼ cup honey to the onion mixture along with 1 tablespoon brown sugar and ⅛ teaspoon cayenne pepper. Marinate and bake the tenderloin as directed, basting once with marinade.

Mix Marinade

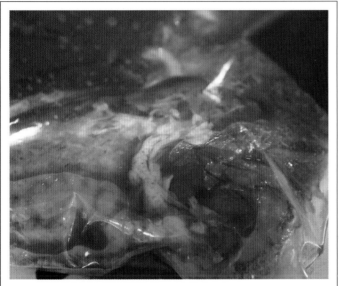

Bake Tenderloin

- Because the marinade is baked along with the pork, it's not necessary to cook the onions and garlic first.

- If you want a caramelized onion flavor, you can sauté the onions in the oil before adding to the marinade.

- The marinade can be made ahead of time; store it covered in the refrigerator up to 3 days.

- Use your own favorite combination of herbs and spices to make the marinade your own.

- For best results use a thermometer in the tenderloin. Insert it before baking.

- Use the type of probe with a wire that attaches the tip to a programmable timer. The timer is placed on the oven.

- Punch in the temperature you want and start cooking. It will beep when the pork is ready.

- Then let the tenderloin stand, covered, 5 to 8 minutes to let the juices redistribute; carve to serve.

PORK

STUFFED CHOPS
Tender pork chops are stuffed with a sweet-and-sour mixture

Stuffed pork chops are a wonderful treat. The stuffing complements the tender texture and slightly sweet flavor of the pork. This is a great recipe for entertaining.

For stuffing, pork chops should be at least 1-inch thick. You can use boneless or bone-in chops. The bone-in chops will have more flavor. Make sure you purchase untreated pork chops.

You can stuff the chops with your favorite stuffing recipe or with any combination of sautéed vegetables or dried fruits. Use your imagination, and when you hit on a winner, be sure to write it down so you can recreate the recipe.

Serve these chops with roasted potatoes drizzled with olive oil, steamed asparagus, and a fruit salad made with grapes and cantaloupe. *Yield: Serves 6*

Ingredients

1 tablespoon unsalted butter

4 cups chopped red cabbage

1 red onion, chopped

3 cloves garlic, minced

2 tablespoons balsamic vinegar

1 tablespoon brown sugar

$\frac{1}{4}$ cup water

6 (1-inch thick) boneless pork chops

2 tablespoons olive oil

1 onion, chopped

$\frac{1}{4}$ cup brown sugar

$\frac{1}{4}$ cup balsamic vinegar

$\frac{1}{4}$ cup water

Calories 367, **% Calories from Fat** 55%, **Fat** (g) 22, **Carbohydrates** (g)17, **Protein** (g) 24, **Sodium** (mg) 69, **Fiber** (g)2, **Saturated Fat** (g) 7, **Cholesterol** (mg) 73

Stuffed Chops

- In large saucepan melt butter. Add cabbage, red onion, and garlic; cook and stir until tender, about 10 minutes.

- Add 2 tablespoons vinegar, 1 tablespoon brown sugar, and ¼ cup water; simmer 10 minutes. Remove and let cool.

- Cut a large slit in the side of the pork chops; stuff with cabbage mixture. Heat olive oil in same pan; brown chops.

- Add onion, ¼ cup each brown sugar, balsamic vinegar, and water. Cover; simmer 25 to 35 minutes, until chops are tender.

Dried Fruit Stuffed Pork Chops: Make recipe as directed, except omit red cabbage. Add ½ cup each golden raisins, dark raisins, and dried currants; 2 teaspoons curry powder; and a small chopped apple to the red onion and garlic mixture. Stuff pork chops, add sauce, and simmer as directed.

Spicy Stuffed Pork Chops: Make recipe as directed, except omit cabbage, all balsamic vinegar, and all brown sugar. Substitute 1½ cups soft fresh bread crumbs for the cabbage. Add 1 serrano and 1 jalapeño pepper—both minced—to the onion mixture. Combine 1 cup salsa with water; pour over chops and simmer.

Prepare Stuffing

- The cabbage will cook down considerably after 10 minutes on the heat. You can substitute green cabbage for the red if you'd like.

- Red onions are sweeter and milder than yellow or white onions. They complement the red cabbage well.

- Chop the cabbage and the onions in fairly small pieces, about the same size so they cook evenly.

- You can make the stuffing ahead of time; refrigerate it until it's time to stuff the chops.

Stuff Chops

- Make the opening into the pork chops as small as possible. Move your knife around inside to enlarge the cavity.

- Be careful to not cut through the chops when you are making the cavity. If you do, the chops will still be delicious, just not as pretty.

- Balsamic vinegar is aged for years and adds a sweet note to the sauce. Buy the best you can afford.

- If there is any leftover stuffing mixture, just spread it on top of the chops after they are browned.

PORK

101

LEMON PORK MEDALLIONS

Medallions, cut from the tenderloin, are juicy in a tart lemon sauce

Medallions are cut from the larger tenderloin, then usually pounded so they are quite thin and cook quickly.

You don't need to pound the medallions; if thicker they will just take longer to cook. Simmer ½-inch-thick medallions 15 minutes, until just slightly pink inside.

Because the medallions are quite small, serve two or three of them per person. You'll need to use the largest skillet you have so the medallions brown evenly and don't steam in their own juices.

The ends of the tenderloin are tapered, so they don't work well for medallions. Cut them off and freeze them to use later in stir-fries.

Serve this dish with a rice pilaf and glazed carrots. *Yield: Serves 6*

Ingredients

1 (2-pound) pork tenderloin

2 tablespoons flour

¹/₂ teaspoon paprika

¹/₈ teaspoon white pepper

2 tablespoons unsalted butter

1 tablespoon olive oil

1 onion, chopped

2 cloves garlic, minced

1 tablespoon minced fresh tarragon

1 cup low-sodium chicken broth

¹/₃ cup lemon juice

1 teaspoon lemon zest

Lemon Pork Medallions

- Cut pork into ½-inch thick medallions. Place, cut side up, on plastic wrap; cover with plastic wrap.

- Pound to ¼-inch thickness. Sprinkle with flour, paprika, and pepper. Heat butter and olive oil in large skillet.

- Brown medallions over medium heat, turning once, about 3 to 4 minutes; remove from heat.

- Add onion, garlic, and tarragon; cook 4 minutes. Add broth; simmer 5 minutes over medium heat. Add pork, lemon juice, and zest; simmer 5 to 6 minutes, until done.

Calories 258, **% Calories from Fat** 40%, **Fat** (g) 11, **Carbohydrates** (g) 5, **Protein** (g) 33, **Sodium** (mg) 172, **Fiber** (g) 1, **Saturated Fat** (g) 5, **Cholesterol** (mg) 109

Curried Pork Medallions: Make recipe as directed, except substitute 1 tablespoon curry powder for the paprika. Brown the medallions as directed. Omit tarragon, lemon juice, and lemon zest. Simmer the medallions in the chicken broth; add ½ cup low-sodium mango chutney and simmer 2 to 3 minutes longer.

ZOOM

Pork tenderloin is cut from the full loin. It is, as its name suggests, very tender. It cooks quickly and can be roasted, pan fried, baked, or grilled. Cook the tenderloin to 155°F; use an instant read meat thermometer to check. Be sure to buy tenderloin that hasn't been injected with brine or marinated.

Pound Medallions

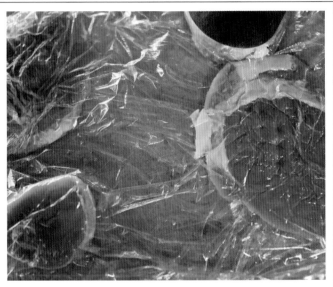

- Since pork tenderloin is such a tender meat, you must use a gentle hand when pounding.

- You'll find that just a few taps with a meat mallet or rolling pin will quickly flatten the slices.

- Pound the medallions so they are all the same thickness. They will cook evenly and remain tender and juicy.

- You can sprinkle the medallions with a combination of flour and your favorite herbs and spices.

Simmer Sauce

- After the medallions have browned, there will be lots of bits and pieces in the pan; these are called pan drippings.

- These drippings have lots of flavor from the browned flour and caramelized pork, so they are incorporated into the sauce.

- Don't drain, wipe out, or wash the pan after the medallions have browned.

- Serve this dish immediately, along with rice or pasta to soak up the delicious sauce.

PORK

BBQ RIBS

Spicy and smoky ribs bake for hours to tender perfection

Sometimes there's nothing more satisfying than biting into a tender and well-flavored pork rib. But if you eat at a restaurant, those ribs are going to be loaded with salt.

Bottled barbecue sauce is also very high in sodium. And as for those marinated pork ribs that are ready to cook? They can have 800 to 1,000 mg of sodium per serving.

Making your own barbecue sauce is really the best solution.

You can make it as mild or as spicy as you'd like; adding spices or subtracting herbs and using your favorite ingredients.

The ribs are simmered before baking to remove some of the fat. And the ribs become meltingly tender when baked in a spicy and sweet barbecue sauce. *Yield: Serves 6*

Ingredients

3 pounds country pork ribs

1 onion, chopped

4 cloves garlic, minced

2 tablespoons olive oil

1 (8-ounce) can no-salt-added tomato sauce

1/4 cup low-sodium chili sauce

1/4 cup low-sodium mustard

1/2 teaspoon celery seed

1 teaspoon paprika

1/4 teaspoon cayenne pepper

1/4 cup brown sugar

2 tablespoons molasses

1/4 cup balsamic vinegar

Calories 597, **% Calories from Fat** 61%, **Fat** (g) 41, **Carbohydrates** (g) 24, **Protein** (g) 34, **Sodium** (mg) 242, **Fiber** (g) 2, **Saturated Fat** (g) 13, **Cholesterol** (mg) 130

BBQ Ribs

- Place ribs in pot; add cold water to cover. Bring to a boil. Reduce heat to low, cover, and simmer 45 minutes.

- While ribs are cooking, cook onions and garlic in olive oil in saucepan 7 to 8 minutes. Add tomato sauce, chili sauce, mustard, and remaining ingredients.

- Simmer 30 to 40 minutes, stirring frequently, until sauce thickens.

- When ribs are done, drain and place in roasting pan; cover with sauce. Bake at 325°F 70 to 90 minutes, basting occasionally, until done.

Slow Cooker Ribs: Prepare recipe as directed, simmering the ribs in water and preparing the sauce. Place 2 to 3 sliced onions in the bottom of a 5- to 6-quart slow cooker. You may need to cut the ribs into portions to fit. Top with the sauce, cover, and cook on low 7 to 9 hours, until tender.

Grilled Ribs: Prepare recipe as directed. When ribs have simmered, drain them. Prepare and preheat a grill. Add the ribs; cook over medium coals 20 to 30 minutes, brushing with sauce after the first turn and frequently thereafter. Place the sauce in a large skillet on the grill; as the ribs finish, add them to the simmering sauce.

Simmer Ribs

Make Sauce

- Country ribs are leaner than regular or baby back ribs because they come from the loin. They can also be meatier.

- The simmering water will draw out excess fat while keeping the meat moist.

- Make sure the water doesn't boil, or the ribs could be tough.

- A simmer means that bubbles rise to the surface of the liquid but break just before reaching the surface.

- You can add any of your favorite spices and herbs to this barbecue sauce.

- For a Tex-Mex sauce, omit the celery seed and add a few minced jalapeño or serrano peppers with some cumin.

- For an Asian-inspired sauce, omit the celery seed and paprika and add five spice powder, star anise, and low-sodium soy sauce.

- You can serve the sauce on the side. Make sure it's been simmered 2 minutes before serving.

PORK

HERBED PORK ROAST

Herbs and garlic melt into a pork loin roast for a delicious meal

A pork roast is a delicious cut of meat that easily serves a crowd. Choose a loin roast; it has the most flavor and is the most tender cut. It's very easy to cook; just season it, place it in the roasting pan, and turn on the oven.

You can season the roast with any herbs or spices that you'd like. Spice blends like curry powder or chili powder, especially if homemade, add wonderful flavor.

The secret to the best roast pork is to make sure it's not overcooked. Use a meat thermometer that is then set to the proper temperature, 150°F. Take the roast out of the oven and let stand 10 minutes, then carve and dig in. *Yield: Serves 8–10*

Ingredients

1 stalk fresh rosemary

3 sprigs fresh thyme

1 (4-pound) boneless pork loin roast

6 cloves garlic, slivered

1 teaspoon paprika

1/4 teaspoon pepper

1/4 teaspoon dry mustard

2 tablespoons olive oil

2 onions, chopped

1/2 cup water

18 baby new red potatoes

1 (16-ounce) package baby carrots

Calories 494 , **% Calories from Fat** 43%, **Fat** (g) 24, **Carbohydrates** (g) 35, **Protein** (g) 33, **Sodium** (mg)139, **Fiber** (g) 5, **Saturated Fat** (g) 8, **Cholesterol** (mg) 89

Herbed Pork Roast

- Break rosemary stalk into 1-inch pieces. Break thyme sprigs into 1-inch pieces.

- Using a sharp knife, make holes in the pork roast; insert rosemary, thyme, and garlic slivers in a regular pattern.

- Mix paprika, pepper, mustard, and oil; brush on roast. Place on onions in roasting pan; add water.

- Roast at 350°F 50 minutes. Add potatoes and carrots; roast another 45 to 55 minutes, until 150°F. Cover roast; let stand 10 minutes, then slice.

Mild Roasted Pork Loin: Make recipe as directed, except omit thyme and rosemary sprigs. Substitute 1 teaspoon each dried sage and dried thyme leaves; mix with paprika, pepper, and oil. Add 2 tablespoons each apple cider vinegar and brown sugar. Substitute 3 red bell peppers, sliced, for the carrots.

Fruity Pork Roast: Make recipe as directed, except omit rosemary sprigs. Omit mustard from rub; add ¼ cup seedless raspberry jam and 1 tablespoon each orange juice and lemon juice. Omit carrots and potatoes; add another onion to the pan. Roast as directed.

Place Herbs in Pork

- You can use other fresh herbs in place of the rosemary and thyme.

- A mixture of chopped fresh sage, minced garlic, and minced jalapeño peppers would be delicious.

- When you make holes in the pork, wiggle the knife a bit to open them enough to easily slide in the garlic and herbs.

- After you brush the paprika mixture on the pork, it can be marinated in the refrigerator, covered, up to 8 hours.

Add Vegetables and Continue Roasting

- Other root vegetables can be used in this recipe. Use sweet potatoes, peeled and cut into cubes, or cubed parsnips.

- If you'd rather use larger potatoes, just scrub them and place around the roast before it goes into the oven.

- The water in the bottom of the pan helps prevent burning. You can use the juices to make a pan sauce.

- Add some low-sodium chicken broth to the roasting pan after the vegetables and roast are removed; boil 2 to 3 minutes.

PORK

GRILLED SALMON

Salmon is grilled on a cedar plank for wonderful flavor and texture

Salmon may be relatively high in fat, but remember, it is good fat. Omega-3 fatty acids, which are prevalent in salmon, are very good for your heart. Don't feel guilty about eating fatty fish; in fact you should eat two servings of this fish a week.

When buying salmon fillets, make sure they feel firm to the touch and smell sweet. Fish that smells fishy isn't fresh and should be avoided.

If there are any tiny pin bones in the salmon, remove them with tweezers. You can find them by running your fingers over the salmon; the bones will feel like tiny bumps.

Salmon can be seasoned with everything from lemon juice to curry powder to dried herbs. *Yield: Serves 6*

Ingredients

1 large untreated cedar plank

1/4 cup orange juice

2 tablespoons olive oil

1 tablespoon fresh dill weed

1/2 teaspoon dill seed

1 tablespoon Dijon mustard

1/4 teaspoon pepper

6 (6-ounce) salmon fillets

1 lemon, sliced

Calories 376, **% Calories from Fat** 56%, **Fat** (g) 24, **Carbohydrates** (g) 2, **Protein** (g) 37, **Sodium** (mg) 113, **Fiber** (g) 0.2, **Saturated Fat** (g) 5, **Cholesterol** (mg) 120

Grilled Salmon

- Make sure the plank is untreated. Soak the plank in plain water for 24 hours.

- Combine orange juice, olive oil, dill weed, dill seed, mustard, and pepper; spread over salmon. Cover and chill 2 to 3 hours.

- Prepare and preheat grill. Place plank on medium coals and cover; cook until plank starts to pop. Turn over.

- Place salmon on plank; top with lemon slices. Cover and grill 10 to 14 minutes, until salmon flakes when tested with fork.

Cedar planks are a great way to grill delicate meats like salmon or other fish fillets. Buy untreated cedar from a hardware or kitchenware store only. You may want to sand it down; in fact after use, sanding will remove the burned part and the plank will be ready to reuse.

Curried Planked Salmon: Make recipe as directed, except for the marinade, combine 1 tablespoon curry powder, ¼ cup orange juice, 1 tablespoon olive oil, ¼ teaspoon dried orange peel, ¼ teaspoon pepper, and 2 tablespoons honey. Prepare plank as directed. Place sliced orange on salmon when grilling.

Prepare Cedar Plank

- Buy your cedar plank at cooking supply stores or at a lumberyard. Be sure the plank is untreated.

- Treated wood is soaked with poisons so insects don't eat it. If you use treated wood near food, you'll get sick.

- The plank can add some flavor, but its main purpose is to shield the salmon from the heat of the grill, cooking it perfectly.

- The plank can be reused many times. Just scrape or sand off the burned parts.

Grill Salmon

- The grill has to be covered when cooking this recipe, whether you are using gas or charcoal.

- When closed, the grill behaves like an oven heated to about 500°F.

- This high, dry heat cooks the fish quickly and keeps it moist and tender on the inside.

- The cedar doesn't really add any flavor to the recipe, but it makes a nice presentation and is fun to use.

GLAZED FISH FILLETS

Fish glazed in a rich garlic and balsamic mixture is hearty and delicious

Fish is one of the healthiest foods you can eat. And fish fillets are low in saturated fat and sodium and high in protein and healthy fats.

Balsamic vinegar is an aged vinegar that has a sweet taste, deep red color, and slightly thickened texture. It is expensive, but a bottle lasts a long time and its flavor is incomparable.

It's difficult to cook fish fillets on the grill, but there are solutions. Use heavy-duty foil, pierced in several places to let the smoke through, or try a silicone grill mat.

You can grill fish fillets directly on the rack if it is very clean and brushed with oil. Some of the fish will stick to the rack, but that's part of the charm of cooking outdoors. *Yield: Serves 6*

Ingredients

1 tablespoon olive oil

4 cloves garlic, minced

$1/4$ cup minced onion

3 tablespoons balsamic vinegar

$1/2$ teaspoon dry mustard

2 tablespoons honey

1 teaspoon dried tarragon

$1/8$ teaspoon pepper

6 (6-ounce) red snapper fillets

Calories 268, **% Calories from Fat** 18%, **Fat** (g) 5, **Carbohydrates** (g) 7, **Protein** (g) 45, **Sodium** (mg) 141, **Fiber** (g) 0.2, **Saturated Fat** (g) 1, **Cholesterol** (mg) 80.7

Glazed Fish Fillets

- In small saucepan heat olive oil over medium heat. Add garlic and onion; cook and stir 5 to 6 minutes, until light golden brown.

- Add vinegar, mustard, honey, tarragon, and pepper; cook and stir until sauce blends.

- Prepare and preheat grill. Place a sheet of heavy-duty foil on the grill; pierce it several times with a knife.

- Place fish on foil; brush with sauce. Cover and grill 5 minutes per inch of thickness, brushing with sauce, until fish flakes. Discard sauce.

Glazed Fish Steaks: Make recipe as directed, except substitute 6 halibut or tuna steaks for the red snapper fillets. Double the sauce and marinate the steaks 4 to 6 hours. Preheat the grill, scrub the rack, and brush with peanut or sunflower oil. Add the steaks; cook 8 to 14 minutes, turning once, until fish flakes.

Glazed Greek Fillets: Make recipe as directed, except omit balsamic vinegar and tarragon. Add 2 tablespoons lemon juice, 1 teaspoon dried oregano leaves, and ⅛ teaspoon cayenne pepper. Prepare grill and place fish fillets on foil; brush with sauce and grill until fish flakes when tested with fork.

Make Sauce

Grill Fish

- The sauce should simmer 2 to 3 minutes, until it comes together and the vinegar blends with the onions.

- Stir the mixture constantly as it cooks so it doesn't burn. The vinegar is fairly high in sugar, which burns easily.

- You can substitute 2 tablespoons red wine or white wine vinegar for the balsamic vinegar if you'd like.

- The sauce can be made ahead of time. Cover and refrigerate it until you're ready to grill; then reheat.

- The fish doesn't need to be turned if it is thinner than 1 inch. Most fillets are about ½-inch thick.

- Make sure you use heavy-duty foil, or use a doubled sheet of regular foil.

- Use a knife to poke several holes in the foil; about 10 per sheet are enough. Don't cut the foil too much.

- The foil can't be reused, so discard it after cooking. Spray the foil with nonstick cooking spray before adding the fish.

FISH

STUFFED FILLETS
Technically not "stuffed," this flavorful dish is easy to make

Fish and stuffing don't automatically go together, but a well-flavored stuffing can add lots of interest to baked fish.

Aromatic vegetables, including onions, garlic, celery, and bell peppers, are great choices for stuffing. Cook them before stuffing the fish, because the filling won't get hot enough to soften the vegetables.

The fish used in this recipe is called lean fish, with about 3 to 4 percent fat. Fatty fish includes salmon, halibut, and tuna. You can substitute salmon or halibut fillets for the lean fish fillets in this recipe; it will be higher in fat.

Serve this recipe with steamed dark leafy greens like kale, drizzled with olive oil, and some sliced tomatoes. For dessert, an apple pie is perfect. *Yield: Serves 6*

Ingredients

1 onion, chopped

4 cloves garlic, minced

1 (8-ounce) package cremini mushrooms, sliced

2 tablespoons olive oil

1 red bell pepper, chopped

2 stalks celery, chopped

2 tablespoons lemon juice

1 tablespoon fresh dill weed

1 teaspoon dried thyme

1 cup soft fresh bread crumbs

12 thin orange roughy fillets

2 tablespoons unsalted butter, melted

1/2 teaspoon paprika

2 tablespoons grated Parmesan cheese

Calories 271, **% Calories from Fat** 36%, **Fat** (g) 11, **Carbohydrates** (g) 12, **Protein** (g) 31, **Sodium** (mg) 171, **Fiber** (g) 1, **Saturated Fat** (g) 4, **Cholesterol** (mg) 120

Stuffed Fillets

- Preheat oven to 350°F. In skillet, cook onion, garlic, and mushrooms in olive oil until liquid evaporates.

- Add bell pepper and celery; cook 3 minutes. Add lemon juice, dill, thyme, and bread crumbs; remove from heat.

- Grease 9- x 13-inch baking dish with unsalted butter. Place 6 fillets in pan. Divide vegetable mixture on top of fillets; top each with a second fillet.

- Mix butter, paprika, and cheese; brush on fillets. Bake 20 to 25 minutes until bottom fillets flake.

White fish fillets are mild in flavor and boneless. The best types of fish for this recipe include tilapia, haddock, cod, walleye, flounder, red snapper, grouper, mahi mahi, and orange roughy. Fresh fish fresh smells slightly sweet and salty, like the sea. A sour flavor is indicative of spoilage.

• • • • RECIPE VARIATION • • • •

Rolled Stuffed Fillets: Make recipe as directed, except cut the filling amounts in half. Add 1 egg white to the filling mixture. Use 6 long, thin mild white fish fillets. Spread the filling on the fillets and roll up. Place in baking dish and pour 2 tablespoons lemon juice into dish. Bake at 400°F 15 to 20 minutes, until done.

Make Filling

- The vegetables should be cooked until they are fairly soft. The mushrooms are cooked until the liquid evaporates.

- If you skip this step, the mushrooms will emit liquid when the fillets are cooking and the stuffing will be soggy.

- You can make the filling ahead of time, but don't add the bread crumbs until you're ready to bake the fish.

- Other vegetables including chopped zucchini or yellow summer squash could be used.

Stuff Fillets

- Spread the vegetable stuffing evenly over the fish. Press down lightly on the stuffing.

- When you add the second fillet, press down gently again to help the stuffing stick to the fish.

- The butter mixture is brushed onto the fish to help keep it moist in the oven and to add flavor.

- Don't stuff the fish ahead of time, as the stuffing will absorb moisture from the fish and may become soggy.

GRILLED FISH KABOBS
This is a delicious and colorful combination of vegetables and fish

Kabobs are a fun and easy way to entertain a crowd. And using lots of herbs and spices makes them delicious and very low in sodium.

There are lots of accessories you can find to help you grill kabobs. From grill mats that protect delicate fish and vegetables to kabob holders that put an end to skewer spinning, you have myriad choices.

You need a sturdy, fairly fatty fish for kabobs. Because the fish is cut into smaller pieces, a delicate white fillet like red snapper will just fall apart when cooked. Halibut, salmon, and tuna are all good choices.

Choose your favorite vegetables to make these kabobs your own. Serve with a rice pilaf, a fruit salad, and some grilled bread.
Yield: Serves 6

Ingredients

1 tablespoon olive oil

4 cloves garlic, minced

¼ cup minced red onion

2 tablespoons grated ginger root

¼ teaspoons ground ginger

2 tablespoons lemon juice

1 teaspoon grated lemon zest

⅛ teaspoon cayenne pepper

1¼ pounds halibut steak

1 (8-ounce) package whole small mushrooms

4 green onions, cut into 2-inch pieces

2 red bell peppers, sliced

Calories 125, **% Calories from Fat** 28%, **Fat** (g) 4, **Carbohydrates** (g) 6, **Protein** (g) 17, **Sodium** (mg) 45, **Fiber** (g) 2, **Saturated Fat** (g) 2, **Cholesterol** (mg) 29

Grilled Fish Kabobs

- In small saucepan cook garlic and onion in olive oil 4 minutes. Add ginger root; cook 3 minutes longer.

- Remove from heat; add ground ginger, lemon juice, zest, and pepper. Place in glass baking dish.

- Cut halibut into 1¼-inch cubes; add to marinade; toss. Cover; chill 4 to 5 hours.

- Prepare and preheat grill; place grill mat on rack. Thread fish, mushrooms, green onion, and bell peppers on 8 metal skewers. Grill, brushing with marinade, 8 to 12 minutes, until done.

• • • • RECIPE VARIATION • • • •

Tex-Mex Fish Kabobs: Make recipe as directed, except omit ginger root and ground ginger. Add 1 minced jalapeño pepper, 1 minced serrano pepper, and 2 teaspoons chili powder. Omit mushrooms; use 1 zucchini, cut into 1-inch pieces. Serve with homemade salsa.

Marinate Fish

- Make sure you prepare the marinade and let it stand while you cube the fish.

- This lets the marinade cool so the fish doesn't start cooking when it's added to the marinade in the baking dish.

- Don't marinate the fish longer than 5 hours, or it will become mushy. Fish flesh is very delicate.

- You can make any type of marinade you'd like. Make one full of fresh herbs for a nice change of pace.

Thread Food onto Skewers

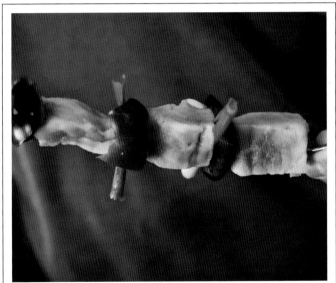

- If it's difficult to thread the food onto skewers, use an awl or sharp chopstick to make a hole in the food.

- Wooden skewers can be used in this recipe, but they may burn too much on the grill.

- If you want to use wooden skewers, soak them in cool water 30 to 60 minutes.

- If you make a lot of kabobs, look for decorative metal skewers in kitchen supply and gourmet stores to add a touch of class to your cookout.

FISH

SHRIMP & FISH SCAMPI
Lemon and garlic are the dominant flavors in scampi

Shrimp is naturally high in sodium, about 55 mg per ounce. So to get a dish that's low in overall sodium amounts, you have to add other ingredients.

Vegetables are a natural addition to shrimp. The beautiful color and sweet flavor of grape tomatoes are perfect in this scampi recipe. Lots of garlic and lemon juice are characteristic of scampi.

Any mild white fish fillet will work well in this recipe. You can choose larger fillets than 6 ounces for heartier servings, but with the onions, garlic, and tomatoes, this recipe is quite filing.

Serve this delicious dish with some cooked pasta tossed with unsalted butter, lemon zest, and parsley and a spinach salad with strawberries. *Yield: Serves 4*

Ingredients

1/4 cup unsalted butter

5 cloves garlic, minced

1 onion, minced

1/3 cup lemon juice

1 teaspoon grated lemon zest

1/8 teaspoon cayenne pepper

2 tablespoons dry white wine

1 teaspoon dried thyme leaves

4 (4-ounce) red snapper fillets

8 ounces medium raw shrimp, peeled

1 cup grape tomatoes

1/3 cup chopped parsley

Shrimp & Fish Scampi

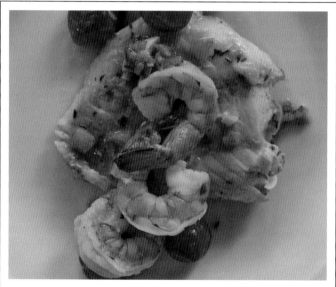

- In large saucepan melt butter over medium-low heat. Add garlic and onion; cook and stir 6 to 8 minutes, until onion starts to brown.

- Add lemon juice, zest, cayenne pepper, wine, and thyme; bring to a simmer. Simmer 2 minutes.

- Add fillets; cook 2 minutes and turn. Add shrimp and grape tomatoes; cover and cook 3 to 5 minutes, shaking pan, until shrimp turn pink.

- Uncover, stir gently, sprinkle with parsley, and serve immediately.

Calories 417, **% Calories from Fat** 34%, **Fat** (g) 16, **Carbohydrates** (g) 8, **Protein** (g) 58, **Sodium** (mg) 238, **Fiber** (g) 1, **Saturated Fat** (g) 8, **Cholesterol** (mg) 200

Shrimp is high in both sodium and cholesterol, but it can be enjoyed in moderation. Other shellfish have high sodium counts, too: One large scallop has 70 mg of sodium, while 3 ounces of lobster has 325 mg. Three ounces of Alaskan crab has 925 mg of sodium; that's the highest of any shellfish.

• • • • RECIPE VARIATION • • • •

Shrimp and Fish Veracruz: Make recipe as directed, except omit thyme leaves. Reduce garlic to 2 cloves and lemon juice to 3 tablespoons. Add ½ teaspoon dried oregano leaves and 1 (14.5-ounce) can no-salt-added diced tomatoes, undrained, in place of the grape tomatoes. Add tomatoes with the lemon juice.

Simmer Sauce

Add Shrimp and Tomatoes

- Don't let the onions and garlic burn; be sure to cook over medium-low heat.

- You'll need to stir this mixture almost constantly. The flavor of burned onions and garlic will ruin the dish, so if they do burn, you'll have to start over.

- You can substitute low-sodium fish stock or clam juice for the white wine if you'd like.

- Other mild fish fillets will work well, including grouper, tilefish, and orange roughy.

- Grape tomatoes are a great choice for any dish, because they are tender, sweet, and perfect year-round.

- You can substitute chopped red or yellow tomatoes for the grape tomatoes if you'd like.

- Make sure the shrimp is peeled and deveined. The vein is a dark line running along the back; make a shallow slit and rinse to remove.

- Serve this dish immediately so the fish and shrimp are both tender.

SALMON WITH ORANGE SAUCE

Salmon cooked with an orange-ginger sauce is a delicious and healthy entree

Salmon with orange is a wonderful combination that doesn't need a grain of salt. Use fresh orange juice for the best flavor. It's easy to squeeze your own with some ripe oranges and a simple glass juicer.

Orange juice and zest, in addition to being delicious, are very good for you. They are high in vitamins C and A, along with antioxidants that fight aging and diseases.

Cook salmon just until it's opaque in the center and a fork inserted in the salmon makes it flake when the fork is twisted.

You can make this recipe using grapefruit juice or lemon juice in place of the orange juice, or use a combination of citrus juices and zest. *Yield: Serves 4*

Ingredients

1 tablespoon unsalted butter

3 cloves garlic, minced

2 tablespoons grated ginger root

³/₄ cup orange juice

1 teaspoon orange zest

1 teaspoon dried tarragon

¹/₈ teaspoon pepper

1 teaspoon reduced-sodium soy sauce

4 (6-ounce) salmon fillets

1 tablespoon cornstarch

1 tablespoon lemon juice

¹/₄ cup white wine

Calories 349, **% Calories from Fat** 49%, **Fat** (g) 19, **Carbohydrates** (g) 10, **Protein** (g) 30, **Sodium** (mg) 135, **Fiber** (g) 0.3, **Saturated Fat** (g) 5, **Cholesterol** (mg) 95

Salmon with Orange Sauce

- In small saucepan heat butter; add garlic and ginger. Cook and stir 4 to 5 minutes, until tender.

- Add orange juice, zest, tarragon, pepper, and soy sauce; simmer 2 minutes.

- Place salmon on broiler rack; brush with some of the orange mixture. Broil under preheated broiler 4 minutes.

- Carefully turn salmon, brush with sauce, and continue broiling. Add cornstarch, lemon juice, and wine to orange sauce; simmer while fish cooks 3 to 5 minutes longer. Serve with fish.

Salmon with Salsa: Make recipe as directed, except omit ginger root, orange juice, zest, tarragon, and soy sauce. Add ½ cup chopped onion and 1 jalapeño, minced; cook until tender. Add 2 red and 1 yellow tomato, both chopped; simmer 5 minutes. Add 2 teaspoons chili powder. Broil salmon, brushing with some salsa, and serve with remaining salsa.

Salmon with Lime Sauce: Make recipe as directed, except substitute ⅓ cup lime juice for the orange juice, and 1 teaspoon lime zest for the orange zest. Omit soy sauce. Add 1 serrano pepper, minced, to the garlic mixture. Broil salmon as directed and serve with sauce.

Simmer Orange Sauce

Broil Salmon

- You can make the orange sauce ahead of time; don't add the cornstarch, lemon juice, and wine until the salmon is broiling.

- Use other dried herbs in this delicious recipe. Dried basil or thyme would work well, as would marjoram leaves.

- Or you can use fresh herbs. Use three times the amount of fresh herbs as dried.

- Add an onion to the sauce for more flavor. Serve this dish with some glazed carrots and a mixed green salad.

- The broiler on most ovens has to be preheated before use. And most ovens require that the oven door be slightly ajar.

- Arrange the oven rack before you turn on the broiler. And spray the broiler rack with nonstick cooking spray.

- If the salmon fillets are thinner than ½ inch, don't turn them. Just brush with more orange sauce; broil 1 minute longer.

- For a smooth finish, mix the cornstarch, lemon juice, and wine with a wire whisk before adding to the sauce.

FISH

BEANS & RICE

This classic recipe uses dried beans for the best texture

Beans and rice is a nutritious and inexpensive dish. These two foods have nourished entire populations for generations. There's really no healthier or more basic food on the planet.

But beans and rice don't have to be boring, and they don't have to be loaded with sodium. Make your own vegetable broth for the lowest sodium count, or look for low-sodium brands in the supermarket.

Turmeric is a potent spice that can prevent some diseases. It turns the rice a beautiful golden color, which looks pretty against the black beans. And the spice adds a rich, slightly nutty taste to the rice.

Serve this dish with some glazed carrots and sugar snap peas, toasted garlic bread, and iced tea. *Yield: Serves 6*

Ingredients

1 cup dried black beans

4 cups water

1 onion, chopped

3 cloves garlic, minced

1 tablespoon olive oil

2$^1/_2$ cups low-sodium vegetable broth

1 teaspoon dried oregano leaves

$^1/_8$ teaspoon pepper

1 cup long grain white rice

1 teaspoon ground turmeric

$^1/_2$ teaspoon cumin

2 cups water

$^1/_8$ teaspoon white pepper

Beans & Rice

- Sort beans and rinse. Cover with 4 cups water and soak, covered, overnight.

- The next day drain beans. In large saucepan cook onion and garlic in olive oil 5 to 6 minutes, until tender.

- Add beans, broth, oregano, and pepper. Bring to a simmer; reduce heat to low, cover, and simmer 60 to 70 minutes, until tender.

- When beans have 25 minutes left to cook, combine rice, turmeric, cumin, water, and white pepper in pan; simmer 20 to 25 minutes, until rice is tender. Serve with beans.

Calories 252 , **% Calories from Fat** 11%, **Fat** (g) 3, **Carbohydrates** (g) 46, **Protein** (g)11, **Sodium** (mg) 235, **Fiber** (g) 6, **Saturated Fat** (g) 1, **Cholesterol** (mg) 0

Prepare Beans

- For a quicker way to prepare the beans, sort them and rinse. Place in a large pot and cover with water.

- Bring the mixture to a boil; boil hard for 2 minutes. Then cover the pot, remove from heat, and let stand 1 hour.

- Drain the beans and continue the recipe as directed. You can use this method with any dried beans.

- Don't cook dried beans with any acidic ingredient, or the beans won't soften properly no matter how long they cook.

Cook Rice

- If you have trouble cooking rice so it turns out tender and moist, invest in a rice cooker. This inexpensive appliance makes perfect rice.

- For more nutrition you could substitute brown rice for the white rice. Cook this rice 35 to 40 minutes until tender.

- Other types of rice that would be delicious in this recipe include basmati, jasmine, Texmati, and Jasmati.

- Place the rice on a serving platter and spoon the bean mixture over; serve immediately.

121

PESTO FETTUCCINE

Pesto is a heady combination of basil, cheese, and garlic

Pesto is an Italian sauce that is not cooked. You must use fresh basil leaves in this recipe; there is really no satisfactory substitution.

This recipe is high in fat, but it's good fat. Olive oil has lots of monounsaturated fatty acids that are heart healthy. It's an integral part of the Mediterranean diet, which has been shown to be one of the healthiest in the world.

You can make pesto in large batches and freeze it for later use. Just divide the pesto into 2-tablespoon or ¼-cup portions and freeze until solid. To use, thaw overnight in the refrigerator and toss with pasta.

Serve this recipe with garlic bread sticks, a mixed fruit salad, and some roasted green beans. *Yield: Serves 4*

Ingredients

2 cups whole fresh basil leaves

2 fresh mint leaves

3 cloves garlic, peeled

1 teaspoon dried basil leaves

¼ cup grated Parmesan cheese

½ cup slivered almonds, toasted

½ cup extra-virgin olive oil

2 tablespoons lemon juice

⅛ teaspoon pepper

3–4 tablespoons water

1 (12-ounce) package fettuccine pasta

½ cup chopped fresh basil

Calories 668, **% Calories from Fat** 50%, **Fat** (g) 37, **Carbohydrates** (g) 68, **Protein** (g) 17, **Sodium** (mg) 103, **Fiber** (g) 5, **Saturated Fat** (g) 6, **Cholesterol** (mg) 6

Pesto Fettuccine

- In food processor combine whole basil leaves, mint, garlic, dried basil, cheese, and almonds; process until minced.

- Gradually add olive oil, lemon juice, pepper, and enough water to make a thick sauce.

- Bring a large pot of water to a boil. Add fettuccine; cook until al dente according to package directions.

- Drain, reserving ⅓ cup cooking water; return pasta to pot. Add pesto and enough cooking water to make a sauce. Toss; garnish with fresh basil.

Process Pesto Ingredients

- To toast almonds, place on a cookie sheet. Bake at 375°F 10 to 15 minutes, stirring once, until brown and fragrant.

- Let the nuts cool completely before chopping in the food processor, or they will become mushy and soft.

- Rinse the basil leaves and shake off the excess water. Tear them into large pieces and place in the food processor.

- The almonds help break up the basil leaves and add a nutty richness to the pesto.

Cook and Toss Pasta

- Pasta should be cooked in a large quantity of rapidly boiling water. Italians like to add a handful of salt to the water.

- But you don't need salt, especially if you use good-quality pasta and serve it with a flavorful sauce.

- Cook the pasta until al dente. This means that when you bite into the pasta, there's a tiny bit uncooked in the center.

- The pasta cooking water is full of starches that help add body to the sauce and make it creamy.

TOFU STIR-FRY

Tofu can be full of flavor when stir-fried with inexpensive ingredients

Tofu is the original health food. Many people shy away from it, thinking it's just too New Age, but it can be very delicious when prepared with spices and aromatic vegetables.

Tofu is soybean curd. Soybeans are unique in the legume world. They provide complete protein, are nutty and sweet tasting, and can help improve heart health because they have lots of antioxidants, selenium, and omega-3 fatty acids.

Choose firm or extrafirm tofu for stir-fries. When drained, these forms will stand up to the heat and tumble of stir-frying. Soft tofu and Silken tofu are used for sauces and desserts.

Serve this stir-fry over hot cooked rice—white, brown, or basmati. All you need is some fruit tossed with mint for dessert, and perhaps some egg rolls for an appetizer. *Yield: Serves 6*

Ingredients

1 (16-ounce) package firm tofu

1 tablespoon low-sodium soy sauce

1/4 teaspoon garlic powder

1 cup low-sodium vegetable broth

1 teaspoon chili paste

1 tablespoons cornstarch

1/4 teaspoon red pepper flakes

2 tablespoons peanut oil

1 tablespoon minced ginger root

6 cloves garlic, minced

1 onion, chopped

1 red bell pepper, sliced

2 cups broccoli florets

Calories 139, **% Calories from Fat** 53%, **Fat** (g) 8, **Carbohydrates** (g) 10, **Protein** (g) 9, **Sodium** (mg) 218, **Fiber** (g) 2, **Saturated Fat** (g) 2, **Cholesterol** (mg) 0

Tofu Stir-Fry

- Drain tofu and press between paper towels to remove excess water. Cut into cubes, drizzle with soy sauce and garlic powder; let stand 10 minutes.

- Combine broth, chili paste, cornstarch, and red pepper flakes.

- In wok or skillet, heat peanut oil. Add ginger root, garlic, and onion; stir-fry 4 to 5 minutes. Add tofu; stir-fry 4 minutes; remove from pan.

- Add bell pepper and broccoli; stir-fry 4 to 5 minutes. Add tofu and broth mixture; stir-fry until thickened, about 4 to 5 minutes.

···· RECIPE VARIATION ····

Curried Tofu Stir-Fry: Make recipe as directed, except substitute 1 tablespoon curry powder for the garlic powder. Omit soy sauce; use 1 tablespoon orange juice. Omit chili sauce and broccoli; add 2 cups cauliflower florets and 1 green bell pepper, chopped. Stir-fry ingredients as directed.

Curry Powder: Curry powder is a blend of aromatic spices; you can vary them as you'd like. For a start, combine 1 tablespoon each ground cumin and coriander, 1 tablespoon turmeric, ½ teaspoon dry mustard powder, ⅛ teaspoon finely ground white pepper, and 1 teaspoon ground ginger.

Prepare Tofu

- Tofu has to be drained before it's marinated or stir-fried, because it contains a lot of water.

- Place the tofu in a strainer or colander and let drain for a few minutes.

- Then press the tofu between kitchen or paper towels. Don't do this ahead of time; the tofu should not marinate long.

- Tofu will absorb flavors easily, so you can marinate it in any mixture you'd like. Use spices or fresh herbs, or onion and garlic.

Stir-Fry Ingredients

- Make sure all the ingredients are ready and waiting for you before you start stir-frying.

- The cooking process is so quick that there will be no time to stop and chop something you forgot.

- To stir-fry, use a sturdy spatula with a long handle. Using a scooping motion, move the food around in the wok or skillet.

- Stir-frying only takes a few minutes. Cut all of the ingredients about the same size so they cook evenly.

MAC & CHEESE

Low-sodium, sharp cheese is the key to this healthy, updated recipe

Macaroni and cheese is the classic children's recipe, but it can be a sophisticated dish. Mac and cheese mixes are full of sodium and artificial ingredients. Make your own for a true comfort-food experience.

Look for low-sodium cheeses that are high in flavor. The sharper the cheese, the less you have to use to get great flavor. Sophisticated cheeses like Havarti, Gruyère, feta, and

Gouda are inexpensive and taste wonderful.

If you've never had homemade mac and cheese, you're in for a treat. Mustard, sour cream, and three kinds of cheeses make this recipe delicious.

Serve with a salad made with romaine lettuce, toasted pecans, and mandarin orange segments; and a chocolate cake for dessert. *Yield: Serves 6*

Ingredients

3 tablespoons unsalted butter

1 onion, chopped

3 cloves garlic, minced

3 tablespoons flour

1/8 teaspoon pepper

1/2 teaspoon dry mustard

1 1/2 cups milk

1/2 cup heavy cream

1/2 cup sour cream

1 1/2 cups shredded low-sodium sharp cheddar cheese

1 cup shredded low-sodium Swiss cheese

1 (12-ounce) package elbow macaroni

1/2 cup ground almonds

2 tablespoons grated Romano cheese

Calories 672, **% Calories from Fat** 53%, **Fat** (g) 39, **Carbohydrates** (g) 55, **Protein** (g) 26, **Sodium** (mg) 98, **Fiber** (g) 3, **Saturated Fat** (g) 22, **Cholesterol** (mg) 106

Mac & Cheese

- Bring a pot of water to a boil. Meanwhile, in saucepan melt butter over medium heat.

- Add onion and garlic; cook and stir 10 minutes until onion browns. Add flour, pepper, and mustard; cook 3 minutes.

- Add milk, cream, and sour cream; cook and stir until thickened. Cook macaroni until al dente; drain.

- Add macaroni with cheeses to sauce; mix well. Pour into greased 2-quart casserole; sprinkle with almonds and Romano. Bake at 400°F 20 to 25 minutes.

YELLOW ● LIGHT

When you're cooking pasta to use in a baked dish, cook it slightly less than al dente. The pasta will absorb liquid from the sauce, and the heat of the oven will help soften it. If you cook the pasta too much in the first step, it will be mushy in the finished dish.

Make Sauce

- Cook the onion until browned to add even more flavor. This step causes caramelization, a complex process that happens over time.

- The flour is then cooked in the fat for a few minutes so it loses its raw flavor and can absorb liquid.

- Use a wire whisk to stir the flour mixture to make sure it's evenly distributed and cooked in the fat.

- For the smoothest sauce, also use a wire whisk to stir the liquid into the onion mixture.

Add Macaroni and Cheeses

- Some companies that make low-sodium cheeses include Tillamook, Primo Taglio, Alpine Lace, and Heluva Good cheese.

- Choose the sharpest cheese you can find for the most flavor; you can use less if the cheese is very strong.

- Stir the mixture gently but thoroughly so the cheeses melt but the pasta doesn't break or fall part.

- You can make the recipe ahead up to this point; cover and refrigerate. Add 10 to 15 minutes to the baking time.

VEGGIE STUFFED SHELLS

Lots of vegetables add flavor and color to jumbo stuffed pasta shells

Large pasta shells are fun to serve and eat. They each hold about 3 tablespoons of filling. Choose the extra large variety for this recipe. Each of these shells is about 2 to 3 inches long.

The shells have to be cooked al dente before being stuffed so they are flexible enough to open up without tearing or breaking.

You can stuff pasta shells with any savory mixture. Sauté any of your favorite vegetables and combine with about a cup of low-sodium pasta sauce, fill the shells, place the shells in a baking pan, cover with more sauce, and then bake until bubbly.

Serve this pretty casserole with a fresh fruit salad made from strawberries, kiwi fruit, orange segments, and raspberries and some toasted garlic bread. *Yield: Serves 6*

Ingredients

1 onion, chopped

4 cloves garlic, minced

2 tablespoons olive oil

1 (8-ounce) package cremini mushrooms, sliced

1 red bell pepper, chopped

1 green bell pepper, chopped

1/4 cup chopped fresh basil

1 tablespoon fresh thyme

1/2 cup sour cream

1/2 cup low-sodium ricotta cheese

2 tablespoons lemon juice

1 cup shredded Swiss cheese

1 (12-ounce) box extra large pasta shells

1 (8-ounce) can no-salt-added tomato sauce

1 teaspoon dried Italian seasoning

Calories 431, **% Calories from Fat** 34%, **Fat** (g) 16, **Carbohydrates** (g) 55, **Protein** (g) 17, **Sodium** (mg) 82, **Fiber** (g) 4, **Saturated Fat** (g) 8, **Cholesterol** (mg) 31

Veggie Stuffed Shells

- Cook and stir onion and garlic in olive oil until light brown, about 9 minutes.

- Add mushrooms; cook and stir until liquid evaporates. Add bell peppers; cook 4 minutes.

- Remove from heat; stir in basil and thyme. Add sour cream, ricotta, lemon juice, and cheese; set aside. Cook shells in boiling water until al dente.

- Stuff shells with vegetable mixture. Mix tomato sauce and seasoning; pour into 2-quart baking dish; top with shells. Bake at 350°F 30 to 40 minutes.

128

• • • • RECIPE VARIATION • • • •

Tex-Mex Stuffed Shells: Make recipe as directed, except substitute 1 chopped poblano pepper for the green bell pepper, omit the mushrooms, and add 2 minced jalapeño peppers to the onion mixture. Add 1 cup frozen corn and ½ cup salsa. Omit basil and thyme. Substitute Pepper Jack cheese for the Swiss.

Mushroom Stuffed Shells: Make recipe as directed, except substitute 1 (8-ounce) package sliced button mushrooms for the green bell pepper. Omit basil and thyme; add 1 tablespoon chopped fresh marjoram and ½ teaspoon dried oregano leaves. Omit Italian seasoning.

Cook Vegetables

- The mushrooms are cooked until the liquid evaporates because they contain a lot of water.

- If that water isn't removed from the mushrooms, it will dilute the sauce and the recipe will be runny.

- Cook and stir the bell peppers until they are tender. Stir frequently so the vegetables don't burn.

- You can cook the vegetables ahead of time if you'd like. Stuff the shells and add another 10 to 15 minutes to the baking time.

Stuff Shells

- Use a small iced teaspoon to fill the shells. Spoon in the filling until the shells are full, but don't overfill them.

- If the vegetables are chopped small enough, you can use a plastic bag to fill the shells.

- Fill the bag and cut a 1-inch hole in the corner. Squeeze the filling to pipe it into the cooked shells.

- If there is any filling mixture left over after stuffing the shells, just spoon it alongside the shells in the baking pan.

SPINACH MANICOTTI
A creamy, flavorful spinach filling stuffs manicotti pasta

Manicotti are large round tubes of pasta that are filled with savory mixtures then baked in pasta sauce. They can be found with the regular pasta in the grocery store.

Manicotti shells can be filled cooked or uncooked. They are a bit easier to stuff when uncooked, because they hold their shape. If you choose to stuff them uncooked, you have to change the way you bake them.

Add 2 cups low-sodium pasta sauce and 1 cup water to the tomato sauce and oregano mixture. Make sure the shells are covered with the sauce. Cover tightly with foil and bake 1 hour; uncover and bake 15 to 20 minutes longer until the shells are tender and the sauce is bubbling. *Yield: Serves 8*

Ingredients

1 tablespoon unsalted butter

1 onion, chopped

4 cloves garlic, minced

1 (10-ounce) package frozen spinach, thawed and drained

1/8 teaspoon fresh nutmeg

1/8 teaspoon pepper

2 tablespoons chopped fresh basil

1 cup sour cream

2 eggs, beaten

1 cup shredded part-skim mozzarella cheese

1/4 cup grated Parmesan cheese

1 (12-ounce) package manicotti shells

1 (15-ounce) can no-salt-added tomato sauce

1 teaspoon dried oregano

Calories 350, **% Calories from Fat** 35%, **Fat** (g) 14, **Carbohydrates** (g) 42, **Protein** (g) 15, **Sodium** (mg) 191, **Fiber** (g) 4, **Saturated Fat** (g) 8, **Cholesterol** (mg) 80

Spinach Manicotti

- Heat butter in saucepan. Add onion and garlic; cook and stir 9 minutes.

- Add spinach; cook and stir until water evaporates. Add nutmeg, pepper, and basil; put in bowl. Add sour cream, eggs, and cheeses.

- Cook manicotti shells in boiling water until al dente; drain and rinse with cold water. Fill with spinach mixture.

- Combine tomato sauce and oregano; pour half into 9- x 13-inch pan. Top with manicotti and remaining sauce. Bake at 350°F 1 hour.

• • • • RECIPE VARIATION • • • •

Mushroom Manicotti: Make recipe as directed, except substitute 3 cups sliced cremini or button mushrooms for the spinach. Cook the mushrooms with the onions and garlic until the moisture evaporates and mushrooms are brown. Omit nutmeg and oregano; add 1 teaspoon dried thyme to tomato sauce.

Mixed Vegetable Manicotti: Make recipe as directed, except substitute 1 red bell pepper and 1 green bell pepper, both chopped, for the spinach. Add 1 cup chopped mushrooms to the onion mixture. Fill shells as directed. Omit nutmeg and oregano; add 1 teaspoon dried basil to the tomato sauce.

Cook Vegetables

Fill Shells

- Frozen chopped spinach is an excellent buy; it takes a lot of fresh spinach to cook down to 2 cups.

- To thaw, place the spinach in a colander and run warm water over it until it thaws.

- Squeeze the spinach between your hands to remove as much water as possible.

- Then press the spinach between paper towels to remove even more water. Sauté until remaining water evaporates.

- Manicotti shells are also called cannelloni shells. Just use the large round open tubes that are about 1½-inch in diameter.

- You do need to stir the shells often as they cook in the boiling water, because they can stick together.

- To fill the shells, use an iced tea spoon. The small bowl and long handle will accommodate the pasta.

- Don't fill the shells too full or press the filling into the pasta or they will rip or break.

UPDATED TUNA CASSEROLE
Fresh tuna instead of canned reduces sodium content

Tuna casserole is everyone's definition of comfort food. The combination of mild tuna with a creamy sauce and tender pasta can be very delicious—and very high In sodium.

Several ingredients in the traditional tuna noodle casserole have lots of salt: canned tuna, canned cream of mushroom soup, and cheese. Substitute fresh tuna for the canned, make a white sauce from scratch instead of using canned soup, and

add more vegetables to turn this recipe into health food.

Tuna steaks are fairly inexpensive and are easy to cook. For this recipe cook them well-done, until they flake when tested with a fork.

Serve this casserole with Peach Gelatin Salad (page 178), *Yield: Serves 6*

Ingredients

- 1 pound tuna steak
- 1 tablespoon olive oil
- 1 tablespoon lemon juice
- 1 onion, chopped
- 3 cloves garlic, minced
- 1 (8-ounce) package cremini mushrooms, sliced
- 2 tablespoons unsalted butter
- 1 red bell pepper, chopped
- 3 tablespoons flour
- 1 teaspoon dried thyme
- 1 teaspoon dried marjoram
- 1/4 teaspoon pepper
- 1 cup low-sodium chicken broth
- 1 cup milk
- 1/2 cup shredded sharp cheddar cheese
- 1 cup frozen peas
- 2 cups egg noodles, cooked
- 3 tablespoons grated Parmesan cheese

Calories 388, **% Calories from Fat** 41%, **Fat** (g) 18, **Carbohydrates** (g) 28, **Protein** (g) 30, **Sodium** (mg) 266, **Fiber** (g) 3, **Saturated Fat** (g) 8, **Cholesterol** (mg) 76

Updated Tuna Casserole

- Brush tuna with oil and lemon juice. Broil 6 inches from heat, turning once, 10 to 12 minutes, until done. Cool 15 minutes.

- In saucepan cook onion, garlic, and mushrooms in butter 7 to 8 minutes. Add red bell pepper; cook 2 minutes.

- Add flour, thyme, marjoram, and pepper; simmer 3 minutes. Add broth and milk; simmer until thickened.

- Remove from heat; add cheddar, peas, noodles, and tuna. Pour into casserole; top with Parmesan. Bake at 375°F 25 to 30 minutes, until bubbly.

Curried Tuna Noodle Casserole: Make recipe as directed, except omit mushrooms and peas. Add 1 tablespoon curry powder to the onion mixture. Add 1 green bell pepper, chopped, and 1 cup chopped celery with the red bell pepper. Omit cheeses. Sprinkle the top with a mixture of 1 cup soft bread crumbs mixed with 1 tablespoon unsalted butter.

Spanish Tuna Noodle Casserole: Make recipe as directed, except omit cheddar cheese and peas. Add 1 teaspoon dried oregano in place of the thyme and marjoram. Stir in 2 red tomatoes, chopped and seeded, along with the egg noodles. Sprinkle top with 3 tablespoons ground unsalted almonds.

Cook Vegetables

- For more texture and a pretty presentation, cut the vegetables into fairly large pieces, about 1-inch cubes.

- You can chop the vegetables ahead of time, but don't cook them until you're ready to make the casserole.

- Use your favorite herbs in this recipe. Other good combinations would be basil and thyme, or dried Italian seasoning.

- Stir the mixture with a wire whisk after you add the flour to make the smoothest sauce.

Broil Tuna

- The current trend with tuna is to cook it until it's still undone in the center, but that just won't work in this recipe.

- There can be a slight bit of pink in the center, but the tuna should flake easily with a fork.

- For even more flavor, you can grill the tuna. Oil the grill rack. Grill 8 to 10 minutes, turning once, until done.

- Or bake the tuna in a preheated 425°F oven 12 to 17 minutes, until the tuna flakes.

ZITI CHICKEN CASSEROLE

Lots of vegetables update the classic chicken casserole

Ziti is a round, hollow pasta that is excellent for casseroles. It's perfect in casseroles because the sauce and ingredients fill the pasta, creating a burst of flavor every time you take a bite.

You can substitute other pastas of about the same size for the ziti in this and any other recipe. Mostaccioli and penne are good choices.

To save time you can substitute 3 cups of your favorite low-sodium pasta sauce for the diced tomatoes and tomato sauce; if you do this, cut back on the herbs.

For even less fat you can substitute low-fat ricotta and sour cream for the full-fat products called for in the recipe. But make sure they aren't higher in sodium. *Yield: Serves 6*

Ingredients

2 tablespoons unsalted butter

4 boneless, skinless chicken breasts

3 tablespoons flour

1 teaspoon paprika

1/4 teaspoon pepper

1 onion, chopped

4 cloves garlic, minced

1 (14.5-ounce) can no-salt-added diced tomatoes

1 (15-ounce) can no-salt-added tomato sauce

1 teaspoon dried oregano

1/4 cup chopped parsley

1 cup ricotta cheese

1 cup sour cream

1 egg

1 cup frozen spinach, thawed and drained

1/8 teaspoon nutmeg

1 1/2 cups shredded mozzarella cheese, divided

1 (12-ounce) package ziti pasta

2 tablespoons grated Romano cheese

Calories 574, **% Calories from Fat** 31%, **Fat** (g) 20, **Carbohydrates** (g) 55, **Protein** (g) 43, **Sodium** (mg) 185, **Fiber** (g) 3, **Saturated Fat** (g) 11, **Cholesterol** (mg) 136

Ziti Chicken Casserole

- Melt butter in large skillet. Dredge chicken in combined flour, paprika, and pepper. Cook in butter until done, 12 to 15 minutes.

- Remove chicken; add onion and garlic to pan; cook 5 minutes. Add tomatoes, tomato sauce, oregano, and parsley; simmer.

- Cube chicken; mix with ricotta, sour cream, egg, spinach, nutmeg, and 1 cup mozzarella. Cook pasta.

- Add pasta to tomato sauce. Layer with chicken mixture in casserole. Top with ½ cup mozzarella and Romano. Bake at 350°F 30 to 40 minutes.

Simmer Sauce

Mix Chicken and Ricotta

- The sauce will simmer about 10 to 15 minutes, until it's thickened.

- Be sure to stir the sauce frequently as it cooks so it doesn't burn on the bottom.

- You can add other vegetables to this sauce as well; think about adding sliced mushrooms or chopped zucchini.

- This recipe is easy to make vegetarian; just omit the chicken and add more vegetables.

- Since the chicken is fully cooked, you can make the dish ahead of time and refrigerate it until you are ready to eat.

- If you do cook the chicken ahead of time, cook the vegetables in the same amount of butter.

- If you'd like, you can mix the chicken and pasta mixtures together.

- You can blend the two mixtures gently to marble, or completely before sprinkling with the cheese.

135

TURKEY TETRAZZINI

Tetrazzini is a creamy sauce filled with pasta, veggies, and turkey

Tetrazzini is actually an American invention. It was supposedly named after Luisa Tetrazzini, an Italian opera star who was famous in the early twentieth century.

Many recipes for turkey or chicken tetrazzini call for bottled Alfredo sauces or canned cream of mushroom soups. This significantly raises the sodium level and hides the true flavors of the dish.

Making your own white sauce is easy to do, and it adds so much flavor to the recipe. Just stir constantly with a wire whisk to prevent lumps.

You can make this recipe as mild or as spicy as you'd like. And it can be made with other meats, including ham and beef meatballs. Enjoy with a glass of white wine. *Yield: Serves 8*

Ingredients

3 tablespoons unsalted butter

1 onion, chopped

3 cloves garlic, minced

1 (8-ounce) package button mushrooms, sliced

2 cups baby spinach

¼ cup flour

¼ teaspoon pepper

½ teaspoon dry mustard

1 teaspoon dried oregano

1 teaspoon dried basil

2 cups low-sodium chicken broth

2 cups light cream or 1 percent milk

1 (16-ounce) package spaghetti

4 cups cubed cooked turkey

1½ cups shredded low-sodium Swiss cheese

3 tomatoes, chopped

2 tablespoons grated Romano cheese

Calories 459, **% Calories from Fat** 30%, **Fat** (g) 15, **Carbohydrates** (g) 42, **Protein** (g) 37, **Sodium** (mg) 135, **Fiber** (g) 2, **Saturated Fat** (g) 8, **Cholesterol** (mg) 85

Turkey Tetrazzini

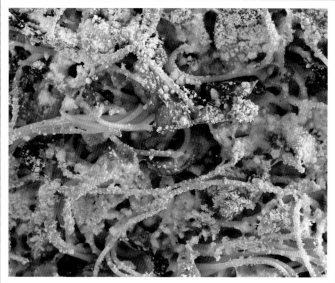

- Melt butter in saucepan; cook onion, garlic, and mushrooms 6 to 7 minutes. Add spinach; cook 2 to 3 minutes, until wilted.

- Add flour, pepper, mustard, oregano, and basil. Simmer 3 minutes. Add broth and cream or milk; simmer until thickened.

- Cook spaghetti according to package directions until al dente; drain. Stir into sauce along with turkey, Swiss cheese, and tomatoes.

- Pour into 13- x 9-inch baking dish. Top with Romano cheese. Bake at 350°F 45 to 55 minutes, until bubbly.

Making your own white sauce is very easy; it just requires some time, patience, and attention to detail. Melt the fat completely first; cook onions in it until tender, if desired. Add the flour and stir with a wire whisk until the mixture bubbles 2 minutes. Then stir with the whisk while you add the liquid.

· · · · RECIPE VARIATION · · · ·

Chicken Tetrazzini: Make recipe as directed, except use 4 cups cooked and cubed boneless, skinless chicken breasts (about 5 breasts). Omit the oregano; add 1 teaspoon dried thyme leaves. And use half part-skim low-sodium mozzarella cheese for half of the Swiss cheese.

Cook Vegetables

Stir in Cheese and Tomatoes

- When you cook fresh spinach, you'll find it wilts and decreases in volume quickly and dramatically.

- Baby spinach is much more tender and milder in flavor than regular spinach, and it doesn't need to be chopped.

- You can caramelize the onions and garlic for more flavor. Sauté 15 to 20 minutes, until brown.

- Using your own homemade chicken stock is better; it will reduce the sodium content dramatically and tastes best.

- You can substitute any variety of low-sodium cheese in this recipe. Just shred it so it melts evenly.

- Use leftover Thanksgiving turkey in this easy recipe, or cook some turkey tenderloins.

- Don't buy roasted turkey from the deli unless you're sure the sodium content is low.

- And don't use packaged cooked diced chicken or turkey; those products are very high in sodium.

VEGETABLE ENCHILADAS

Spicy enchiladas can be filled with lots of vegetables for a healthy twist

Enchiladas are made of corn or flour tortillas, rolled around a filling and baked in a spicy sauce topped with cheese.

If you order enchiladas at a restaurant, particularly a fast-food restaurant, there's a good chance you're going to be consuming close to 1,000 mg of sodium in each serving. Frozen enchilada dinners are no better. So make your enchiladas

from scratch; it's easy, and they taste wonderful.

Enchiladas are, naturally, quite spicy. You can regulate the heat by omitting the jalapeño peppers and reducing the chili powder. Or make it spicier by adding more!

These enchiladas are a one-dish meal; all you need is a fruit or green salad for a hearty dinner. *Yield: Serves 8*

Ingredients

1 poblano pepper

1 red bell pepper

1 green bell pepper

2 onions, chopped

4 cloves garlic, minced

2 jalapeño peppers

1 tablespoon olive oil

1 yellow summer squash, chopped

1 (8-ounce) package cremini mushrooms, sliced

1 (15-ounce) can no-salt-added tomato sauce

1 cup low-sodium salsa

1 tablespoon chili powder

1 teaspoon chile paste

8 (7-inch) flour tortillas

1 cup shredded sharp low-sodium cheddar cheese

Calories 290, **% Calories from Fat** 34%, **Fat** (g) 11, **Carbohydrates** (g) 40, **Protein** (g) 10, **Sodium** (mg) 310, **Fiber** (g) 6, **Saturated Fat** (g) 4, **Cholesterol** (mg) 14

Vegetable Enchiladas

- Broil peppers, turning frequently until skin blackens. Place in paper bag, let cool.

- Skin, seed, and chop peppers. Cook onion, garlic, and jalapeños in oil 5 minutes.

- Add squash and mushrooms; cook 6 minutes. Add peppers; remove from

pan. Add sauce, salsa, chili powder, and chile paste to pan; simmer.

- Add ½ cup sauce to pepper mixture; fill tortillas. Put 1 cup sauce in 13- x 9-inch pan; top with filled tortillas, remaining sauce, and cheese. Bake at 350°F 30 to 40 minutes.

Homemade Chili Powder: In small bowl, combine 2 tablespoons each paprika, ground chiles, and dried oregano, 1 tablespoon each ground cumin, garlic powder, and onion powder, 2 teaspoons cayenne pepper, and ½ teaspoon black pepper. Blend well; store in airtight container.

Vegetable Burritos: Make recipe as directed, except add the cheese to the vegetable filling. Use 10-inch tortillas; after they are filled and rolled, brush the exterior with peanut oil. Place on baking sheet and bake in 400°F oven 25 to 30 minutes, turning once, until tortillas are crisp and filling is hot.

Broil Peppers

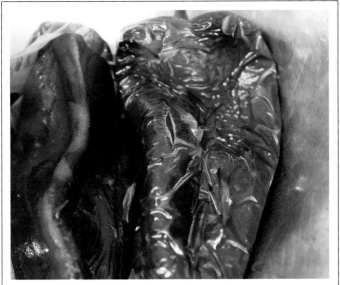

Fill Tortillas

- The skin of the peppers really should turn black when they are broiled. This adds flavor to the recipe.

- The skin is peeled off, so you don't have to worry about consuming any burned food.

- The skin will peel off easily after the peppers have been steamed in the paper bag.

- Peel off as much skin as you can. Don't worry if it doesn't all come off; it does add flavor and texture.

- You can use flour or corn tortillas in this recipe. Be sure to check the sodium content on the label.

- Corn tortillas come in several colors. Blue tortillas are made from blue corn, while red tortillas are colored with chile peppers.

- Flour tortillas also are available in different flavors and colors. Vary them for a celebratory dish.

- You can prepare this recipe ahead of time; cover and refrigerate up to 24 hours, then bake, adding 10 to 20 minutes baking time.

CHILES RELLENOS

Broiled poblano peppers are the base for this spicy Tex-Mex casserole

Chile rellenos are stuffed chile peppers. In fact, that's what the words mean! Many of the traditional recipes call for battering and frying the chiles. Baking them in a spicy tomato sauce is much healthier and just as tasty.

The chiles are roasted, then typically filled with a seasoned cheese mixture. Using ground beef, brown rice, and onion adds interest and nutrition to the dish.

You can substitute Anaheim or pasilla chiles for the poblano peppers. Anaheims are just about as mild, but the pasilla peppers can be quite spicy.

Serve this dish with more sour cream and some guacamole to top each serving and a fruit salad made from apples and pears. For dessert make ice-cream sundaes. *Yield: Serves 6*

Ingredients

12 poblano peppers

$1/2$ pound 90 percent lean ground beef

1 onion, chopped

4 cloves garlic, minced

2 jalapeño peppers, minced

1 chipotle pepper, minced

1 tablespoon chili powder

1 cup cooked long grain brown rice

$1/2$ cup sour cream

$1 1/2$ cups low-sodium salsa, divided

1 (8-ounce) can no-salt-added tomato sauce

1 cup grated sharp low-sodium cheddar cheese

Calories 260, **% Calories from Fat** 39%, **Fat** (g) 11, **Carbohydrates** (g) 28, **Protein** (g) 15, **Sodium** (mg) 49, **Fiber** (g) 4, **Saturated Fat** (g) 6, **Cholesterol** (mg) 41

Chiles Rellenos

- Broil poblano peppers, turning often, until blackened. Place in paper bag 10 minutes. Peel peppers, open, remove stems, seeds.

- Cook ground beef, onion, garlic, and peppers until beef is done; drain. Add chili powder, rice, sour cream, and $1/2$ cup salsa.

- Fill peppers with ground beef mixture; place in 2-quart casserole. Mix remaining salsa with tomato sauce.

- Pour salsa mixture over filled peppers; sprinkle with cheese. Bake at 350°F 40 to 45 minutes, until bubbly.

Turkey Chiles Rellenos: Make recipe as directed, except use ¾ pound ground turkey breast in place of the ground beef. Add ½ teaspoon dried marjoram leaves and ⅛ teaspoon white pepper to the filling. Substitute 1 cup grated low-sodium Swiss cheese for the cheddar cheese.

Pork Chiles Rellenos: Make recipe as directed, except use ½ pound lean ground pork in place of the ground beef. Add ½ teaspoon ground cumin and ¼ teaspoon pepper to the filling. Omit the brown rice; add ½ cup chopped dark raisins and ¼ cup toasted pine nuts to the filling.

Prepare Peppers

- When the peppers are roasted, they will become tender and pliable. Let them cool until you can handle them.

- Remove the seeds by inserting a small spoon into the slit and gently scrape out the seeds and membrane.

- You can leave the stems on the peppers or remove them. They do add visual appeal.

- If you choose to remove the stems, you don't have to cut a slit in the peppers. Fill from the top.

Fill Peppers

- Use that same small spoon to add the filling. Make sure the chiles are stuffed completely, but don't overstuff them.

- If you add too much filling, the peppers will split as they bake. The dish will still be tasty, but not as pretty.

- If there is any leftover filling, spoon it on top of the peppers, or mix it with the salsa and tomato sauce.

- This dish can be made ahead of time, since the ground beef is completely cooked. Refrigerate until you're ready to bake.

LASAGNA

Lasagna is a classic layered casserole made to serve a crowd

Everyone loves lasagna. Combine pasta, a seasoned ground beef tomato sauce, and cheese— what's not to love?

Traditional lasagna recipes are usually very high in sodium because of the tomato sauce and cheese. This recipe is much healthier and just as delicious. The layers in lasagna are made up of lasagna noodles, a meat sauce, a sauce made with ricotta cheese, and shredded mozzarella cheese.

Lasagna is a great recipe to freeze. Cool completely, wrap in freezer wrap, label, and freeze up to 4 months. Let the lasagna thaw in the refrigerator overnight, then bake, adding 15 to 20 minutes to the baking time.

Enjoy this lasagna with some dry red wine and a spinach salad topped with croutons. *Yield: Serves 10*

Ingredients

- 1 pound 90 percent lean ground beef
- 1 onion, chopped
- 4 cloves garlic, minced
- 2 (14.5-ounce) cans no-salt-added diced tomatoes
- 1 (15-ounce) can no-salt-added tomato sauce
- 1 teaspoon dried oregano
- 1 teaspoon dried basil
- 1/2 teaspoon fennel seeds
- 1/4 cup unsalted butter
- 1/4 cup flour
- 1/4 teaspoon white pepper
- 2 1/2 cups homemade chicken stock
- 1 cup milk
- 1 cup ricotta cheese
- 1 egg
- 1 (10-ounce) package frozen spinach, thawed and drained
- 1 cup shredded part-skim mozzarella cheese
- 12 lasagna noodles
- 1/4 cup grated Romano cheese

Calories 451, **% Calories from Fat** 40%, **Fat** (g) 20, **Carbohydrates** (g) 44, **Protein** (g) 24, **Sodium** (mg) 246, **Fiber** (g) 4, **Saturated Fat** (g) 10, **Cholesterol** (mg) 83

Lasagna

- Cook beef, onion and garlic; drain. Add tomatoes, tomato sauce, oregano, basil, and fennel; simmer.

- In another pan, melt butter; add flour and pepper. Cook 3 minutes. Add chicken stock and milk; simmer until thickened; remove from heat. Add ricotta, egg,

- spinach, and mozzarella.

- Cook noodles al dente. In 9- x 13-inch greased baking dish, place 1/3 beef mixture.

- Layer 1/3 noodles, spinach mixture, and beef mixture; repeat. Top with Romano. Bake at 375°F 40 to 50 minutes.

········· GREEN ● LIGHT ·········

You can make lasagna without cooking the noodles. Look for no-boil noodles in the grocery store; be sure to check the sodium label. Or layer uncooked noodles in the recipe; add another ½ cup water to the beef mixture. Refrigerate overnight; bake covered 1 hour. Uncover; bake 15 minutes.

· · · · RECIPE VARIATION · · · ·

Tex-Mex Lasagna: Make recipe as directed, except substitute 1 pound lean ground pork for the ground beef. Add 1 minced serrano pepper to the onion mixture and 1 cup salsa with the tomato sauce. Omit ricotta mixture; blend 1 (15-ounce) can refried beans with ½ cup salsa as a substitute.

Simmer Tomato Sauce

- Simmer the tomato sauce until it is slightly thickened; this only takes a few minutes.

- You can substitute 4 red tomatoes, chopped, for the canned tomatoes if you'd like.

- Fennel seeds are the traditional flavoring for Italian pasta sauce. You can omit them or use celery seeds instead.

- Substitute fresh herbs for the dried. Use 2 tablespoons chopped fresh basil and 1 tablespoon oregano leaves.

Layer Ingredients

- Layer the ingredients three times, starting with noodles and ending with the beef mixture

- Spread the different layers evenly over each other. Each should be of an even thickness.

- Bake the lasagna until the casserole bubbles and the cheese on top browns.

- Let the lasagna stand 10 to 15 minutes after it comes out of the oven. This will let the layers set so you can cut neat squares.

GROUNDNUT STEW

Peanut butter adds nutrition and flavor to this hearty stew

This recipe, from Africa, is quite different from other chicken stews. Peanuts are called "groundnuts" in that country. This term also applies to other seeds that ripen underground, including legumes.

This stew, with peanut butter melted in at the end, is a fabulous combination of textures and flavors. The sweet potato, onion, and eggplant are traditional ingredients, but you can use any fresh vegetables that you like.

Don't omit the garnishes; they add wonderful texture, color, flavor, and temperature contrast to the dish.

Serve this dish over hot cooked rice, either brown or white, to soak up the delicious sauce. Some pita breads or whole wheat tortillas on the side, along with some fresh fruit, are good accompaniments. *Yield: Serves 6*

Ingredients

2 tablespoons unsalted butter

1 onion, chopped

3 cloves garlic, minced

1 (8-ounce) package cremini mushrooms, sliced

1 sweet potato, peeled and cubed

1 cup peeled and cubed eggplant

1 serrano pepper, minced

6 boneless, skinless chicken thighs, cut into strips

1 teaspoon paprika

1 teaspoon dried marjoram

1/4 teaspoon pepper

1/8 teaspoon cayenne pepper

5 cups low-sodium chicken broth, divided

1 (14.5-ounce) can no-salt-added diced tomatoes

1/2 cup no-salt-added peanut butter

1/4 cup chopped unsalted peanuts

1/2 cup chopped green onion

1 green bell pepper, chopped

Calories 360, **% Calories from Fat** 58%, **Fat** (g) 23, **Carb** (g) 20, **Protein** (g) 22, **Sodium** (mg) 90, **Fiber** (g) 5, **Saturated Fat** (g) 6, **Cholesterol** (mg) 63

Groundnut Stew

- Melt butter in large pot. Cook onion, garlic, and mushrooms 8 minutes. Add sweet potato, eggplant, and serrano.

- Cook and stir 8 minutes. Add chicken, paprika, marjoram, pepper, and cayenne pepper; cook 3 to 4 minutes.

- Add 4 cups chicken broth and tomatoes; simmer 25 minutes, until chicken is done.

- Blend peanut butter with remaining 1 cup broth; add to stew. Simmer 10 minutes. Garnish with chopped peanuts, green onions, and green bell pepper.

Cook Vegetables

Add Peanut Butter

ETHNIC DELIGHTS

- Sweet potatoes are full of vitamin A and rich flavor. Peel them and cut into cubes as you would a russet potato.

- To prepare eggplant, wash it well and cut off the ends. Cut the vegetable in half, then place cut side down on the work surface.

- Cut into strips, then cut those strips into cubes. You can peel the eggplant or leave the skin on for more fiber.

- The eggplant will absorb the fat as it cooks. Don't be put off by this; that's just its character.

- You can use crunchy or creamy peanut butter in this easy stew; just make sure it's low in sodium.

- The peanut butter is blended with the broth in a process called "tempering."

- This makes the peanut butter melt easily into the stew and makes the finished dish very smooth.

- Other traditional garnishes include unsalted peanuts, fresh chopped lettuce, tomatoes, and sliced bananas.

145

CHICKEN DIVAN

Chicken with broccoli in a sherried cream sauce is elegant

Chicken divan was first made in a New York restaurant called the Divan Parisienne. The word *divan* in recipe lingo has come to refer to meats cooked with broccoli and served with a cream sauce.

Many updated recipes for chicken divan use canned cream of mushroom or chicken soup. This adds lots of sodium to the recipe and just doesn't taste as good as a homemade sauce.

This rich dish is perfect for entertaining. You can make it ahead of time, since the chicken is completely cooked in the first step. Cover and refrigerate up to 8 hours; add 10 to 15 minutes to the baking time to make up for the chill.

Serve with biscuits, hot from the oven, and a rice pilaf made with chopped walnuts and thyme. *Yield: Serves 6*

Ingredients

¼ cup unsalted butter

4 boneless, skinless chicken breasts, sliced

1 teaspoon paprika

¼ teaspoon white pepper

1 onion, chopped

3 cloves garlic, minced

¼ cup flour

¼ cup dry sherry

2 cups low-sodium chicken broth

½ cup heavy cream or 1 percent milk

1½ pounds broccoli, cut into florets

2 tablespoons lemon juice

1 cup shredded low-sodium Swiss cheese

2 tablespoons grated Parmesan cheese

Calories 296, **% Calories from Fat** 46%, **Fat** (g)15, **Carbohydrates** (g) 10, **Protein** (g) 27, **Sodium** (mg) 115, **Fiber** (g) 1, **Saturated Fat** (g) 9, **Cholesterol** (mg) 86.0

Chicken Divan

- Melt butter in large pan. Sprinkle chicken with paprika and pepper; cook in butter about 9 to 11 minutes; remove.

- Add onion and garlic to pan; cook 5 minutes. Add flour; simmer 3 minutes. Add sherry; cook 4 minutes.

- Add broth and cream or milk; simmer until thickened. Put broccoli in sprayed 9- x 13-inch pan; drizzle with lemon juice; add chicken.

- Stir Swiss cheese into sauce; pour over broccoli and chicken. Top with Parmesan. Bake at 350°F 25 to 35 minutes until bubbly.

Pork Divan: Make recipe as directed, except use 1½ pounds pork tenderloin, sliced ½-inch thick, in place of the chicken breasts. Omit paprika; season the pork with ½ teaspoon ground cumin. Add 2 cups sliced cremini or button mushrooms to the onion mixture.

Turkey Divan: Make recipe as directed, except use 1½ pounds turkey tenderloin in place of the chicken breasts. Slice the tenderloin and sauté in butter as directed, just until done. Add 1 cup chopped leeks to the onion mixture. Omit sherry; add 2 tablespoons Dijon mustard to the sauce mixture.

Cook Chicken

- Cook the chicken until it's no longer pink inside. Be careful to not overcook it.

- Don't use cooking sherry in this or any other recipe, because contains a lot of salt. Use a good quality dry sherry in this low-sodium dish.

- The sherry adds a wonderful smoky depth of flavor to the sauce, but you can omit it if you'd like.

- Add another ¼ cup heavy cream or milk to the sauce if you do omit the sherry; or use dry white wine.

Simmer Sauce

- This sauce is made with a roux, which is a combination of flour and fat cooked until bubbly.

- The cooking process removes the raw taste of the flour and prepares the flour to soak up the liquid.

- A wire whisk is your best

choice for this task, as it evenly and quickly combines small amounts of food and liquid.

- The sauce will bubble and the top will turn brown when the dish is done. Let cool 5 minutes, then serve.

ETHNIC DELIGHTS

SOUVLAKI

Marinated pork is grilled on skewers with onions and bell peppers

Souvlaki is the Greek word for "skewer." This dish is made of meats and vegetables threaded onto a skewer and grilled until brown and juicy.

Kalamaki (or "little reed") is a skewer made of meat, cut into small cubes and skewered on wooden skewers. In both recipes the meat is marinated in a mixture of lemon, garlic, olive oil, wine, and lots of herbs.

Lamb is traditionally used for this recipe, but you can use pork, chicken breasts, or chicken thighs. The meat is always boneless and is marinated before grilling.

Serve Souvlaki with Tzatziki Sauce (page 149), made from sour cream and cucumber; a rice pilaf flavored with oregano and mint; a cucumber and tomato salad; and lemon meringue pie. *Yield: Serves 8*

Ingredients

2 lemons

3 tablespoons olive oil

2 tablespoons balsamic vinegar

2 tablespoons red wine

1 teaspoon dill seed

1/4 teaspoon dried mint leaves

1/4 teaspoon pepper

1 tablespoon fresh oregano

2 pounds pork tenderloin

2 red onions

3 green bell peppers

Calories 190, **% Calories from Fat** 49%, **Fat** (g) 10, **Carbohydrates** (g) 4, **Protein** (g) 20, **Sodium** (mg) 48, **Fiber** (g) 1, **Saturated Fat** (g) 3, **Cholesterol** (mg) 62

Souvlaki

- Remove zest from lemons and juice. Combine juice, zest, olive oil, vinegar, wine, dill, mint, pepper, and oregano in large bowl.

- Cut pork into 1½-inch cubes and add to marinade. Cover and chill 8 to 24 hours.

- Remove pork from marinade; reserve marinade. Cut onions into 8 wedges each; cut bell peppers into strips. Thread food onto skewers.

- Grill 6 inches from medium coals 12 to 15 minutes, brushing with marinade, until pork registers 155 °F. Discard remaining marinade. Serve with Tzatziki Sauce.

Tzatziki Sauce: Peel cucumber and cut in half lengthwise; remove seeds. Shred cucumber, drain on paper towels. Mix with 1 cup sour cream; 2 tablespoons lemon juice; 2 cloves garlic, minced; 1 tablespoon fresh dill weed; and ¼ teaspoon pepper. Serve with Souvlaki.

Lamb Souvlaki: Make recipe as directed, except use 2 pounds lean lamb shoulder instead of the pork tenderloin. Omit dried mint; add 1 tablespoon minced fresh mint leaves. Omit balsamic vinegar; add 2 tablespoons orange juice. Marinate as directed and grill as directed.

Prepare Marinade

Thread on Skewers

- This marinade is quite variable and tolerant. You can use lime juice instead, add garlic, or omit the mint.

- Use other fresh herbs, omit the balsamic vinegar, and add hot minced chile peppers.

- You can make the marinade ahead of time. Store it in the refrigerator up to 2 days.

- If you change the marinade and love the results, be sure to write down your formula. Soon you'll have a notebook full of tried-and-true recipes.

- Metal skewers are the best choice for this type of recipe, because the food grills longer than 7 to 8 minutes.

- The onions may be a little bit difficult to skewer. If that's the case, use a sharp knife to start a hole.

- You can assemble the skewers ahead of time; cover and refrigerate up to 8 hours.

- It's okay to marinate the pork longer than 24 hours but not longer than 48; the meat will be very flavorful and tender.

ETHNIC DELIGHTS

149

KUNG PAO CHICKEN

Chicken is stir-fried with vegetables in a super spicy sauce

"Kung pao" is a Chinese phrase that comes from the governor's title *Gong Bao,* or palatial guardian. This dish is spicy! It originated in the Sichuan area of China and is part of the Szechuan cuisine.

Lots of garlic, hot chile peppers, chile paste, and onions add wonderful flavor to chicken breasts. You can substitute chicken thighs for the breasts if you'd like; just increase the

chicken cooking time to 8 to 10 minutes.

You can also make the recipe with cubed pork tenderloin or pork chops, or cubed turkey tenderloin. Make the dish as spicy or as mild as you'd like, but note that the basic premise of the dish is quite spicy.

Serve with a mixed fruit salad, some green tea, and chopsticks! *Yield: Serves 6*

Ingredients

2 tablespoons rice wine vinegar

1 tablespoon low-sodium soy sauce

2 tablespoons sesame oil

1 teaspoon hot chile paste

2 tablespoons cornstarch

$1/2$ teaspoon red pepper flakes

2 cups low-sodium chicken broth

6 boneless, skinless chicken breasts, cubed

2 tablespoons peanut oil

2 onions, chopped

5 cloves garlic, minced

2 jalapeño peppers, minced

2 red bell peppers, chopped

1 cup sliced shiitake mushrooms

Calories 276, **% Calories from Fat** 37%, **Fat** (g) 11, **Carbohydrates** (g) 14, **Protein** (g) 30, **Sodium** (mg) 146, **Fiber** (g) 2, **Saturated Fat** (g) 2, **Cholesterol** (mg) 68

Kung Pao Chicken

- Combine vinegar, soy sauce, sesame oil, chile paste, cornstarch, red pepper flakes, and broth in large bowl. Add chicken; cover and chill 8 to 24 hours.

- Drain chicken, reserving marinade. Heat peanut oil in skillet or wok. Add chicken; stir-fry 6 to 7 minutes, until

done; remove from wok.

- Add onions, garlic, jalapeños, red bell peppers, and mushrooms to wok; stir-fry 6 to 7 minutes, until crisp-tender.

- Stir marinade and add to wok along with chicken; stir-fry 3 to 4 minutes. Serve over hot cooked rice.

For the best stir-frying results, follow a few rules. Always prepare all the ingredients ahead of time so you can add them to the wok or skillet without pausing. Heat the wok or skillet over high heat, then add the oil. Keep the food moving using a large spatula or spoon.

Kung Pao Pork: Make recipe as directed, except substitute 6 boneless, skinless pork loin chops for the chicken breasts. Marinate the pork the same way. Stir-fry the pork like the chicken, cooking it 8 to 9 minutes. Omit shiitake mushrooms; add 2 cups sliced cremini mushrooms.

Marinate Chicken

Stir-Fry Vegetables

ETHNIC DELIGHTS

- You can find low-sodium soy sauce right next to the regular soy sauce in the grocery store.

- Compare brands and flavors to see which one has the lowest content. It takes only a little bit to add great smoky flavor to your stir-fry.

- The marinade can be made ahead of time and stored, covered, in the refrigerator up to 3 days.

- You can marinate the vegetables with the chicken, but keep the marinating time to 8 hours or less.

- Keep the food moving constantly as it cooks. This prevents burning and lets the food cook evenly.

- Once you start stir-frying, you can't stop, or the food will be undercooked or overcooked.

- Keep all the food in bowls, lined up in the order you'll add them to the pan.

- This dish must be served with lots of hot white rice to soak up the sauce and provide a neutral, cooling complement to the spicy sauce and chicken.

SHEPHERD'S PIE
This comforting English dish is hearty and easy to make

Shepherd's pie is made of ground meat cooked with spices and onions and topped with mashed potatoes. Updated recipes usually use a potato topping made with potato flakes and a meat mixture made with condensed soups.

But when all parts of this recipe are made from scratch, not only does it taste wonderful, but the dish lower in sodium and fat and much healthier.

Lots of herbs make this dish delicious without salt. Marjoram adds a complex and deep richness to beef, and thyme adds a light, lemony note. You can use other combinations of your own favorite herbs, or substitute fresh for the dried.

Serve this filling pie with some bread sticks and a spinach salad with apples. *Yield: Serves 8*

Ingredients

5 potatoes, peeled and cubed

2 onions, chopped

6 cloves garlic, minced

3 tablespoons unsalted butter

$1/2$ cup light cream or 1 percent milk

2 tablespoons Dijon mustard

$1/2$ cup shredded extra sharp cheddar cheese

1 pound 90 percent lean ground beef

1 teaspoon dried thyme leaves

1 teaspoon dried marjoram

1 (8-ounce) package mushrooms, sliced

1 red bell pepper, chopped

3 tablespoons flour

$1/4$ teaspoon pepper

2 cups low-sodium beef broth

$1/2$ cup low-sodium ketchup

1 teaspoon Worcestershire sauce

2 cups frozen peas and carrots

Calories 334, **% Calories from Fat** 41%, **Fat** (g) 15, **Carbohydrates** (g) 35, **Protein** (g) 17, **Sodium** (mg) 186, **Fiber** (g) 4, **Saturated Fat** (g) 8, **Cholesterol** (mg) 53

Shepherd's Pie

- Boil potatoes 15 minutes, until tender. Cook onion and garlic in butter.

- Drain potatoes; add half of onion mixture; mash. Add cream, mustard, and cheese; beat well and set aside.

- Add ground beef to remaining onion mixture; cook until done; drain. Add thyme, marjoram, mushrooms, and bell pepper; cook 3 minutes.

- Add flour and pepper; cook 3 minutes. Add remaining ingredients; simmer 10 minutes. Pour into $2\frac{1}{2}$-quart casserole; top with potatoes. Bake at 375°F 35 to 45 minutes, until browned.

Lamb Shepherd's Pie: Make recipe as directed, except substitute 1 pound lean ground lamb for the ground beef. Omit marjoram; add ½ teaspoon each dried mint leaves and dried oregano leaves. Use 3 sweet potatoes, peeled and cubed, for the regular potatoes in the topping.

Spicy Turkey Shepherd's Pie: Make recipe as directed, except substitute 1 pound ground turkey for the ground beef. Add 1 tablespoon chili powder to the potato mixture. Add 2 minced jalapeño peppers to the onion mixture. Omit thyme and marjoram; add 1 teaspoon dried oregano leaves and ½ teaspoon dried cumin.

ETHNIC DELIGHTS

Prepare Potatoes

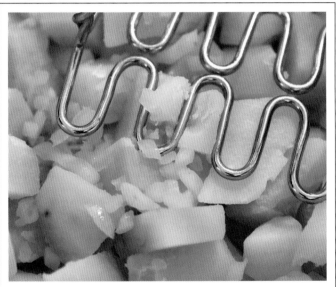

Simmer Beef Mixture

- Don't peel the potatoes ahead of time; they will turn brown because of enzymatic oxidation.

- You can use russet potatoes, Yukon Gold potatoes, or red potatoes for the topping.

- The potatoes are done when a knife slips easily into and out of the flesh.

- Mashing the potatoes with fat first helps make them fluffy, because it coats the starch granules.

- When the beef has cooked with the onions, drain it well to remove any fat.

- When you're cooking with low-fat beef products, any liquid created by browning will be mostly water.

- The sauce mixture should be simmered until thickened and well blended; stir frequently.

- You can make this recipe ahead of time; cover and refrigerate 24 hours, then bake, adding 20 to 25 minutes to the baking time.

SHRIMP GUMBO

A flour and oil roux, cooked until brown, is the secret to the best gumbo

Gumbo is a Cajun recipe that originated in the bayous of Louisiana. It's a thick stew made with a dark brown roux, vegetables, and lots of seafood.

The roux, or flour and oil mixture, is cooked until deep golden brown. This adds great smoky and rich flavor to the gumbo without any sodium at all.

Gumbo always starts with the "holy trinity" of vegetables: green bell pepper, onion, and celery. This combination is fresh tasting and adds great texture and flavor to the gumbo. Garlic is usually added, but you can leave it out if you'd like.

Serve the gumbo with hot cooked rice. *Yield: Serves 6*

Ingredients

¹/₃ cup peanut oil

¹/₃ cup flour

2 onions, chopped

4 stalks celery, chopped

5 cloves garlic, minced

2 green bell peppers, chopped

1 tablespoon chili powder

¹/₈ teaspoon pepper

¹/₂ teaspoon crushed red pepper flakes

1 teaspoon Creole seasoning

4 cups low-sodium chicken broth

3 tomatoes, peeled, seeded, and chopped

1 bay leaf

2 cups frozen okra, if desired

1 pound medium raw shrimp, shelled and deveined

Calories 273, **% Calories from Fat** 51%, **Fat** (g) 16, **Carbohydrates** (g) 21, **Protein** (g) 16, **Sodium** (mg) 164, **Fiber** (g) 4, **Saturated Fat** (g) 2, **Cholesterol** (mg) 110

Shrimp Gumbo

- In large heavy pot, cook oil and flour together until browned, stirring constantly, about 9 to 12 minutes.

- Carefully add onion, celery, garlic, and bell peppers; cook 4 to 5 minutes. Add chili powder, pepper, red pepper flakes, and Creole seasoning.

- Stir in broth, chopped tomatoes, and bay leaf. Cover and simmer 45 minutes.

- Add okra; simmer 15 minutes. Add shrimp; simmer 5 minutes. Remove bay leaf and serve over hot cooked rice.

A good brown roux can take 35 to 40 minutes to cook to the proper color. Gumbos can be made with brown roux or dark brown roux. The aroma of this mixture is strong and sharp, with a nutty flavor like toast. Don't overcook the roux or let it burn; if it burns, you'll have to start over.

Seafood Gumbo: Make recipe as directed, except reduce shrimp to ⅓ pound. Add ⅓ pound bay or sea scallops, cut in half, and ½ pound mild white fish fillets, cut into cubes, along with the shrimp. Simmer until the fish flakes, the scallops are opaque, and the fish is white and flakes with a fork.

Make Roux

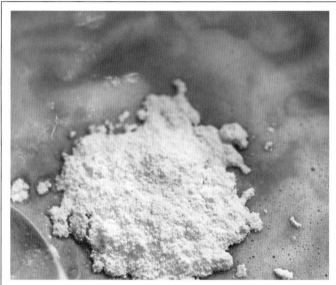

- Be sure to watch the roux carefully as it cooks. Stir very frequently so it doesn't burn.

- Making a good brown roux for gumbo takes patience and low heat.

- If you like making gumbo or other Cajun dishes, you can make a lot of roux at once.

- Freeze it in ⅓- or ½-cup portions up to 6 months. Let thaw in the refrigerator, then gently heat and continue with the recipe.

Make Sauce

- Okra is an unusual vegetable that has a substance called mucilage that is sticky and can be slimy.

- Overcooking okra can make it slimy. Don't cook it as long and it will stay crisptender.

- The shrimp should be simmered just until it turns pink and curls.

- It's easy to overcook shrimp; then it becomes tough and rubbery. Watch the mixture carefully and remove from heat the second the shrimp is done.

ETHNIC DELIGHTS

CLASSIC BAKED BEANS

This old-fashioned recipe is traditionally served with brown bread

Baked beans are nutritious and delicious and one of the most inexpensive and filling recipes you can make.

But canned baked beans, even though labeled low-sodium, are really high in salt. Baked beans are easy to make from scratch, and you can make the whole dish for under $5 or $6. If you've never had these beans made from scratch, you're in for a treat!

Navy beans are traditionally used in baked beans, but you can use kidney beans or great northern beans. Since the beans cook in a tomato sauce, they have to be soaked overnight in order to soften properly.

Serve these savory and warm beans with Brown Bread, a classic quick bread that's easy to make and also low in sodium. *Yield: Serves 8*

Ingredients

1 1/2 pounds dry navy beans

6 cups water

2 onions, chopped

4 cloves garlic, minced

2 tablespoons unsalted butter

1/2 cup molasses

1 teaspoon dry mustard

1/2 cup brown sugar

1 (8-ounce) can no-salt-added tomato sauce

1/4 cup low-sodium chili sauce

1 teaspoon dried marjoram

1/4 teaspoon pepper

Classic Baked Beans

- Sort and rinse beans and place in bowl; cover with 8 cups water; let stand overnight.

- In the morning drain beans. Place in pot, add 6 cups water, and simmer 1 hour, until beans are tender. Cook onion and garlic in butter until tender, about 6 to 7 minutes.

- Place beans, onion mixture, and remaining ingredients in casserole coated with cooking spray; stir well.

- Cover and bake at 325°F 2 hours. Uncover; bake 1 to 2 hours longer, until tender.

Calories 378, **% Calories from Fat** 10%, **Fat** (g) 4, **Carbohydrates** (g) 69, **Protein** (g) 18, **Sodium** (mg) 18, **Fiber** (g) 20, **Saturated Fat** (g) 2, **Cholesterol** (mg) 8

Slow Cooker Baked Beans: Soak beans as directed. The next morning drain and simmer as directed. Cook onions and garlic until tender as directed. Combine all ingredients except tomato sauce and chili sauce in 4-quart slow cooker; cook on low 8 hours. Add sauces; cook on low 1 to 2 hours longer, until tender.

Brown Bread: Preheat oven to 350°F; spray a 9- x 5-inch loaf pan with nonstick baking spray. Combine 1½ cups whole wheat flour, 1½ cups all-purpose flour, ½ cup brown sugar, 1 teaspoon baking soda, ½ cup molasses, and 1½ cups buttermilk. Pour into pan; bake 50 to 60 minutes, until done.

Cook Onion and Garlic

Combine Ingredients in Casserole

- The onion and garlic are cooked before mixing with the beans so they are very tender.

- You can add other vegetables to the baked beans, like sliced or chopped mushrooms or chopped bell peppers.

- Cook those vegetables along with the onions and garlic so they melt into the beans.

- The beans are first baked covered so they steam in all the liquid.

- Then the cover is removed, and the beans are baked until tender, with a delicious crusty top.

- You can stir the beans once or twice during baking time if you'd like.

- Serve the beans with brown bread to make a complete protein. This is a wholesome and inexpensive vegetarian meal.

BLACK BEAN CHILI

Smoky and spicy chili is just the thing for a cold winter day

Chili is the perfect recipe for a cold day. Cooking it in the slow cooker means the house will be filled with a fabulous aroma when you get home. It warms you up immediately.

Making chili with canned beans means a high sodium content. Even if you rinse the beans or simmer them in some plain water, 70 percent of the sodium content will remain.

In the slow cooker it's easy to make chili using dried beans. For best results the beans should soak overnight. This helps them soften properly and helps reduce digestive discomfort by removing sugars from the beans.

Adding rice to the chili helps provide complete protein. Wild rice is actually a grass seed. *Yield: Serves 6*

Ingredients

1 pound dry black beans

1 cup wild rice

2 onions, chopped

4 cloves garlic, minced

1 tablespoon olive oil

2 jalapeños peppers, minced

2 tablespoons chili powder

1 teaspoon cumin

2 teaspoons dried oregano

1 bay leaf

8 cups water

2 (14.5-ounce) cans no-salt-added diced tomatoes

1 (8-ounce) can no-salt-added tomato sauce

1 tablespoon balsamic vinegar

Calories 370, **% Calories from Fat** 9%, **Fat** (g) 4, **Carbohydrates** (g) 68, **Protein** (g) 19, **Sodium** (mg) 17, **Fiber** (g) 13, **Saturated Fat** (g) 1, **Cholesterol** (mg) 0

Black Bean Chili

- Sort black beans and rinse. Cover with cold water and soak overnight.

- In the morning, drain beans. Place in 4- to 5-quart slow cooker with wild rice. Cook onions and garlic in olive oil; add to beans.

- Add jalapeño peppers, chili powder, cumin, oregano, bay leaf, and water. Cover; cook on high 4 hours.

- Turn slow cooker to low. Add tomatoes, tomato sauce, and vinegar. Cover and cook on low 2 to 3 hours, until blended; remove bay leaf.

Classic Stovetop Chili: Make recipe as directed, except don't use a slow cooker. Soak beans overnight and drain. Heat olive oil in stockpot; add onions and garlic; cook 5 minutes. Add rice, beans, and remaining ingredients, except vinegar; simmer 2 hours, until beans are tender. Stir in vinegar.

White and Red Chili: Make recipe as directed, except omit wild rice. Use ¾ pound each dried navy beans and dried red kidney beans. Soak as directed, then cook in slow cooker as directed, cooking the beans on high first, then adding tomatoes and vinegar and cooking on low.

Mix Ingredients

Add Tomatoes

- The wild rice adds a wonderful texture, lots of fiber, and a nutty taste to this special chili.

- Rinse the wild rice before you add it to the rest of the ingredients. Choose wild rice with the longest grains you can find.

- For very intense heat and spice, substitute habañero or Scotch Bonnet chiles for the jalapeño peppers.

- But be sure you know just how hot these peppers are! They are not for the faint of heart.

- The tomato products and the vinegar are held back and added at the end of cooking time.

- Acidic ingredients like tomatoes slow down the softening of beans. It's difficult to get soft beans when they are cooked with tomatoes, especially in a slow cooker.

- The recipe will still have a rich tomato flavor, because it's cooked for several hours longer on low.

- Serve this chili with some cheese crackers or corn bread and a fruit and lettuce salad.

SLOW COOKER BEANS

Canned dried beans are very high in sodium, so make your own with ease in the slow cooker

Canned beans, while nutritious, are very high in sodium. Even reduced-sodium varieties still have more than someone on a low-salt diet should consume.

So make your own beans! This method in the slow cooker is very easy. You could even make beans and freeze some; use them in recipes like Roasted Garlic Dip.

Beans are high in fiber, especially soluble fiber, which helps regulate cholesterol levels. They are a natural plant food and should be included regularly in a healthy diet. The beans are mildly seasoned with onions, but you can add any other vegetable, herb, or spice you'd like. *Yield: Makes 8 cups*

Ingredients

1 pound dry kidney, navy, or black beans

8 cups water

¹/₈ teaspoon pepper

1 onion, quartered

Slow Cooker Beans

- Sort beans and rinse; drain. Place in slow cooker with water, pepper, and onion.

- Cover and cook on low 8 to 9 hours, until beans are tender. Use filtered water, not hard water, which will prevent softening.

- When beans are tender, remove and discard onion. Drain beans if necessary.

- Divide beans into 1¾-cup amounts. Use within 4 days, or freeze for longer storage.

Calories 159, **% Calories from Fat** 2%, **Fat** (g) 0.4, **Carbohydrates** (g) 29, **Protein** (g) 11, **Sodium** (mg) 12, **Fiber** (g) 12, **Saturated Fat** (g) 0.1, **Cholesterol** (mg) 0

········· GREEN ● LIGHT ·············

· · · · RECIPE VARIATION · · · ·

Stovetop Beans: Make recipe as directed, first soaking the beans in water overnight. Drain the beans the next morning, then combine with 5 cups water, 1 tablespoon olive oil, pepper, and 3 cloves garlic, minced, in a large pot. Cover and bring to a boil; reduce heat to low and simmer 1½ to 2 hours, until tender.

Sort Beans

Cook Beans

- To sort beans, spread them out on your countertop in a single layer.

- Run your fingers through the beans, removing any that are shriveled or that seem very light in weight.

- Also remove and discard any beans that are split in half. They will cook too quickly and will become mushy.

- To save time, sort beans by the bag, then decant them into glass or plastic containers. Label them and store up to 6 months.

- Check the beans at the 8-hour mark to see if they are tender. Taste one to check for doneness.

- You can also blow on the beans. If the skins split, the beans are ready to be taken off the heat and used in your recipes.

- If you plan to freeze the beans, undercook them slightly, as freezing will soften them.

- Leave some space at the top of the freezer container for expansion; this is called head space.

BEAN RECIPES

LENTILS & RICE

This classic vegetarian recipe cooks nicely in your slow cooker

Lentils are also known as pulses or *daal*. The lentil seeds grow in pods. Lentils are just as good for you as beans, with one major advantage: They don't need to be soaked before cooking.

The little round seeds are very high in protein and have lots of soluble fiber, vitamin B (especially folate), and iron. They are nutty and tender and have a slightly sweet, smoky flavor.

When combined with rice, especially brown rice, lentils offer complete protein. The lentils are deficient in two amino acids that the rice contains. And they taste wonderful together.

You can flavor lentils and rice any way you'd like. They are delicious served plain, seasoned with onions and garlic, or dressed up with lots of fresh herbs. *Yield: Serves 6*

Ingredients

1 tablespoon olive oil

1 onion, chopped

4 cloves garlic, minced

1¹/₂ cups long grain brown rice

1¹/₂ cups lentils

6 cups low-sodium vegetable broth

1 tablespoon fresh thyme

1 teaspoon dried oregano

Pinch salt

¹/₈ teaspoon pepper

¹/₄ cup chopped cilantro

1 cup shredded low-sodium Swiss cheese

Lentils & Rice

- Heat olive oil in saucepan; cook onions and garlic until tender, about 5 to 6 minutes. Add rice; cook 3 to 4 minutes longer.

- Sort lentils; rinse and drain. Add to onion mixture with vegetable broth, thyme, oregano, salt, and pepper.

- Bring to a simmer; reduce heat to low, cover, and simmer 45 to 55 minutes, until rice and lentils are tender.

- Uncover; cook 10 minutes. Add cilantro and cheese and stir. Cover and let stand 10 minutes, then stir and serve.

Calories 471, **% Calories from Fat** 20%, **Fat** (g) 11, **Carbohydrates** (g) 69, **Protein** (g) 26, **Sodium** (mg) 81, **Fiber** (g) 16, **Saturated Fat** (g) 4, **Cholesterol** (mg) 17

Lentil Brown Rice Salad: Make recipe as directed, except when the rice and lentils are tender, drain mixture if necessary. In bowl combine ⅓ cup each olive oil and lemon juice, 1 minced garlic clove, 3 tablespoons Dijon mustard, and 1 teaspoon dried thyme; mix. Pour over lentil mixture and mix; chill 4 to 6 hours before serving.

Rice and Lentil Soup: Prepare onions and garlic as directed; add brown rice and lentils. Increase vegetable broth to 8 cups; add 2 cups water. Cook until lentils and rice are tender, about 35 minutes. Omit cheese; add 2 cups baby spinach leaves and cilantro during the last 5 minutes of cooking time.

Cook Onion and Garlic

Simmer Ingredients

- Feel free to add even more onions and garlic to this classic recipe if you like them.

- You can cook the vegetables until tender, or cook them longer, stirring frequently, until the onions start to caramelize.

- Other vegetables would be good in this dish too, like sliced or chopped mushrooms or sweet bell peppers.

- The rice is sautéed with the vegetables for a few minutes to help it maintain an al dente texture in the finished dish.

- Substitute your favorite low-sodium cheese for the Swiss, and use parsley instead of cilantro for a change.

- This dish doesn't take very long to cook, which makes it ideal for a last-minute vegetarian meal.

- Keep these ingredients on hand in your cupboard or pantry to quickly put together a healthy low-sodium meal.

- Serve this dish with some toasted garlic or cheese bread, a spinach salad with poppyseed dressing, and glazed carrots.

BEAN RECIPES

MANY BEAN STEW

Use any combination of dry beans in this hearty and healthy stew

Bean stews are fun to make and taste delicious. If you are trying to eat a vegetarian diet at least once a week, beans are a great substitute for meat.

Dried beans and other legumes have a wonderful nutty, meaty taste and a texture that is very similar to meat.

You can also add meat to this recipe; just be sure that it's low sodium. Lean ground beef, cooked and drained, is a great addition, as is low-sodium pork sausage or even cubes of beef tossed in some flour and paprika.

Beans you can use in this recipe include navy beans, black beans, kidney beans, pink beans, pinto beans, black-eyed peas, brown speckled cow beans, cannellini beans, and cranberry beans. *Yield: Serves 6–8*

Ingredients

1 cup dry navy beans

1 cup dry black beans

1 cup dry kidney beans

1 cup dry pinto beans

1 onion, chopped

3 cloves garlic, minced

1 tablespoon unsalted butter

3 carrots, sliced

2 stalks celery, sliced

8 cups low-sodium vegetable broth

1 tablespoon fresh thyme

1 bay leaf

$1/2$ teaspoon dry mustard

1 teaspoon dried marjoram

1 (14.5-ounce) can no-salt-added diced tomatoes

1 tablespoon lemon juice

$1/4$ teaspoon pepper

Calories 403 , **% Calories from Fat** 9%, **Fat** (g) 4, **Carbohydrates** (g) 68, **Protein** (g) 27, **Sodium** (mg) 108, **Fiber** (g) 21, **Saturated Fat** (g) 2, **Cholesterol** (mg) 4

Many Bean Stew

- Sort over beans, rinse, and drain. Place in large bowl, cover with water, and let stand overnight.

- In the morning drain beans; place in 4- to 5-quart slow cooker. Cook onion and garlic in butter; add to beans.

- Add carrots, celery, and broth; mix well. Add thyme, bay leaf, mustard, and marjoram. Stir well, cover, and cook on high 4 hours.

- Add tomatoes, lemon juice, and pepper. Cover and cook on low 3 to 4 hours or until stew is blended. Remove bay leaf and serve.

Mix Beans in Slow Cooker

- Beans are one of the most inexpensive sources of protein in the supermarket, so stock up.

- Browse through your supermarket occasionally to see if newer heirloom beans, like the Jackson wonder bean, are available.

- A combination of fresh and dried herbs adds to the depth of flavor in this easy recipe.

- You can use any combination of herbs that you'd like. Oregano and marjoram, or basil and thyme would be delicious.

Add Tomatoes and Lemon Juice

- If you'd like to use fresh tomatoes in place of the canned, substitute 1¾ cups chopped tomatoes and their juice.

- One tablespoon apple cider vinegar is a good substitute for lemon juice, or you can add orange or lime juice.

- Be sure the beans are fairly tender before you add the tomatoes; taste one to be sure.

- Serve this stew with a green salad and some corn bread or scones hot from the oven.

BEAN RECIPES

BBQ BEANS

Spicy and sweet beans are the perfect side dish for a summer cookout

Barbecued beans are a staple at summer cookouts. Canned barbecued beans are loaded in sodium, and even home-made recipes that start with canned beans are beyond reach if you're watching your salt intake.

So start with dried beans and add tons of flavor with spices, onions, garlic, molasses, and vinegar. These beans bake in the oven, but they work just as well made in the slow cooker.

Since this recipe is so low in sodium, you can add a couple of slices of low-sodium bacon, crisply cooked and crumbled. That will increase the sodium content to 40 mg per serving.

The beans can be made with pinto beans, navy beans, or kidney beans. Or use a combination of dried beans for your own personal recipe. *Yield: Serves 6–8*

Ingredients

1 pound dry navy beans

6 cups water

2 onions, chopped

3 cloves garlic, minced

1 tablespoon unsalted butter

1/2 cup brown sugar

1 tablespoon chili powder

1/4 cup molasses

1/4 cup honey

1 (8-ounce) can no-salt-added tomato sauce

3 tablespoons apple cider vinegar

1/2 teaspoon hot pepper sauce

Calories 320, **% Calories from Fat** 7%, **Fat** (g) 2, **Carbohydrates** (g) 65, **Protein** (g) 12, **Sodium** (mg) 19, **Fiber** (g) 13, **Saturated Fat** (g) 1, **Cholesterol** (mg) 4

BBQ Beans

- Sort beans, rinse, and drain. Place in saucepan with water to cover. Boil 2 minutes, cover, remove from heat, and let stand 1 hour.

- Drain and rinse beans and return to saucepan. Cover with 6 cups water. Simmer 1 hour, until tender.

- Cook onion and garlic in butter. Add remaining ingredients; simmer.

- Combine beans with their cooking liquid and onion mixture in 2½-quart baking dish. Cover and bake at 350°F 30 minutes; uncover and bake 30 minutes longer.

Slow Cooker BBQ Beans: Make recipe as directed, except boil the sorted beans 2 minutes, then let stand, covered, 2 hours. Drain well and place in slow cooker with all ingredients except tomato sauce and vinegar. Cover and cook on low 7 to 8 hours, until tender. Add tomato sauce and vinegar; cook 1 to 2 hours longer.

BBQ Beans on the Grill: Make recipe as directed, except use a cast-iron pot or one made for cooking on the outdoor grill. Cook beans and vegetables as directed; combine in the pot. Place over medium coals, cover, and simmer 90 to 100 minutes, stirring frequently, until the beans are tender.

Simmer Beans

Simmer Mixture

- Because there's no way to avoid cooking the beans with high acidic ingredients, they have to be simmered before baking.

- Don't worry: The beans will still absorb lots of flavor while baking in the sauce.

- If you have hard water that is softened, think about cooking the beans in bottled water, which has fewer minerals.

- Water that contains lots of minerals can slow the softening of the beans.

- You can caramelize the onions in this recipe for even more flavor. Cook them 15 to 20 minutes, stirring frequently.

- It's important to simmer the tomato mixture until it's blended and slightly thickened, about 10 to 15 minutes.

- For a fresh flavor, you can add 1 to 2 chopped red tomatoes to the sauce if you'd like.

- In fact any other vegetable can be added to this dish. Try sliced mushrooms or sweet or hot peppers.

SPINACH SALAD

Tender baby spinach is served with a sweet-and-sour salad dressing

Salads can be boring, or delicious. They can be a side dish or a main dish. They are nutritious, beautiful, and enjoyable to eat. But the main problem with salads is the dressing.

Most salad dressings are loaded with sodium. Making your own is so easy, and you can flavor them any way you'd like.

Most salad dressings are high in fat because oil is very high in calories. But if you use olive oil or another heart-healthy monounsaturated oil in your homemade dressing, don't worry about it. You do need good fat in your diet.

Add some cooked cubed chicken or turkey to this salad to make it a main dish salad. Or serve with some broiled salmon for the perfect and healthy lunch. *Yield: Serves 6*

Ingredients

¹/₃ cup sugar

¹/₄ cup minced red onion

¹/₂ teaspoon paprika

¹/₄ cup cider vinegar

2 tablespoons lemon juice

3 tablespoons olive oil

¹/₈ teaspoon salt

¹/₈ teaspoon pepper

8 cups baby spinach leaves

2 cups sliced strawberries

3 tablespoons toasted pine nuts

Spinach Salad

- In small bowl combine sugar, red onion, paprika, vinegar, lemon juice, oil, salt, and pepper.

- Whisk well until mixture is blended and sugar dissolves.

- In serving bowl combine spinach, strawberries, and pine nuts. Add dressing, toss to coat, and serve.

- Toss to mix. If making ahead of time, place strawberries on bottom of bowl and top with spinach. Add pine nuts just before serving.

Calories 173 , **% Calories from Fat** 57%, **Fat** (g) 11, **Carbohydrates** (g)19, **Protein** (g) 2, **Sodium** (mg) 34, **Fiber** (g) 2, **Saturated Fat** (g) 1, **Cholesterol** (mg) 0

• • • • • RECIPE VARIATION • • • • •

Spinach Mandarin Orange Salad: Make recipe as directed, except omit paprika and use 2 tablespoons lime juice in place of the lemon juice. In place of the strawberries, use 1 (15-ounce) can drained mandarin oranges. Instead of the pine nuts, use toasted chopped pecans.

Mix Dressing

- It's important to mix the salad dressing until the sugar dissolves, or the salad will be sugary.

- The sugar makes the dressing sweet-and-sour. You can reduce the sugar to 3 tablespoons if you'd like.

- Or substitute honey for the sugar for a more natural dressing.

- You can season the dressing any way you'd like. Add lots of fresh herbs or use spice blends like curry powder or chili powder.

Prepare Ingredients

- Spinach is grown in sandy soil, so there will be a lot of sand lurking in those green leaves.

- Rinse the spinach well if it has been prewashed. If it hasn't, immerse the spinach in cold water and let the sand sink to the bottom.

- To prepare strawberries, rinse them well, then shake off excess water.

- Cut off the tops and slice the strawberries into ⅓-inch slices. Don't rinse the strawberries until you're ready to use them.

SALADS

MIXED FRUIT SALAD

Your favorite fruits, mixed with a lemony dressing, make a delicious and healthy salad

A combination of fresh fruits drizzled with a simple dressing is one of the best foods to eat, no matter what the season.

During the spring and summer months, use strawberries, peaches, cherries, and raspberries. During the fall and winter months, use apples, pears, oranges, and kiwifruit. Use the fruits that look best in the market.

These salads are usually best when served immediately. You can let the salad chill in the refrigerator for an hour or two, but the soft fruits such as the strawberries will get soggy, and the hard fruits such as the apples and pears will turn brown.

This is the perfect salad for a summer cookout with grilled chicken or steak. *Yield: Serves 6*

KNACK LOW-SALT COOKING

Ingredients

¹/₄ cup honey

¹/₃ cup lemon juice

1 teaspoon grated lemon zest

1 tablespoon Dijon mustard

1 tablespoon fresh thyme leaves

2 tablespoons minced green onion

¹/₄ cup olive oil

Pinch salt

¹/₈ teaspoon pepper

2 cups sliced strawberries

2 pears, chopped

2 oranges, peeled and cubed

3 cups melon balls

Calories 227, **% Calories from Fat** 38%, **Fat** (g) 10, **Carbohydrates** (g) 38, **Protein** (g) 2, **Sodium** (mg) 86, **Fiber** (g) 5, **Saturated Fat** (g) 1, **Cholesterol** (mg) 0

Mixed Fruit Salad

- In small bowl combine honey, lemon juice and zest, mustard, thyme, green onion, olive oil, salt, and pepper.

- Whisk dressing well until the sugar dissolves. You can refrigerate the dressing up to 6 hours at this point.

- When ready to eat, prepare fruits. Sprinkle pears with some of the dressing as you work.

- Drizzle dressing over the salad and toss gently to coat. Serve immediately.

Poppyseed Dressing: In blender or food processor, combine ⅓ cup each sugar and lemon juice, 2 tablespoons chopped red onion, 1 tablespoon Dijon mustard, ⅛ teaspoon white pepper, and ½ cup canola oil; blend until thick. Add 2 tablespoons poppy seeds and mix.

Raspberry Vinaigrette: In blender or food processor, combine ½ cup rinsed raspberries, ¼ cup vegetable oil, ¼ cup sugar or honey, and 2 teaspoons Dijon mustard. Blend or process until smooth and thickened. Season with ⅛ teaspoon white pepper and 2 teaspoons minced fresh mint leaves.

Whisk Dressing

- You can prepare the salad dressing by combining all the ingredients in a small jar with a screw-top lid.

- Shake the jar until the dressing is well blended. You can refrigerate the dressing in the jar up to 4 days.

- Or combine the ingredients in a blender or food processor; blend or process until smooth and thickened.

- The salad dressing can be made ahead of time. Don't keep it longer than 4 days.

Prepare Fruit

- Leave the skin on the pears if it's pretty. If the skin is spotty, peel using a swivel-bladed vegetable peeler.

- The skin on pears has lots of fiber and adds great texture and visual interest to the salad.

- To prepare oranges, remove the peel, then remove as much of the white pith as you can.

- For the melons, wash first, then cut in half. Gently scoop out the seeds, then use a melon baller to make as many balls as you can.

SALADS

BROCCOLI SALAD

Broccoli, onion, and raisins in a sweet salad dressing is delicious

This salad is a favorite in the Midwest. It's flavorful and full of texture and very good for you, too. It adds a sweet and tangy flavor to broccoli; even broccoli haters will love it.

Broccoli belongs to the cruciferous family of vegetables, along with cauliflower and brussels sprouts. The vegetable has many phytonutrients, antioxidants, and chemicals called indoles, which protect against cancer.

When broccoli is properly cooked in lots of water, with no cover, it does not have a bitter or sulfurous taste. And when mixed with low-sodium bacon and a flavorful dressing, it's downright delicious.

This salad is excellent served with grilled or roasted chicken or at a summer cookout of hamburgers and grilled corn on the cob. *Yield: Serves 6–8*

Ingredients

2 (20-ounce) packages frozen broccoli, thawed

4 slices low-sodium bacon

1 red onion, chopped

3 cloves garlic, minced

1/4 cup low-sodium, low-fat mayonnaise

1/2 cup vanilla yogurt

1/3 cup sugar

1/4 teaspoon pepper

3 tablespoons lemon juice

1/2 cup golden raisins

1/2 cup unsalted sunflower seeds

Broccoli Salad

- Thaw the broccoli in the refrigerator overnight or place under cool running water. Then drain broccoli and dry in a kitchen towel; place in large bowl.

- Cook bacon until crisp; drain, crumble, and set aside. Drain fat from pan; do not wipe. Add onion and garlic; cook 5 to 6 minutes.

- Add onion and garlic to broccoli. In separate bowl combine mayonnaise, yogurt, sugar, pepper, and lemon juice.

- Add dressing to broccoli with bacon, raisins, and seeds. Chill 2 to 3 hours.

Calories 203, **% Calories from Fat,** 34%, **Fat** (g) 8, **Carbohydrates** (g) 30, **Protein** (g) 8, **Sodium** (mg) 96, **Fiber** (g) 6, **Saturated Fat** (g) 1, **Cholesterol** (mg) 7

Prepare Broccoli

- You can use fresh broccoli in place of the frozen if you'd like.

- Choose dark green bunches with tightly closed heads. The flowers should not be yellow, and the broccoli should feel heavy and firm.

- Rinse the broccoli well, cut

off the ends, then cut off the tops. Separate the tops into florets. You can cut the stems into pieces and save for later use.

- Cook the fresh broccoli in boiling water 4 to 6 minutes, until tender, then run under cold water a few minutes.

Mix Dressing

- You can make the dressing ahead of time; cover it and store in the refrigerator up to 3 days.

- Add fresh herbs to the dressing for even more flavor. A tablespoon or two of fresh thyme or basil would be nice.

- The salad will become more watery the longer it's kept refrigerated.

- Just use a slotted spoon to scoop out the solid ingredients, or drain the salad in a sieve, then place in a serving bowl.

SALADS

173

CAPRESE SALAD

Fresh mozzarella, critical to this salad, is very low in sodium

This salad, straight from Italy, is technically called *Insalata Caprese*. This salad can be made only with the very best, most tender vine-ripened tomatoes.

Look for *bocconcini*, or fresh mozzarella balls, at the deli of large supermarkets, at cheese shops, or in Italian markets. It's very different from the part-skim mozzarella cheese you buy to shred and put on pizza.

Fresh mozzarella is silky smooth and is very mild, with a sweet, fresh, milky flavor. Paired with sweet and tart tomatoes, this is the perfect summer salad.

Serve this salad with some fresh ears of corn and unsalted butter, a grilled rib eye steak, and some chocolate chip cookies (low sodium, of course!) for dessert. *Yield: Serves 8*

Ingredients

¹/₂ pound fresh mozzarella balls (bocconcini)

6 ripe red tomatoes, sliced

3 cloves garlic, minced

¹/₄ cup minced red onion

2 tablespoons extra-virgin olive oil

1 tablespoon lemon juice

2 tablespoons balsamic vinegar

¹/₂ teaspoon dried basil

¹/₈ teaspoon pepper

12 fresh basil leaves

Caprese Salad

- Arrange mozzarella and tomatoes on a serving platter. Alternate each slice to make a pretty pattern.

- In small bowl combine garlic with onion, olive oil, lemon juice, vinegar, dried basil, and pepper; mix well.

- Drizzle over the tomatoes and cheese. Tear half the basil leaves and sprinkle over salad.

- Arrange remaining basil leaves on top. Cover and chill 2 to 3 hours before serving.

Calories 111, **% Calories from Fat** 68%, **Fat** (g) 8, **Carbohydrates** (g) 3, **Protein** (g) 5, **Sodium** (mg) 83, **Fiber** (g) 0, **Saturated Fat** (g) 4, **Cholesterol** (mg) 20

Arrange Tomatoes and Cheese

- Alternate slices of tomato and the cheese, overlapping slightly.

- You can arrange the slices in a circle or any pretty pattern; just fiddle with them until they look the way you'd like.

- You can substitute yellow or heirloom tomatoes for some or all the red tomatoes; just make sure they're perfectly ripe.

- This is a beautiful dish for a summer evening, or to bring to a potluck party.

Drizzle Dressing over Salad

- Extra-virgin olive oil is essential to the taste of this salad. It has a rich and fruity flavor important to its authenticity.

- You can substitute fresh basil for the dried in the dressing; in fact, the classic recipe demands it.

- A combination of fresh and dried basil adds a wonderful depth of flavor to the dressing.

- You can assemble the salad ahead of time, but don't hold it longer than 3 hours.

SALADS

POTATO SALAD

Classic potato salad is made of tender potatoes in a creamy mustard dressing

Everyone loves potato salad. You probably have a favorite recipe from your mother or aunt.

The best potato salads are made with boiled or roasted potatoes that are seasoned or added to the dressing while they are still very warm. The potatoes absorb flavor from these ingredients and make the potato salad outstanding.

For boiling, red potatoes are your best choice, because they hold their shape better. You can roast russet potatoes, cut into cubes and drizzled with a bit of olive oil, at 400°F 55 to 65 minutes, until they are tender.

Make extra dressing to add to the salad in case your potatoes absorb a lot of it. Just add to taste and stir gently. *Yield: Serves 8*

Ingredients

3 pounds red potatoes

2 sweet potatoes

3 tablespoons cider vinegar

1/2 cup low-sodium mayonnaise

1 cup yogurt

1/4 cup sour cream

3 tablespoons Dijon mustard

1/2 teaspoon dry mustard powder

1/4 cup milk

1/4 teaspoon pepper

2 tablespoons fresh dill weed

3 stalks celery, sliced

1/2 cup chopped green onion

Calories 312, **% Calories from Fat** 32%, **Fat** (g) 11, **Carbohydrates** (g) 45, **Protein** (g) 7, **Sodium** (mg) 210, **Fiber** (g) 5, **Saturated Fat** (g) 3, **Cholesterol** (mg)19

Potato Salad

- Peel the potatoes and cut into cubes. Bring a large pot of water to a boil. Add sweet potatoes; simmer 5 minutes.

- Add red potatoes; simmer 8 to 12 minutes longer, until both types of potatoes are tender.

- While potatoes are cooking, make dressing. In large bowl, combine vinegar, mayonnaise, yogurt, sour cream, mustard, dry mustard powder, milk, pepper, and dill.

- Drain potatoes and add to dressing; mix well. Add celery and green onion. Chill 4 to 5 hours before serving.

Homemade Mayonnaise: You should use pasteurized eggs in this recipe for food safety reasons. Separate 1 pasteurized egg; freeze the white. Place yolk and 1 more whole pasteurized egg in blender; blend in 2 tablespoons lemon juice, then, with the blender on, slowly drizzle in 1¼ cups olive or canola oil until thick and creamy. Store, covered, in fridge up to 5 days.

Classic Potato Salad: Make recipe as directed, except use 5 pounds russet potatoes, scrubbed and cubed. Drizzle with 2 tablespoons olive oil; roast at 400°F 55 to 65 minutes, until tender. Combine dressing ingredients; add hot potatoes and stir. Cover and chill before serving.

Cook Potatoes

- You can roast the potatoes in the oven if you'd like. Peel, cut into cubes, and roast at 400°F 45 to 55 minutes.

- Turn the potatoes once with a large spatula halfway during roasting time.

- The potatoes are tender when a knife slips easily in and out of the flesh of the potato.

- Make sure the dressing is ready and waiting for the potatoes. Hot potatoes will soak up the flavors of the dressing.

Make Dressing

- You can use any fresh herbs or your favorite spices in this salad.

- Basil, thyme, marjoram, sage, or oregano are all good choices. Add 1 to 2 tablespoons for lots of flavor.

- You can make the dressing ahead of time and store it, tightly covered, in the refrigerator up to 2 days.

- Potato salad gets better the longer it's refrigerated. It will keep 3 to 4 days, if it lasts that long without being devoured.

SALADS

PEACH GELATIN SALAD

Tender canned peaches in a sweet and tart gelatin make a delicious retro salad

Gelatin salads may be old-fashioned, but they are fun to make and eat and are good for you, so it's time for their comeback. Unflavored gelatin is very different from the flavored gelatins you mix with water and let set. Unflavored gelatin is pure gelatin—no water, flavorings, or artificial ingredients. It comes in small envelopes, found in the baking aisle of the supermarket. This type of gelatin must be made in specific steps. First the gelatin is softened in cool water. Then, after it "blooms," hot or boiling water is added to dissolve it.

Serve this delicious salad with a roast chicken, asparagus, and crisp bread sticks. *Yield: Serves 8*

Ingredients

2 (0.25-ounce) packages unflavored gelatin

¹/₃ cup sugar

2 (15-ounce) cans sliced peaches

1¹/₂ cups peach nectar

2 eggs

¹/₃ cup sugar

1 cup orange juice

2 tablespoons flour

¹/₂ cup heavy cream, whipped

Calories 181, **% Calories from Fat** 34%, **Fat** (g) 7, **Carbohydrates** (g) 27, **Protein** (g) 4, **Sodium** (mg) 34, **Fiber** (g) 2, **Saturated Fat** (g) 4, **Cholesterol** (mg) 73

Peach Gelatin Salad

- Mix gelatin and sugar in bowl. Drain peaches, reserving juice. Add peach nectar to juice to equal 3 cups.

- Pour 1 cup peach nectar mixture over gelatin; let stand 5 minutes. Heat remaining nectar to boiling.

- Add heated nectar to gelatin; stir until gelatin and sugar dissolve. Add peaches; place in fridge.

- In saucepan, beat eggs, sugar, orange juice, and flour; cook until thick. Cool 30 minutes; fold into peach mixture with whipped cream; pour into 6-cup mold. Cover; chill 5 to 6 hours.

If you can find it, leaf or sheet gelatin is a great substitute for powdered gelatin. It comes in clear, stiff sheets that look like windowpanes. All you do is soak it in water to cover for a few minutes, then squeeze out the water from the soft mass and add to the other liquids.

• • • • RECIPE VARIATION • • • •

Pear Gelatin Salad: Make recipe as directed, except substitute 2 cans sliced pears in water and 1½ cups pear nectar for the sliced peaches and peach nectar. Add 1 teaspoon fresh mint leaves to the egg mixture; refrigerate as directed.

Stir Gelatin

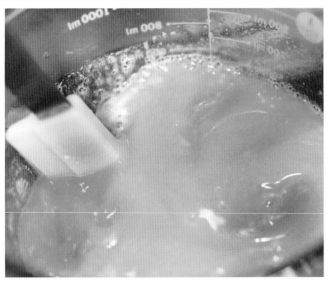

- The gelatin must completely dissolve before you go on to the next step.

- Stir 4 to 5 minutes, until you can no longer see grains of sugar or gelatin in the spoon when you scoop up a small amount.

- If the gelatin or sugar isn't completely and thoroughly dissolved, the finished salad will be grainy.

- Don't boil the gelatin, or it may become tough or lose its thickening power altogether.

Fold Mixtures Together

- Fold the two mixtures together using an up and over motion with your spoon. Don't overmix.

- To remove a gelatin salad from a mold, first make sure it's very well set.

- Then remove from the fridge and place a serving platter on top. Drape a hot, wrung-out towel on the mold.

- Invert the mold and plate together and shake vigorously; the salad should slip right out. If it doesn't, repeat the hot towel application.

HASH BROWN POTATOES

Shredded potatoes, onion, garlic, and egg make crisp hash brown patties

Hash brown potatoes, that staple of breakfast diners, are easy to make at home and contain much less sodium than the frozen patties. Most frozen patties have about 55 to 60 mg of sodium per serving, which makes them a low-sodium food.

But making your own is fun, and nothing tastes better than crisply fried hash browns right out of the pan.

Grate the potatoes on a box grater or in a food processor. Work quickly, as the enzymes in the potatoes will cause them to change color quickly. If there are some potatoes that turn pink or light brown, don't worry about it.

Serve these hash browns with some scrambled eggs, a fruit salad, and lots of orange juice. *Yield: Serves 6*

KNACK LOW-SALT COOKING

Ingredients

3 russet potatoes, peeled

2 tablespoons lemon juice

8 cups water

1 onion, minced

3 cloves garlic, minced

1 egg

2 tablespoons fresh thyme

¹/₂ teaspoon dry mustard

¹/₃ cup flour

¹/₄ teaspoon pepper

1 cup peanut oil

Calories 175, **% Calories from Fat** 29%, **Fat** (g) 6, **Carbohydrates** (g) 27, **Protein** (g) 4, **Sodium** (mg) 21, **Fiber** (g) 1, **Saturated Fat** (g) 1, **Cholesterol** (mg) 35

Hash Brown Potatoes

- Shred potatoes directly into a mixture of lemon juice and water. When all are shredded, drain.

- Squeeze potatoes dry between your hands, then in a kitchen towel.

- Combine potatoes with onion, garlic, egg, thyme, mustard, flour, and pepper in large bowl.

- Heat oil in large shallow saucepan until 375°F. Using a ½-cup measure, drop potato mixture into skillet, four patties at a time. Fry, turning once, 5 to 6 minutes per side. Drain on paper towels and serve.

When buying potatoes, look for firm potatoes that are heavy for their size. There should be few brown spots and no wet or soft spots, and the potatoes should be fairly clean. To prepare, all you have to do is scrub them under cool running water until all the dust is removed.

• • • • RECIPE VARIATION • • • •

Spicy Hash Brown Potatoes: Make recipe as directed, except add 1 jalapeño and 1 serrano pepper, both minced, to the onion mixture. Omit dry mustard and fresh thyme; add 1 tablespoon chili powder, ½ teaspoon ground cumin, and ½ teaspoon dried oregano to the potatoes.

Shred Potatoes

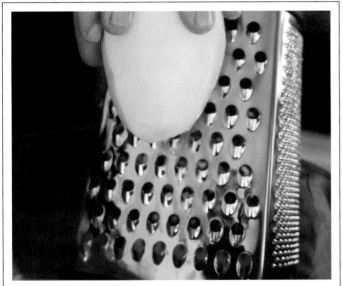

Cook Hash Browns

- Use the shredding disk on the food processor, or the large holes on your box grater, to shred the potatoes.

- If you're pressed for time, you can use frozen shredded loose-pack hash brown potatoes.

- Just thaw them in the refrigerator overnight or according to package directions, and drain well before mixing with the other ingredients.

- Be sure to read the label to make sure the sodium content on the frozen potatoes is low.

- The oil will splatter as you add the wet potato mixture, so be careful and stand back a bit.

- Use hot pads to protect your hands and arms as the potatoes cook.

- Drain the hash browns on paper or kitchen towels for

about 1 minute after they come out of the pan.

- This will help remove excess oil. The potatoes will absorb about 10 percent of the oil as they cook as long as the cooking temperature is correct.

OVEN FRIES

Crisp baked potatoes are better than fried

French fries seem to be the classic "bad for you food," ubiquitous at fast-food joints and greasy spoon restaurants. They are delicious when fried, but baking them in the oven can yield surprisingly good and crisp results.

To make crisp and brown french fries in the oven, you have to make sure the potatoes are arranged in a single, even layer on the cookie sheet and bake them at a high temperature.

Lemon juice, pepper, good olive oil, and Parmesan cheese add delicious flavor to these fries. And with very little salt, you can actually taste the flavor of the potatoes!

Serve these crisp fries with some low-sodium ketchup, a grilled steak or grilled salmon, and a fresh fruit salad. *Yield: Serves 6*

Ingredients

3 russet potatoes

2 tablespoons lemon juice

2 tablespoons olive oil

¹/₃ cup grated Parmesan cheese

¹/₄ teaspoon pepper

¹/₂ teaspoon paprika

Pinch salt

3 tablespoons flour

Oven Fries

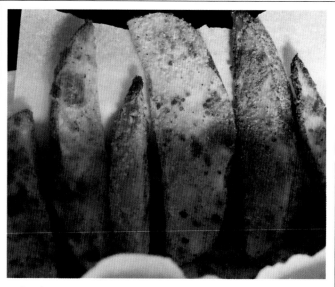

- Scrub potatoes, cut each into 12 wedges, and pat dry with paper towels.

- Sprinkle with lemon juice and olive oil and toss to coat. In bowl mix cheese, pepper, paprika, salt, and flour.

- Toss potatoes with flour mixture until coated. Place in single layer on baking sheet.

- Bake at 425°F 15 minutes; turn with spatula. Bake 15 to 25 minutes longer, until golden brown and crisp.

Calories 161, **% Calories from Fat** 35%, **Fat** (g) 6, **Carbohydrates** (g) 22, **Protein** (g) 5, **Sodium** (mg) 119, **Fiber** (g) 2, **Saturated Fat** (g) 2, **Cholesterol** (mg) 5

Spicy Oven Fries: Make recipe as directed, except add ½ teaspoon garlic powder, ½ teaspoon onion powder, and 1 tablespoon chili powder to the flour mixture. Omit olive oil; melt 3 tablespoons unsalted butter in jelly roll pan. Add coated potatoes in a single layer. Bake, turning once, until browned and crisp.

Curried Oven Fries: Make recipe as directed, except omit the Parmesan cheese and paprika. Add 1 tablespoon plus 1 teaspoon curry powder to the flour mixture along with 2 teaspoons sugar. Toss in lemon juice and oil, then in flour mixture. Bake as directed, turning once, until brown and crisp.

Toss Potatoes with Lemon Juice

Turn Potatoes with Spatula

- The lemon juice stops enzymatic browning. This helps keep the potatoes from changing color as they are exposed to air.

- The juice also adds a nice flavor to the potatoes in the absence of salt.

- You can make the flour mixture ahead of time, but don't prepare the potatoes ahead of time.

- If you can find frozen potato wedges or fries with little or no sodium, you can substitute them for the raw potatoes.

- Remove the pan from the oven and place it on a heat-proof work surface.

- Use a heavy-duty spatula and work under the potatoes to turn them.

- Move the potatoes around gently so they stay as whole as possible. Some will break; don't worry about that.

- Place the potatoes in a paper towel–lined serving bowl, to keep them both dry and warm.

SCALLOPED POTATOES

Creamy scalloped potatoes are perfect for the holidays

Scalloped potatoes are a wonderful dish for company or for serving your family a homey meal.

You can find scalloped potato mixes in the supermarket, but these products are almost always very high in sodium. And nothing tastes better than fresh potatoes baked in a richly seasoned homemade cream sauce.

For a very special occasion, substitute heavy cream for the light cream in this recipe. Each serving will then have 18.2 grams of fat.

If you're feeding a crowd, make two or three pans of this recipe. Store them well covered in the refrigerator up to 8 hours. Then bake as directed, adding 15 to 20 minutes to the baking time. *Yield: Serves 6–8*

Ingredients

¹/₄ cup unsalted butter

1 onion, chopped

5 cloves garlic, minced

¹/₄ cup flour

¹/₂ teaspoon dry mustard

¹/₈ teaspoon salt

¹/₄ teaspoon pepper

1 tablespoon fresh oregano

2 cups 1 percent milk

1 cup light cream

¹/₃ cup sour cream

6 russet potatoes, peeled and sliced ¹/₈-inch thick

Calories 286, **% Calories from Fat** 45%, **Fat** (g) 14, **Carbohydrates** (g) 35, **Protein** (g) 6, **Sodium** (mg) 88, **Fiber** (g) 2, **Saturated Fat** (g) 9, **Cholesterol** (mg) 42

Scalloped Potatoes

- In saucepan, melt butter over medium heat. Add onion and garlic; cook and stir 7 minutes.

- Add flour, mustard, salt, and pepper; cook and stir 5 minutes. Add oregano, milk, and cream; bring to a simmer.

- Simmer sauce until thickened, stirring constantly. Add sour cream.

- Layer ¹/₃ potatoes in greased 2-quart baking dish; top with ¹/₃ sauce; repeat layers. Bake at 325°F 60 to 70 minutes until potatoes are tender.

··········· GREEN ● LIGHT ··············

To cut potatoes for scalloped potatoes, peel and place them in a bowl of ice water. You can use a mandoline or food processor to slice the potatoes about ⅛-inch thick. Or use a sharp knife, working carefully, and add the sliced potatoes back to the water as they are finished.

· · · · RECIPE VARIATION · · · ·

Cheesy Scalloped Potatoes: Make recipe as directed, except omit oregano. Add 1 tablespoon fresh thyme leaves or 1 teaspoon dried thyme leaves to the flour mixture. Layer 1½ cups shredded low-sodium Swiss cheese with the potatoes and sauce mixture. Top with 2 tablespoons grated Parmesan cheese and bake as directed.

Cook Sauce

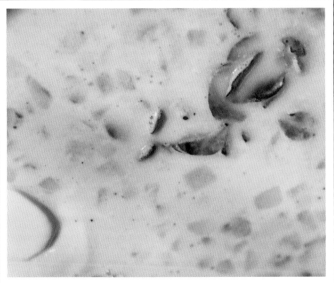

- Cook the onions and garlic until very tender, because they won't soften when cooked with the potatoes.

- Stir with a wire whisk while the flour mixture is cooking to make sure the flour is well blended with the butter.

- For the smoothest sauce, use a wire whisk again when adding the liquid to the flour mixture.

- Add your favorite herbs and spices to the sauce to make the recipe your own.

Layer Potatoes and Sauce

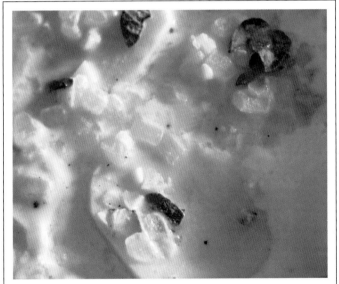

- The potatoes have to be cut to the same thickness so they cook in the same amount of time.

- You can use other potatoes in this recipe. Yukon Gold potatoes are a great substitution, because they naturally taste buttery.

- Make sure the potatoes are in even layers so they all come in contact with the sauce.

- You can sprinkle the top of the scalloped potatoes with a little bit of grated cheese for a browned and crusty top.

HASSELBACK POTATOES

It's the preparation method, not the ingredients, that makes these potatoes special

Hasselback Potatoes are a fun way to serve this sturdy, basic vegetable. A simple cutting method makes the potatoes look very fancy, perfect for a special dinner.

The name comes from Hasselbacken, the name of the Swedish restaurant where the recipe originated.

You'll need a very large spoon for this recipe, one that the potatoes will fit into snugly. The potatoes are placed in the spoon, then thinly sliced crosswise. The potato is uncut at the bottom, so the slices fan out.

This creates lots of surface area so the flesh becomes crisp and absorbs all of the seasonings. *Yield: Serves 6*

KNACK LOW-SALT COOKING

Ingredients

6 russet potatoes

8 cups water

2 cups ice

6 cloves garlic, minced

¼ cup unsalted butter

2 tablespoons lemon juice

1 teaspoon dried Italian seasoning

¼ teaspoon pepper

3 tablespoons grated Parmesan cheese

1 cup panko bread crumbs

Calories 323, **% Calories from Fat** 27%, **Fat** (g) 10, **Carbohydrates** (g) 52, **Protein** (g) 8, **Sodium** (mg) 186, **Fiber** (g) 5, **Saturated Fat** (g) 6, **Cholesterol** (mg) 23

Hasselback Potatoes

- Peel potatoes, placing in a mixture of water and ice cubes as you work.

- Cook garlic in butter 4 to 5 minutes over low heat. Remove from heat.

- Place potatoes in large spoon. Make crosswise slices across the potato, ⅛-inch apart and not all the way through.

- Place potatoes in pan. Mix juice, garlic butter, seasoning, and pepper; drizzle on potatoes. Bake at 400°F 40 minutes. Mix cheese and bread crumbs; sprinkle on potatoes. Bake 25 to 35 minutes until golden.

•••• RECIPE VARIATION ••••

Herbed Hasselback Potatoes : Make recipe as directed, except omit dried Italian seasoning. Combine ½ teaspoon each dried thyme, dried marjoram, and dried basil in place of the Italian seasoning. Then add 1 tablespoon each minced fresh basil, marjoram, and thyme to the bread crumb mixture.

Onion Hasselback Potatoes: Make recipe as directed, except omit dried Italian seasoning and reduce the number of garlic cloves to 2. Finely mince 1 large onion. Cook the onion in butter until very tender and just starting to turn brown on the edges, then continue with the recipe.

Slice Potatoes

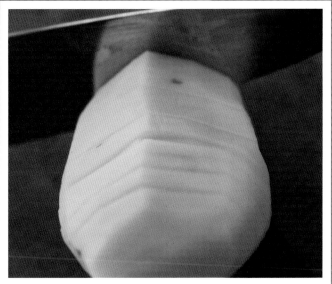

Sprinkle with Crumbs

- You can slice the potatoes on a work surface if you're careful to not cut through to the bottom and cut the slices apart.

- Cut a thin slice off the side of the potato so it will sit firmly, then place a chopstick on either side of the potato.

- Work slowly and carefully so the potatoes stay together and you don't cut yourself.

- You can leave the skin on the potatoes for more nutrition; they will just look more rustic.

- Panko bread crumbs are a special type of crumb that is very light and crisp. Look for them in the international foods aisle of the supermarket.

- If you can't find them, dried bread crumbs will work just as well. But don't use packaged dry bread crumbs; they are high in sodium.

- Make bread crumbs using well-toasted bread in your food processor.

- Make sure the Parmesan cheese is very finely grated so this small amount goes further.

SWEET POTATO CASSEROLE

Mashed tender sweet potatoes are topped with a pecan streusel

Sweet potatoes are so good—and so good for you. They can be purchased year-round, although their fresh season is November and December.

True yams are not sweet potatoes. In the United States any potato labeled "yam" must have the words "sweet potato" added to it. True yams are very moist with dark brown skin. They are very different vegetables.

The sweet potato is a powerhouse in nutrition, with more than 250 percent Daily Value of Vitamin A in a single tuber. They have lots of antioxidants, vitamin C, fiber, potassium, and iron.

They are also delicious! A sweet potato doesn't need a lot of help, but adding warm spices turns this vegetable into a decadent dish perfect for the holidays or company. *Yield: Serves 8*

Ingredients

4 sweet potatoes, peeled and cubed

3 tablespoons unsalted butter, melted

1/2 cup milk

1 teaspoon vanilla

1/3 cup brown sugar

2 tablespoons lemon juice

1 tablespoon thyme leaves

1/4 cup unsalted butter, melted

2/3 cup coarsely chopped pecans

1/2 cup flour

3/4 cup oatmeal

1 cup brown sugar

1 teaspoon cinnamon

1/4 teaspoon cardamom

1/8 teaspoon nutmeg

Calories 373, **% Calories from Fat** 47%, **Fat** (g) 18, **Carbohydrates** (g) 50, **Protein** (g) 4, **Sodium** (mg) 56, **Fiber** (g) 4, **Saturated Fat** (g) 7, **Cholesterol** (mg) 27

Sweet Potato Casserole

- Place potatoes in water to cover; simmer 20 to 25 minutes, until tender. Drain potatoes; return to hot pot.

- Add 3 tablespoons melted butter; mash potatoes, leaving some chunky. Beat in milk, vanilla, 1/3 cup brown sugar, lemon juice, and thyme. Place in greased 2 1/2-quart casserole.

- In small saucepan, melt 1/4 cup butter; add pecans; toast until fragrant.

- Combine remaining ingredients; add butter and pecans; mix until crumbly. Sprinkle on potatoes. Bake at 350°F 30 to 40 minutes.

•••• RECIPE VARIATION ••••

Spicy Sweet Potato Casserole: Make recipe as directed, except omit vanilla, brown sugar, and streusel topping. Melt ¼ cup butter; add 1 onion, 2 minced jalapeño peppers, and 3 cloves garlic, minced; cook 5 minutes. Add 1 tablespoon chili powder. Place in casserole; sprinkle with 3 tablespoons grated Cotija cheese; bake.

Classic Sweet Potato Casserole: Make recipe as directed, except do not mash the sweet potatoes Simmer potatoes until tender, then drain and mix with butter; 2 tablespoons each light cream, and brown sugar; 1 tablespoon lemon juice, and 1 teaspoon vanilla; place in casserole. Omit streusel topping; sprinkle with pecans and bake.

Mash Potatoes

Mix Streusel Topping

- When purchasing sweet potatoes, look for smooth and heavy tubers with no wet or soft spots.

- Peel sweet potatoes using a sharp paring knife; they are very bumpy, so they are not easy to peel with a swivel-bladed peeler.

- Sweet potatoes are much harder than russet or red potatoes, so be careful when cubing them.

- The potatoes are returned to the hot pot after draining to remove excess moisture. This makes the potatoes fluffy.

- You can make the topping ahead of time; store it in a tightly covered container in a cool, dry place.

- Use regular or quick-cooking oatmeal in the streusel. Regular oatmeal is less processed for a chewier topping.

- You can reduce the number of pecans to ½ cup for less fat, or choose another type of nut, like walnuts.

- Bake the casserole until the topping is deep golden brown and crisp.

BAKED STUFFED POTATOES

Tender potatoes are filled with caramelized onions and sour cream

Stuffed potatoes are a delicious side dish with a grilled steak, salmon, or roasted chicken, or they can be a complete meal when served with a light green salad.

The secret to making the best stuffed baked potatoes is to mash the flesh, while hot, first with butter and olive oil, then with dairy products like sour cream or milk. This makes the filling fluffy and creamy.

Prepare all the filing ingredients while the potatoes are in the oven. Let the potatoes cool just enough so you can handle them, cut them in half, and scoop out the flesh. Then proceed with the recipe. *Yield: Serves 8*

Ingredients

4 large russet potatoes

2 tablespoons unsalted butter

2 tablespoons olive oil

1 onion, chopped

5 cloves garlic, minced

1/2 cup low-fat sour cream

1/4 cup Dijon mustard

1 tablespoon fresh thyme

1/4 cup chopped parsley

1/4 teaspoon pepper

Baked Stuffed Potatoes

- Prick potatoes several times with fork. Bake at 400°F 55 to 65 minutes, until potatoes are tender. Let cool 10 minutes.

- Melt butter and olive oil in skillet; add onion and garlic. Cook and stir 15 to 20 minutes, until browned. Add to potatoes; mash.

- Cut potatoes in half; scoop out flesh, leaving 1/4-inch of the flesh and skins intact.

- Add sour cream, mustard, thyme, parsley, and pepper; mix well. Stuff skins. Bake potatoes 20 to 30 minutes longer, until browned.

Calories 235, **% Calories from Fat** 33%, **Fat** (g) 8, **Carbohydrates** (g) 37, **Protein** (g) 5, **Sodium** (mg) 104, **Fiber** (g) 3, **Saturated Fat** (g) 3, **Cholesterol** (mg) 14

• • • • RECIPE VARIATION • • • •

Stuffed Sweet Potatoes: Make recipe as directed, except use 3 large sweet potatoes. Bake them as directed, then cut in half. Omit mustard, thyme, and parsley; add ¼ cup brown sugar, 1 teaspoon cinnamon, and ½ teaspoon ground nutmeg to filling. Bake at 400°F 30 to 40 minutes, until browned.

Spicy Stuffed Potatoes: Make recipe as directed, except add 1 minced serrano pepper to the onion mixture. Don't caramelize the onions; cook them 5 to 6 minutes, until tender. Omit mustard and thyme; add 1 tablespoon chili powder, 1 teaspoon dried oregano, and 1 teaspoon chile paste. Add ¼ cup grated Parmesan cheese.

Remove Flesh from Potatoes

Mix Filling

- Use a kitchen towel to hold the potato in your less dominant hand while you use a large spoon to remove the flesh.

- Scoop into the flesh, leaving about a ¼-inch layer of potato attached to the skin so the potato holds together.

- The potato flesh will break apart as you remove it. Use a potato masher to mash the onion mixture into the potatoes.

- If the skin breaks, that's okay; just stuff the broken pieces and reserve them for lunch for the next day.

- You can substitute ricotta cheese, plain yogurt, or cream cheese for the sour cream.

- Use coarse-ground mustard, yellow mustard, or low-sodium chili sauce in place of the Dijon mustard.

- Any combination of herbs will be delicious in this recipe. Add basil or marjoram to the thyme or use oregano and basil.

- You can prepare the potatoes ahead of time. Refrigerate them, covered, up to 8 hours, then bake, adding 10 minutes to the baking time.

CHICKEN STOCK
Low-sodium chicken broth is easy to make

Homemade chicken stock tastes so much better than any canned or boxed stock—they aren't even comparable. And since even low-sodium canned stocks contain a lot of sodium, making your own lets you control what your family eats.

Stock is easy to make; just combine meat, vegetables, water, and herbs or spices and let them simmer away until the liquid tastes rich.

Stock is made from bones and meat, while broth is made from just meat or just vegetables. Either one is a good substitute for the other.

Stock freezes very well. To substitute for a 14-ounce can of ready-to-use chicken or beef stock, freeze the liquid in 1¾-cup portions up to 4 months. Thaw in the microwave or refrigerator overnight to use. *Yield: Makes 8 cups*

Ingredients

2 pounds bone-in, skin-on chicken thighs

2 tablespoons olive oil

8 cups water

1 onion, quartered

3 carrots, cut in half

3 stalks celery, cut in half

¼ teaspoon pepper

1 tablespoon fresh thyme

½ bunch parsley

3 whole cloves

1 bay leaf

Calories 38, **% Calories from Fat** 81%, **Fat** (g) 3, **Carbohydrates** (g) 2, **Protein** (g) 0.2, **Sodium** (mg)12.5, **Fiber** (g) 0, **Saturated Fat** (g) 1, **Cholesterol** (mg) 0

Chicken Stock

- Brown chicken thighs, skin side down, in olive oil 6 to 7 minutes, until chicken releases.

- Place in 5-quart slow cooker. Add remaining ingredients.

- Cover and cook on low 6 hours. Take chicken out of slow cooker; remove meat from bones and keep for later use.

- Return bones and skin to slow cooker; cook on low 2 to 3 hours longer, until broth tastes rich. Strain and chill. Refrigerate overnight; remove fat. Freeze in 1- or 1¾-cup portions.

•••• RECIPE VARIATION ••••

Beef Stock: Make recipe as directed, except substitute 2 pounds meaty beef bones for the chicken. Place bones, onions, and carrots in roasting pan; drizzle with olive oil and roast at 400°F 1 hour. Combine all ingredients in slow cooker and cook as directed.

Vegetable Broth: Make recipe as directed, except omit chicken. Chop onions; add 3 tablespoons minced garlic. Cook in olive oil with carrots until starting to brown. Add 1 cup each sliced fresh mushrooms and chopped celery root to the vegetable mixture. Cook as directed in slow cooker.

Brown Chicken

- For the richest and deepest stock, it's important to brown the chicken very well before cooking.

- You can also roast the chicken, onions, and carrots in a 400°F oven 45 minutes, until browned.

- You can make the recipe without browning the chicken first; the broth will still be rich, but lighter in color.

- The vegetables can be quartered or chopped; it depends on how much work you want to do.

Cook Stock

- You can cook the stock on the stovetop. Place in a large pot and simmer on low heat 2 hours.

- As the stock simmers, skim off the foam and scum that rise to the top and discard.

- The slow cooker is a great choice for cooking stock, because you don't have to pay attention to it.

- Refrigerate the stock overnight before using or freezing to remove the fat. You can save the fat for recipes calling for schmaltz.

LENTIL SOUP

Lentils cooked in homemade chicken broth make a delicious soup

Lentil soup is a classic easy and inexpensive soup that is nourishing and delicious. Lentils, unlike other dried legumes, are easy to prepare, because they cook quickly without soaking or precooking.

The lentils melt into the soup and thicken it. If you'd like to see more discrete lentils in the finished product, reserve some and add them during the last 30 minutes of cooking time.

Any vegetables, herbs, and spices are delicious in this soup. Try adding sliced or chopped mushrooms, red or green bell peppers, or poblano or Anaheim peppers for more spice.

This soup can be made vegetarian by using vegetable broth in place of the chicken broth or stock.

Serve with corn bread or scones, hot from the oven. *Yield: Serves 6*

Ingredients

1 tablespoon unsalted butter

1 tablespoon olive oil

1 onion, chopped

3 cloves garlic, minced

1 1/2 cups lentils

7 cups homemade chicken stock

4 tomatoes, peeled, seeded, and chopped

2 carrots, shredded

1 teaspoon dried marjoram

1 bay leaf

2 tablespoons lemon juice

1/4 teaspoon pepper

Calories 275, **% Calories from Fat** 29%, **Fat** (g) 9, **Carbohydrates** (g) 37, **Protein** (g) 14, **Sodium** (mg) 26, **Fiber** (g) 17, **Saturated Fat** (g) 2, **Cholesterol** (mg) 5

Lentil Soup

- In large pot heat butter and olive oil over medium heat. Add onion and garlic; cook and stir 5 minutes.

- Add lentils, stock, tomatoes, carrots, marjoram, and bay leaf. Bring to a simmer over medium-low heat.

- Cover and simmer soup 55 to 65 minutes, until lentils are tender. Remove bay leaf; add lemon juice and pepper.

- Puree some of the lentils, if desired, for thicker soup. Stir well and serve.

···· RECIPE VARIATION ····

Lentil Stew: *Make recipe as directed, except reduce the chicken stock to 6 cups. Add 2 peeled and chopped potatoes with the tomatoes and carrots. Omit marjoram; add 1 teaspoon dried thyme leaves. Partially puree some of the lentils and potatoes.*

Lentil Spinach Soup: *Make recipe as directed, except add 2 stalks celery, chopped, with leaves, to the soup with the shredded carrots. In the last 5 minutes of cooking time, add 3 cups washed and coarsely chopped baby spinach leaves. Cook 8 minutes; add lemon juice and finish soup.*

Cook Onion and Garlic

- Chop the onions by peeling them, then cut in half from stem to root. Place cut side down on work surface.

- Cut the onions in one direction, then, holding the slices together, cut perpendicular to the first slices to make cubes.

- To prepare the garlic, place on work surface, top with the side of a chef's knife blade, and push down with your hand.

- Remove the peel and mince the garlic, moving your knife back and forth, until it's finely chopped.

Simmer Soup

- You can use any color lentils you want. You can buy red, green (also known as Puy lentils), black, or brown lentils.

- Or mix different types of lentils for more interest and a colorful soup.

- To cook in the slow cooker, combine all ingredients except lemon juice in a 4-quart slow cooker.

- Cover and cook on low 6 to 7 hours, until lentils and vegetables are tender. Puree if desired before serving.

CHICKEN NOODLE SOUP

This is a classic and homey soup, just like Grandma used to make

Chicken noodle soup is "good for what ails you." It is nature's penicillin, proven by scientific study to reduce the symptoms of a cold or flu.

If you want to make the soup with raw chicken, cube 3 to 4 boneless, skinless chicken breasts and brown in the olive oil. Remove chicken and add onions, garlic, and ginger root; cook vegetables. Return chicken to soup with carrots and celery and simmer as directed.

You can use chicken breasts or thighs in this recipe. The thighs add more fat, but they also make the flavor richer.

Serve this soup with toasted garlic bread or corn bread or biscuits hot from the oven. A spinach salad is a nice complement. *Yield: Serves 6*

Ingredients

1 tablespoon olive oil

1 onion, chopped

3 cloves garlic, minced

1 tablespoon grated ginger root

2 carrots, sliced

2 stalks celery, sliced

1 teaspoon dried oregano

1 teaspoon dried thyme

$1/4$ teaspoon pepper

6 cups reduced-sodium chicken broth

2 tablespoons lemon juice

2 cups egg noodles

1 cup frozen peas

3 cups chopped cooked chicken

$1/2$ cup light cream

Calories 299, **% Calories from Fat** 38%, **Fat** (g) 13, **Carbohydrates** (g) 20, **Protein** (g) 26, **Sodium** (mg) 118, **Fiber** (g) 3, **Saturated Fat** (g) 4, **Cholesterol** (mg) 83

Chicken Noodle Soup

- Heat olive oil in large saucepan. Add onion, garlic, and ginger root; cook and stir 6 to 7 minutes.

- Add carrots, celery, oregano, thyme, and pepper; cook 4 to 5 minutes. Add broth; bring to a simmer.

- Simmer soup 30 to 40 minutes, until vegetables are tender. Stir in lemon juice and egg noodles.

- Simmer 8 to 11 minutes, until noodles are almost tender. Add peas, chicken, and cream; heat through until hot and steaming; do not boil.

Slow Cooker Chicken Noodle Soup: Make recipe as directed, except substitute 3 boneless, skinless raw chicken breasts for the cooked cubed chicken. Brown chicken in olive oil with the onions and garlic. Combine in 4- to 5-quart slow cooker. Cover and cook on low 7 to 8 hours, then add noodles, peas, and cream and cook 15 to 20 minutes longer.

Curried Chicken Noodle Soup: Make recipe as directed, except add 1 tablespoon curry powder with the onions, garlic, and ginger root. Omit oregano and thyme; add ¼ teaspoon dried mint leaves. In place of the egg noodles, use 1½ cups orzo pasta; cook 10 to 14 minutes, until tender; proceed with recipe.

Cook Vegetables

Add Egg Noodles

- Other vegetables that would be good in this soup include sliced button or cremini mushrooms or red bell peppers.

- You can substitute fresh herbs for the dried. Add them along with the peas, chicken, and cream.

- Use 1 tablespoon each fresh thyme and oregano leaves. The leaves are small enough that they don't need to be minced.

- Sage and thyme would also be a good combination of herbs for this soup.

- The noodles will take slightly longer to cook in the soup than they do in plain water.

- Add the peas while frozen. Frozen peas have more nutrients than fresh, because they are processed as soon as they are harvested.

- If the soup isn't thick enough, you can combine 2 tablespoons cornstarch with the cream; cook 3 to 4 minutes, until thickened.

- This soup improves upon standing. Refrigerate overnight, then gently reheat and simmer 2 to 3 minutes before serving.

PUMPKIN SOUP

Pumpkin makes a rich and creamy soup with a gorgeous color

Pumpkins make a wonderful soup, rich and flavorful, with a color perfect for fall parties and celebrations.

If you've never had pumpkin soup, you're in for a treat. The flavor is intense, smoky, and sweet, accented with onions, garlic, and lots of spices. Pumpkins are good for you, with lots of beta-carotene, vitamin C, and vitamin A.

You can substitute 2 pounds butternut or acorn squash for the sugar pumpkins if you can't find them.

Canned pumpkin is usually used to make this type of soup. Make sure you buy pure pumpkin, not pumpkin puree. Substitute 1 can solid-pack pumpkin for the sugar pumpkins for an easier recipe.

Serve this soup with a spinach salad and some crisp bread sticks. *Yield: Serves 6*

Ingredients

2 small (1-pound) sugar pumpkins

2 tablespoons butter

1 onion, chopped

3 cloves garlic, minced

3 tablespoons brown sugar

2 tablespoons flour

1 teaspoon ground ginger

¼ teaspoon cinnamon

⅛ teaspoon cardamom

⅛ teaspoon nutmeg

¼ teaspoon pepper

4 cups low-sodium chicken broth

1 tablespoon lemon juice

½ cup 1 percent milk

¼ cup roasted pumpkin seeds

Calories 193, **% Calories from Fat** 51%, **Fat** (g) 11, **Carbohydrates** (g) 22, **Protein** (g) 6, **Sodium** (mg) 73, **Fiber** (g) 2, **Saturated Fat** (g) 4, **Cholesterol** (mg) 12

Pumpkin Soup

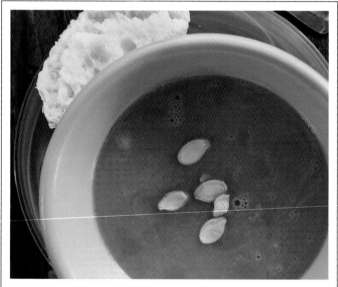

- Peel pumpkins, cut in half, scoop out seeds. Cube flesh.

- Melt butter in pot; cook onion and garlic 5 minutes.

- Add brown sugar, flour, ginger, cinnamon, cardamom, nutmeg, and pepper; cook 3 minutes. Add broth; bring to a simmer.

- Add pumpkin; simmer, covered, 20 to 25 minutes, until pumpkin is tender. Mash most of the soup, leaving some pieces.

- Add juice and milk to soup; heat through until soup steams; do not boil. Garnish with pumpkin seeds.

•••• RECIPE VARIATION ••••

Spicy Pumpkin Soup: Make recipe as directed, except omit the brown sugar and all the spices except pepper. Add 2 minced jalapeño or serrano peppers to the mixture with the onions and garlic. Add 1 teaspoon ground chiles, ½ teaspoon ground cumin, and ⅛ teaspoon cayenne pepper with the ¼ teaspoon black pepper. Continue with recipe as directed.

ZOOM

Preparing pumpkins or hard winter squash takes some time and patience. First peel the pumpkin using a sharp paring knife, then use a chef's knife to cut the vegetables in half. Use a stainless steel spoon to scoop out the seeds. You can save the seeds and roast them to eat as snacks or garnish the soup.

Simmer Pumpkin in Soup

- Stir the flour mixture with a wire whisk to make sure all the flour cooks evenly in the butter.

- When you add the broth to the onion mixture, stir it with a wire whisk so the liquid blends with the flour.

- This helps thicken the soup. The pumpkin flesh, when mashed, will also thicken the soup.

- When the pumpkin is tender, a sharp knife will slip easily in and out of the flesh.

Mash Vegetables

- Mash the vegetables using a handheld vegetable masher or an immersion blender.

- You can make the soup as smooth or as chunky as you'd like. Blend it partially or completely.

- Stir in light cream or heavy cream instead of the milk for a special occasion.

- To roast pumpkin seeds, rinse, pick off pulp, then dry in a paper towel and spread on cookie sheet. Roast at 325°F 15 to 25 minutes.

VEGETABLE BARLEY SOUP
Tender vegetables simmered with nutty barley make a great soup

Barley is another whole grain that is so good for you. It has a wonderful nutty taste and chewy texture that pairs beautifully with tender vegetables in this healthy soup.

Barley is full of fiber, especially soluble fiber, which is important in maintaining heart and intestinal health. It helps lower cholesterol and reduce the risk of diabetes. And it tastes absolutely delicious, especially when cooked in a soup with vegetables.

Use your favorite vegetables in this soup. A variety of mushrooms adds nice texture and flavor interest. Think about using dried mushrooms, which are very low in sodium. Soak the mushrooms in liquid, strain, and cut off the stem before adding to the soup. Serve this soup with corn bread or bread sticks. *Yield: Serves 8*

Ingredients

2 tablespoons olive oil

2 onions, chopped

4 cloves garlic, minced

1 (8-ounce) package cremini mushrooms, sliced

4 carrots, sliced

3 stalks celery, sliced

1 bay leaf

1 teaspoon dried marjoram

1 teaspoon dried thyme

1/4 teaspoon pepper

6 cups low-sodium beef broth

1 (14.5-ounce) can no-salt-added diced tomatoes

1 cup barley

1 cup frozen peas, thawed

1 cup frozen corn, thawed

1 tablespoon balsamic vinegar

Calories 214, **% Calories from Fat** 23%, **Fat** (g) 5, **Carbohydrates** (g) 35, **Protein** (g) 10, **Sodium** (mg) 117, **Fiber** (g) 7, **Saturated Fat** (g) 1, **Cholesterol** (mg) 0

Vegetable Barley Soup

- Heat oil in large pot. Add onions, garlic, and mushrooms; cook and stir until mushrooms are browned, about 8 to 9 minutes.

- Add carrots and celery; cook 4 to 5 minutes longer. Add bay leaf, marjoram, thyme, and pepper; simmer 2 minutes.

- Add broth, tomatoes, and barley; bring to a simmer. Simmer, covered, 25 to 35 minutes until barley is tender.

- Add peas, corn, and balsamic vinegar. Simmer 3 to 4 minutes longer, until hot and blended; remove bay leaf.

ZOOM

Barley comes in several types, depending on how processed it is. Hulled barley, or groats, just has the outer hull removed. Pearl barley is most easily found; it is missing the bran layer. Pot or Scotch barley has the endosperm layer left on, which makes it more nutritious than pearl barley.

• • • • RECIPE VARIATION • • • •

Slow Cooker Barley Soup: Make recipe as directed, except cook the soup in a 4-quart slow cooker. Cook the onions and garlic in the oil, then combine in slow cooker with remaining ingredients except corn, peas, and vinegar. Cover and cook on low 8 to 9 hours. Stir in corn, peas, and vinegar; cook 1 hour longer.

Cook Mushrooms and Onions

- Cooking mushrooms until they are brown and their liquid evaporates concentrates the flavor.

- Since this is a soup, and a bit more water won't affect the recipe, you can cook the mushrooms just until tender.

- Add other vegetables like sweet bell peppers, chopped zucchini, or sliced summer squash.

- The marjoram and thyme accent the beefy flavor of the mushrooms, but you can use other herbs.

Add Broth and Barley

- If you use pearl barley, simmer for about half an hour. If you choose to use regular barley, the soup will need to simmer for an hour.

- Quick-cooking barley isn't recommended for this dish, because it cooks in about 10 minutes.

- Other frozen vegetables you could add instead of the peas and corn include broccoli or cauliflower florets or sugar snap peas.

- Serve this hearty soup with a green or spinach salad made with sliced strawberries, raspberries, and toasted almonds.

CARIBBEAN BLACK BEAN SOUP
Black beans combine with limes and chiles for a fresh soup

Black beans make an elegant soup that can be flavored so many ways. The ingredients that make this soup "Caribbean" include ginger root, jalapeño, allspice, sweet potatoes, and lime juice.

The combination of black beans and sweet potatoes is a nutritional powerhouse. They are both high in fiber, and sweet potatoes contain lots of vitamins A and C.

If you make Slow Cooker Beans (page 160) and freeze them, you can substitute 4 cups of that recipe for the dried black beans and make this recipe in about an hour.

Garnish this soup with lime slices or wedges and some chopped fresh cilantro. Serve with toasted garlic bread or dinner rolls brushed with a bit of honey. *Yield: Serves 8*

Ingredients

1 pound dry black beans

1 tablespoon olive oil

1 onion, chopped

1 red onion, chopped

4 cloves garlic, minced

1 jalapeño pepper, minced

1 tablespoon grated ginger root

1/8 teaspoon cardamom

1/4 teaspoon allspice

1/4 teaspoon pepper

3 cups water

3 cups low-sodium vegetable broth

2 sweet potatoes, peeled and cubed

2 tablespoons brown sugar

2 tablespoons lime juice

Calories 235, **% Calories from Fat** 14%, **Fat** (g) 4, **Carbohydrates** (g) 41, **Protein** (g) 11, **Sodium** (mg) 27, **Fiber** (g) 9, **Saturated Fat** (g) 1, **Cholesterol** (mg) 0

Caribbean Black Bean Soup

- Sort beans, rinse, and drain. Cover with water and soak overnight. Drain and rinse again.

- In large pot cook onions, garlic, jalapeño, and ginger root in oil 7 to 8 minutes, until tender.

- Add beans, cardamom, allspice, pepper, water, and vegetable broth. Simmer, covered 1½ hours, until beans are almost tender.

- Add sweet potatoes and brown sugar; simmer 25 to 35 minutes longer, until beans and potatoes are tender. Add lime juice and serve.

Slow Cooker Black Bean Soup: *Make recipe as directed, except use 4- to 5-quart slow cooker. Soak the beans as directed. Sauté onions and garlic in olive oil, then combine with the drained beans and all ingredients except lime juice in slow cooker. Cover and cook on low 8 to 9 hours; add lime juice and serve.*

Spicy Black Bean Soup: *Make recipe as directed, except omit ginger root, cardamom, and allspice. Add 1 minced serrano pepper to the onion mixture. Add 1 tablespoon chili powder (preferably homemade) and omit brown sugar. Stir in 2 cups frozen corn in the last 10 minutes of cooking time.*

SOUPS

Cook Onions and Garlic

- This simple soup can be made with lightly sautéed onions and garlic,

- Or you can cook the onions and garlic until caramelized; in that case, hold back the jalapeño and ginger until you add the beans.

- Cardamom is an expensive spice. You can omit it and increase the allspice to ½ teaspoon if you'd like.

- Other vegetables for this soup include chopped celery or green bell pepper.

Add Sweet Potatoes

- You can substitute russet, red, or Yukon Gold potatoes for the sweet potatoes if you'd like.

- Use 3 russet potatoes, 4 Yukon Gold potatoes, or 6 to 7 red potatoes, depending on the size.

- The lime juice is added at the very end so it doesn't prevent the beans from softening properly.

- Some freshly chopped cilantro would be a nice addition to the soup at the last minute.

CHICKEN CHEESE PITAS

Tender chicken and Swiss cheese are delicious in a pita sandwich

These sandwiches are full of flavor and are fun to eat. Oregano, lemon, garlic, onion, and sour cream make this recipe special.

Homemade pita breads are really necessary for this sandwich if you need to eat a very low-sodium diet. If you use purchased pita breads, the sodium count will be close to 300 mg per serving. There are some brands, especially the

organic varieties, that are low in sodium. Just read labels!

You can substitute boneless, skinless chicken thighs for the breasts in this recipe; use 6 of them. The recipe will be higher in fat, but more flavorful.

Serve these sandwiches with iced green tea and some sliced fresh fruit. *Yield: Serves 6*

Ingredients

3 boneless, skinless chicken breasts, cut into strips

1 teaspoon dried oregano

1/2 teaspoon grated lemon peel

1/4 teaspoon pepper

1/4 teaspoon onion powder

1 tablespoon unsalted butter

2 garlic cloves, minced

1 tablespoon lemon juice

1/2 cup sour cream

2 tablespoons plain low-fat yogurt

1 cup shredded Swiss cheese

1 red bell pepper, chopped

2 carrots, shredded

1/4 cup toasted pine nuts

6 Homemade Whole Wheat Pitas (page 71)

2 cups baby spinach leaves

Calories 290, **% Calories from Fat** 59%, **Fat** (g) 16, **Carbohydrates** (g) 14, **Protein** (g) 22, **Sodium** (mg) 127, **Fiber** (g) 2, **Saturated Fat** (g) 8, **Cholesterol** (mg) 65

Chicken Cheese Pitas

- Toss chicken with oregano, lemon peel, pepper, and onion powder; set aside.

- Melt butter in medium pan; add garlic; cook 2 minutes. Add chicken; cook and stir until chicken is done, about 6 to 8 minutes. Place in bowl.

- Add lemon juice; toss and let stand 10 minutes. Add sour cream and yogurt; mix well.

- Add cheese, bell pepper, carrots, and pine nuts. Cut pita breads in half; line with baby spinach and fill with chicken mixture.

Tex-Mex Chicken Pitas: Make recipe as directed, except reduce oregano to ½ teaspoon. Add 1 minced jalapeño pepper and 2 teaspoons chili powder to the chicken mixture. Omit sour cream, yogurt, and carrots; add 1 cup chunky spicy salsa. Substitute Pepper Jack cheese for the Swiss.

To safely pack lunch boxes, follow this rule: hot foods hot, cold foods cold. Use insulated lunch boxes and thermoses. Pack hot food while it's very hot and cold food while it's very cold. Rinse the thermos with hot or cold water, depending on if you're adding hot or cold liquid.

Cook Chicken

Fill Pitas with Chicken

- Cook the chicken just until done. When the chicken is cut into even pieces, it doesn't take very long to cook.

- Cut open a piece of the chicken to check doneness. It should not be pink on the inside.

- You can cook the chicken ahead of time; refrigerate until ready to eat, then combine with the other ingredients.

- Or use precooked chicken; about 2 cups is the equivalent of three boneless chicken breasts.

- When you cut the pitas in half, a pocket should naturally open; if it doesn't, cut one open. Don't overfill the sandwiches, or the pita breads will split.

- You can serve this as a cold sandwich, which is great for lunch boxes.

- Make the chicken mixture, toss with the lemon juice, then add sour cream and yogurt; cool completely in refrigerator.

- When cool, add cheese, bell pepper, and carrots. Pack with pine nuts and pita breads; assemble at lunch.

TUNA SALAD SANDWICHES

Fresh tuna makes all the difference in these classic sandwiches

Tuna salad sandwiches are the traditional sandwiches that most noncooks depend on. Mix canned tuna with some mayonnaise and mustard and slap it between bread slices and you're ready to go.

As delicious as that sandwich is, this one is better. It starts with fresh tuna, so not only is the sandwich lower in sodium, it tastes like a treat from a gourmet shop.

Herbs help make this classic sandwich something special. Basil, marjoram, thyme, and summer savory are great accents for the rich, meaty taste of tuna. You can make the sandwich with vegetables or omit the mustard and cheese and add some red grapes.

Serve this sandwiches with unsalted potato chips, pear and apple slices, and chocolate chip cookies. *Yield: Serves 6*

Ingredients

2 tuna steaks

2 tablespoons lemon juice

1 tablespoon olive oil

2 garlic cloves, minced

1/2 cup mayonnaise

1/4 cup plain low fat yogurt

2 tablespoons Dijon mustard

1 teaspoon dried basil

2 stalks celery, chopped

1/4 cup chopped green onion

1/4 cup grated Parmesan cheese

1 round French Bread loaf (page 66)

2 tablespoons unsalted butter

6 leaves butter lettuce

Calories 484, **% Calories from Fat** 29%, **Fat** (g) 16, **Carbohydrates** (g) 44, **Protein** (g) 42, **Sodium** (mg) 322, **Fiber** (g) 6, **Saturated Fat** (g) 6, **Cholesterol** (mg) 137

Tuna Salad Sandwiches

- Drizzle tuna with lemon juice and olive oil; refrigerate 30 minutes.

- Heat olive oil in pan; add garlic; cook 2 minutes. Add tuna steaks; cook, turning once, until done, 8 minutes.

- Let tuna cool 15 minutes; flake into large pieces. In bowl, mix mayonnaise, yogurt, and mustard.

- Add basil, celery, green onion, cheese, and tuna. Slice French bread in half to make two equal rounds; spread cut sides with butter. Make sandwiches with bread, lettuce, and tuna mixture.

Curried Tuna Sandwiches: Make sandwiches as directed, except sprinkle the tuna before cooking with 2 teaspoons curry powder. Then cook until done. Omit mustard and cheese; add 2 teaspoons curry powder and ½ cup mango chutney to the mayonnaise mixture.

Open-Face Hot Tuna Sandwiches: Make recipe as directed, except omit the Parmesan cheese. Cut the loaf in half, spread with butter, and toast. Divide tuna mixture among the halves of bread; sprinkle with 1½ cups grated low-sodium Swiss cheese. Broil 6 inches from heat 7 to 10 minutes, until golden.

Cook Tuna

Mix Filling

- The tuna should be cooked until it flakes with a fork and is completely opaque, with no red in the center.

- Don't cook it until medium or medium rare unless you really like tuna cooked this way.

- This is a great recipe to make when you have leftover grilled tuna or salmon from the night before.

- Always grill an extra fillet or steak or two, refrigerate, then use in this or any sandwich recipe.

- The mayonnaise mixture can be made ahead of time; in fact it's a great sandwich spread.

- Store it, covered, in the refrigerator up to 4 days and use with any sandwich, from roasted chicken to roast beef.

- Mix the filling ingredients together gently to keep the chunks of tuna large.

- Use a serrated knife to easily cut the large sandwich into pieces to serve.

HOAGIE SANDWICHES

A hoagie can be made with anything from a vegetable to mixed meats

Hoagie sandwiches are made on hoagie buns, which are oblong instead of round. The buns can be soft or crusty; the choice is up to you.

Like most commercially made breads, hoagie buns can be very high in sodium. You can make your own from any bread recipe; just form the dough into 5- x 2-inch oblongs and flatten with your hand. Let rise and bake until golden.

Traditional hoagies are made with lots of preserved meats and cheeses, which makes them very high in sodium. But you can enjoy this treat with some judicious substitutes.

These sandwiches can be served hot or cold. To serve them hot, wrap in foil and bake at 375°F 15 to 25 minutes, until hot. *Yield: Serves 4*

Ingredients

3 tablespoons extra-virgin olive oil

1 red onion, chopped

2 cloves garlic, minced

1 (8-ounce) package mushrooms, sliced

2 cups sliced cooked homemade turkey

1 teaspoon fennel seeds

$1/2$ teaspoon dried oregano

$1/4$ teaspoon pepper

$1/8$ teaspoon cayenne pepper

2 tablespoons lemon juice

6 Hoagie Buns (page 69)

4 slices provolone cheese, low-sodium if possible

2 cups shredded lettuce

2 teaspoons fresh oregano

Calories 446, **% Calories from Fat** 32%, **Fat** (g) 29, **Carbohydrates** (g) 45, **Protein** (g) 26, **Sodium** (mg) 238, **Fiber** (g) 3, **Saturated Fat** (g) 24, **Cholesterol** (mg) 103

Hoagie Sandwiches

- Heat olive oil in saucepan; add onion, garlic, and mushrooms; cook and stir until browned, about 10 minutes.

- Add turkey; sprinkle with fennel, oregano, pepper, and cayenne pepper.

- Cook over low heat, turning turkey several times, until turkey is hot and tender; sprinkle with lemon juice.

- Toast Hoagie Buns if desired. Pile meat mixture onto the buns. Top with provolone cheese, lettuce, and fresh oregano. Press sandwiches together with the palm of your hand and serve.

Very Low-Sodium Hoagie Sandwiches: Make recipe as directed, except instead of precooked or leftover turkey, use 1 pound thinly sliced raw turkey cutlets. After the onion mixture has browned, add the turkey and sprinkle with seasonings. Cook 5 to 6 minutes, turning once, until turkey is cooked. Proceed with recipe.

Mixed Hoagie Sandwiches: Make recipe as directed, except use half cooked turkey and half cooked thinly sliced roast beef. Warm both meats as directed. Add 1 to 2 slices fresh tomato to each sandwich and use shredded romaine lettuce.

Prepare Turkey

Assemble Sandwiches

- Slice the turkey about ⅓-inch thick so it will warm through quickly and not overcook.

- You can substitute sliced cooked chicken, pork, or salmon for the sliced cooked turkey.

- Add other vegetables to this delicious sandwich, including sliced red or green bell peppers or sliced zucchini.

- Other herbs would be good too; use a combination of dried and fresh for the most flavor.

- Make sure to get some of the oil and juices from the turkey and vegetables onto the buns.

- This will add lots of flavor and help keep the sandwich together as you eat it.

- You can cut the sandwiches in half and serve more people. The individual sandwiches are very hearty servings.

- These sandwiches really don't hold well, so don't make them ahead of time.

CRISP SALMON SALAD

Fresh salmon is the key to this low-sodium salad

A delicious salad for lunch is always welcome. And salmon, especially when it's fresh, makes this salad spectacular.

Salmon is a fatty fish; that means it has more fat than other fish fillets or steaks. But the fat in this fish is good fat. You should eat a serving of fatty fish at least two times a week.

Salmon is rich in omega-3 fatty acids, which help promote heart health, reduce the inflammation that could be the cause

of heart disease and cancer, lower lipid levels, and increase the good cholesterol in your body. And it's delicious!

Since salmon naturally tastes so rich and decadent, it doesn't need salt. Enjoy the taste of the fresh fish in this easy salad. *Yield: Serves 6*

Ingredients

2 (8-ounce) salmon steaks

2 tablespoons olive oil

2 tablespoons lemon juice

2 tablespoons orange juice concentrate

$1/2$ teaspoon paprika

$1/2$ teaspoon cumin

$1/4$ teaspoon pepper

3 stalks celery, chopped

1 apple, chopped

$1/4$ cup chopped green onions

$1/4$ cup unsalted sunflower seeds

1 avocado, peeled and cubed

3 cups baby spinach leaves

Calories 299, **% Calories from Fat** 63%, **Fat** (g) 16, **Carbohydrates** (g)10, **Protein** (g) 14, **Sodium** (mg) 57, **Fiber** (g) 4, **Saturated Fat** (g) 3, **Cholesterol** (mg) 27

Crisp Salmon Salad

- Broil salmon 6 inches from heat for 8 to 9 minutes, turning once, until just cooked. Let cool 10 minutes.

- Combine oil, lemon juice, orange juice concentrate, paprika, cumin, and pepper in bowl; whisk to blend.

- Flake salmon into large pieces; add to dressing with celery, apple, and green onions; toss.

- Cover and refrigerate 2 to 4 hours. When ready to serve, top with sunflower seeds and avocado and serve on spinach leaves.

Salmon Vegetable Salad: Make recipe as directed, except omit orange juice concentrate and apple. Add 2 tablespoons Dijon mustard to the dressing. Add 1 red and 1 green bell pepper, both chopped, to the salad, and add 2 tablespoons chopped fresh basil. Refrigerate salad as directed.

· · · · · · · · · GREEN ● LIGHT · · · · · · · · ·

Salmon is very high in vitamin D, which may help prevent some kinds of cancer. The salmon you buy is either wild or farm raised. Whenever you can, look for wild salmon. It has a more intense flavor, and the food the salmon eats in the wild helps increase the omega-3 content.

Mix Dressing

- This dressing is a good basic salad dressing you can use for everything from pasta salad to plain green salads.

- The dressing will keep in the refrigerator, well covered, up to 4 days. Shake or stir it before using.

- You can omit the paprika and cumin and add fresh or dried herbs instead.

- Try thyme, basil, oregano, marjoram, sage, and a bit of mint, or use some minced jalapeño peppers.

Mix Salad

- Mix the salad gently so the salmon stays in large pieces. You can cook the salmon well-done or medium.

- If you cook the salmon to medium, it won't flake; cut it apart into large pieces.

- This salad is great for box lunches. Just chill it overnight; in the morning, portion into a small container.

- Place in an insulated lunch box with some frozen juice or a frozen gel pack to keep the food cool.

211

ROASTED VEGGIE SANDWICHES

Grilled vegetables soak up lemon dressing in a delicious sandwich

Roasted vegetables, so good for you, are delicious in a pressed sandwich. A pressed sandwich is, well, pressed! Wrap the sandwich tightly in plastic wrap. You can weigh the sandwiches down with some heavy cans or place a cookie sheet on top and add cans to that.

The sandwiches can marinate at room temperature if you don't add any cheese. Any kind of low-sodium cheese can be added just before the sandwiches are served.

Use any of your favorite vegetables in this easy sandwich, including different types of mushrooms, zucchini, and even chopped cauliflower.

These sandwiches are perfect for a picnic, especially if you leave out the cheese. And that will reduce the fat content, too! *Yield: Serves 6*

Ingredients

1 red bell pepper, sliced

1 green bell pepper, sliced

1 yellow bell pepper, sliced

1 yellow summer squash, sliced

1 red onion, sliced

3 portobello mushrooms, sliced

2 tablespoons olive oil

2 tablespoons lemon juice

$1/4$ teaspoon pepper

1 teaspoon dried tarragon

1 teaspoon dried thyme

$1/4$ cup chopped parsley

6 French Bread Rolls (page 67)

6 slices fresh mozzarella

Calories 328, **% Calories from Fat** 27%, **Fat** (g) 10, **Carbohydrates** (g) 47, **Protein** (g) 15, **Sodium** (mg) 158, **Fiber** (g) 7, **Saturated Fat** (g) 4, **Cholesterol** (mg) 66

Roasted Veggie Sandwiches

- Preheat oven to 425°F. Place bell peppers, squash, onion, and mushrooms on a roasting pan.

- Drizzle with olive oil, lemon juice, and pepper; toss to coat. Roast 8 to 11 minutes, until vegetables are tender, turning once with spatula.

- Add tarragon, thyme, and parsley and mix gently. Let cool 20 minutes. Layer vegetables and juices on split rolls.

- Top with mozzarella cheese, press together, and wrap in plastic wrap. Refrigerate 3 to 4 hours before serving.

Roasted Veggie Salad: Make recipe as directed, except double all the ingredients. Omit rolls. When all the vegetables are roasted, add ½ cup plain yogurt and ¼ cup low-sodium mayonnaise; mix gently. Add cubed mozzarella cheese, cover, and refrigerate 4 to 5 hours to blend flavors.

Roasted Antipasto: Make recipe as directed, except slice the vegetables into large slices. Roast as directed, adding 5 to 10 minutes to the roasting time. Arrange vegetables on platter and top with thin strips of cheese. Sprinkle with fresh herbs and serve immediately.

Roast Vegetables

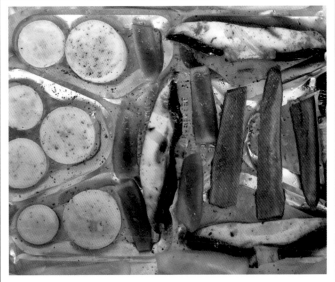

Assemble Sandwiches

- The vegetables in this recipe are all tender, which means they will cook at about the same time.

- If you want to use vegetables like potatoes, carrots, or sweet potatoes, they need to be cooked separately, for about 45 minutes.

- You can add minced garlic to the vegetables; sprinkle it on along with the olive oil and lemon juice.

- Other vegetables like snap peas, snow peas, or sliced zucchini can be added.

- If you use a different bread, choose a low-sodium variety with a fairly coarse texture. The bread will soak up some of the juices from the vegetables.

- A sturdy bread is necessary, or the sandwiches will fall apart after being refrigerated.

- If the sandwich is wrapped tightly in plastic wrap, it doesn't have to be weighted.

- Don't refrigerate the sandwiches longer than 4 hours or the bread will become soggy.

213

GYROS SANDWICHES

Tender slow cooker lamb makes wonderful sandwiches with a yogurt sauce

A gyro is a recipe from Greece, consisting of lamb, pork, or beef cooked with lots of seasonings and served with Tzatziki Sauce and pita bread.

In the traditional version, the lamb is grilled over an open flame or roasted over hot coals. This easier version is cooked on the stovetop.

Pita breads are perfect for this sandwich because they offer an intense taste without getting soggy.

You can also make this recipe with cubed pork or beef. *Yield: Serves 6*

Ingredients

2 tablespoons olive oil

2 tablespoons lemon juice

1 pound lamb shoulder, cubed

1 onion, chopped

5 cloves garlic, minced

1/2 teaspoon crushed red pepper flakes

1 teaspoon cumin

1 teaspoon dried oregano

1/2 cup sour cream

1/4 cup thick Greek yogurt

1 tablespoon fresh dill weed

1 teaspoon grated lemon zest

2 tomatoes, seeded and chopped

1/4 cup shredded Parmesan cheese

4 Pita Breads (page 71), split

Calories 497, **% Calories from Fat** 47%, **Fat** (g) 26, **Carbohydrates** (g) 6, **Protein** (g) 21, **Sodium** (mg) 154, **Fiber** (g) 1, **Saturated Fat** (g) 12, **Cholesterol** (mg) 78

Gyros Sandwiches

- Combine olive oil, lemon juice, and lamb in bowl; cover and refrigerate 8 to 12 hours.

- Place lamb mixture in saucepan; add onion and garlic. Cook and stir until lamb is done, about 9 to 12 minutes.

- Place in bowl; add red pepper flakes, cumin, and oregano; let cool 20 minutes. Add sour cream, yogurt, dill, zest, tomatoes, and cheese.

- Cover and chill 2 to 3 hours before using. Use in pita breads for sandwiches.

Grilled Gyros Sandwiches: Make recipe as directed, except cut onion into 8 to 10 wedges. Add minced garlic to olive oil and lemon juice marinade. Thread onions and lamb on skewers. Grill over medium coals 7 to 9 minutes, turning once, until done. Proceed with recipe.

Gyro Salad: Make recipe as directed, through cooking the lamb, adding the seasonings, sour cream, and tomatoes. Cover and chill as directed. When ready to serve, toss 6 cups baby spinach with 1 tablespoon lemon juice and 1 tablespoon olive oil; top with lamb mixture and serve.

Cook Lamb

Mix Filling

- Make sure to trim the excess fat from the lamb before cutting it into cubes.

- The cubes should be about 1½ inches in diameter. Make them the same size so they marinate and cook evenly.

- Lamb should be cooked medium rare to medium. It will be a light pink color inside.

- Cook the lamb to the doneness you prefer. Check the lamb as it is cooking and take it off the heat when it's perfect.

- If you can't find Greek yogurt, regular yogurt will work. You might want to drain it first so it's thicker.

- To drain yogurt, place in a cheesecloth-lined sieve, then place that in a bowl in the refrigerator overnight.

- Let the yogurt drain. Use the thick yogurt in recipes; the whey can be added to bread doughs or soups.

- You can use the filling hot. Just mix the sour cream, yogurt, dill, zest, tomatoes, and cheese; use that to top the hot lamb in the pita breads.

CHOCOLATE CHUNK COOKIES

Rich chocolate chunk cookies are full of even more chocolate

Even when you're trying to eat a healthy diet, you need to have dessert occasionally. And when you do, make it the best you can find or make, and make sure it's low in sodium.

These cookies are very special, because they have three kinds of chocolate. Cocoa powder is in the dough along with ground white chocolate, which gives the cookies a creamy

texture and rich taste. And semisweet chocolate chunks are the finishing touch.

These are the perfect cookies to tuck into a lunch box or to serve with a glass of cold milk as an after-school snack. They freeze very well; to thaw just let stand at room temperature until they are soft. *Yield: Makes 48 cookies*

Ingredients

1 cup unsalted butter, softened

1 cup brown sugar

1/2 cup sugar

1/2 cup cocoa powder

2 eggs

2 egg yolks

2 teaspoons vanilla

1 cup white chocolate chips, ground

2 1/2 cups flour

1 teaspoon baking soda

2 cups semisweet chocolate chunks

Calories 139, **% Calories from Fat** 51%, **Fat** (g) 8, **Carbohydrates** (g) 17, **Protein** (g) 2, **Sodium** (mg) 118, **Fiber** (g)1, **Saturated Fat** (g) 5, **Cholesterol** (mg) 30

Chocolate Chunk Cookies

- Beat butter with brown sugar and sugar until light and fluffy. Add cocoa powder and mix well.

- Add eggs, egg yolks, and vanilla; beat until smooth. Add ground white chocolate chips.

- Add flour and baking soda; mix just until dough forms. Add semisweet chocolate chunks.

- Chill dough, covered, 2 to 3 hours. Drop by tablespoons onto cookie sheets. Bake at 325°F 12 to 17 minutes, until set. Cool on wire racks.

For the perfect cookies, measure the flour carefully. Most people scoop the measuring cup into the flour; this will result in too much flour, which makes tough cookies. Lightly spoon the flour into the measuring cup, then level it off with the back of a knife. And always chill the dough before baking.

Peanut Butter Chocolate Chunk Cookies: Make recipe as directed, except substitute ½ cup unsalted peanut butter for half the butter. Omit cocoa powder. Continue making the batter. Add 1 cup coarsely chopped unsalted peanuts along with the chocolate chunks. Chill and bake cookies as directed.

Grind White Chocolate

Mix Dough

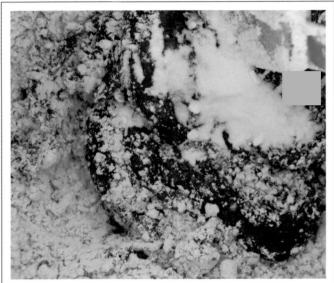

- To grind the white chocolate, place it in a food processor. Pulse the chocolate until the particles are very fine.

- You can use white chocolate chips, also called vanilla milk chips, or a white chocolate candy bar cut into pieces.

- The ground chocolate chips will melt into the cookies, becoming part of the batter.

- Don't substitute any other kind of chocolate for the white chocolate, as it doesn't have the same texture.

- Don't overmix cookie dough, or the gluten will develop and the cookies will be tough.

- Chilling the dough helps ensure that the cookies are tender, because it gives the protein a chance to relax.

- For the most even cookies, use a small ice cream scoop to scoop out the dough.

- Bake the cookies on ungreased cookie sheets. There's enough fat in the dough to prevent sticking.

MERINGUE BAR COOKIES

A chocolate crust is covered with crisp meringue in these bars

Bar cookies are great time savers. You make a dough and press or pour it into a large pan, bake the cookies, then cut them into squares.

These cookies are very special. The meringue that bakes on top becomes chewy and crisp, while the tender base is rich and chocolaty. In between, toffee bits and white chocolate add flavor and texture.

Whenever you bake, measure the flour carefully and have the ingredients at room temperature so they combine easily.

Don't microwave the butter to soften, because parts of it almost always melt, which changes the structure of the cookies. Let the butter stand at room temperature for an hour before using. *Yield: Serves 24*

Ingredients

1 cup brown sugar

1/2 cup unsalted butter, softened

1/3 cup cocoa powder

3 egg yolks

2 teaspoons vanilla

1 2/3 cups flour

1 teaspoon baking soda

1 cup toffee bits

1 cup white chocolate chips

3 egg whites

1/2 cup sugar

Calories 169, **% Calories from Fat** 43%, **Fat** (g) 8,**Carbohydrates** (g) 24, **Protein** (g) 2, **Sodium** (mg) 78, **Fiber** (g) <1, **Saturated Fat** (g) 5, **Cholesterol** (mg) 29

Meringue Bar Cookies

- In bowl combine brown sugar and butter; beat until fluffy. Add cocoa powder, egg yolks, and vanilla; beat well.

- Add flour and baking soda. Spread dough into bottom of greased 13- x 9-inch pan.

- Sprinkle with toffee bits and white chocolate chips.

- In bowl, beat egg whites until foamy; add sugar gradually; beat until stiff. Spread over bars. Bake at 325°F 30 to 35 minutes, until meringue is light brown. Cool on wire rack.

Lemon Meringue Bar Cookies: Make recipe as directed, except use granulated sugar in place of the brown sugar and omit the cocoa powder. Add 1 teaspoon grated lemon rind to the cookie base. Add 1 tablespoon lemon juice to the egg whites before you start beating, then fold in ½ teaspoon grated lemon zest.

Separate eggs while they are cold; the best tool is your fingers. Break the egg into one hand and let the whites slip through your fingers into a bowl. Place the yolk in another bowl. Be sure that no part of the egg yolk gets into the whites, or they will not form peaks.

Make Meringue

- When beating the meringue, start the beater at low speed. When the egg whites foam, increase the speed.

- Add the sugar gradually so it dissolves and your meringue is smooth, not grainy.

- The meringue should be beaten until stiff peaks form. This means when you lift the beater, the egg mixture stands up in peaks.

- Let the bars cool completely on a wire rack before cutting them. Store covered at room temperature.

Assemble Bars

- Beating the butter with the sugar creates small holes in the fat that fill with carbon dioxide produced by the baking powder.

- This makes the texture of the cookies light and tender. Do not substitute baking powder for baking soda.

- This soft dough will press easily into the pan. You may need to flour your fingers to prevent sticking.

- Use unsalted butter, solid shortening, or nonstick baking spray to grease the pan.

DESSERTS

ICE CREAM PIE

A rich chocolate cookie crust holds ice cream and toppings; yum

Ice cream pies are the perfect summer dessert. Not only are they easy to make, they are fun to serve and a cooling and delicious finish to a meal on a hot night.

The best crust for an ice cream pie is a cookie crust. The crunch of the cookies is the perfect foil against the smooth cold creaminess of the ice cream, marshmallow crème, and fudge topping.

You can use low-fat varieties of all these ingredients, and the pie will still be delicious. In fact most people won't know they're eating a lower-fat dessert.

Let the frozen pie stand at room temperature 10 to 15 minutes before slicing; this makes serving, and eating, easier. *Yield: Serves 8*

Ingredients

8 homemade Chocolate Chunk Cookies (page 216)

¼ cup unsalted butter

½ cup chopped pecans

1 cup marshmallow crème

2 cups chocolate ice cream

2 cups low-fat vanilla ice cream

1 cup hot fudge topping

Calories 508, **% Calories from Fat** 43%, **Fat** (g) 24, **Carbohydrates** (g) 70, **Protein** (g) 6, **Sodium** (mg) 205, **Fiber** (g) 3, **Saturated Fat** (g) 12, **Cholesterol** (mg) 61

Ice Cream Pie

- Place cookies in food processor; process until crumbs form. Add butter and pecans; mix until crumbly.

- Press crumb mixture into 9-inch pie pan. Spoon marshmallow crème onto the crust.

- Soften ice cream by letting it stand at room temperature 10 to15 minutes. Layer ice cream and hot fudge topping on crust.

- Cover and freeze 4 to 6 hours, until firm. To serve, let stand at room temperature 15 to 20 minutes.

Ice Cream Tartlets: Make recipe as directed, except increase cookies to 10. Then press cookie mixture into the bottom and up the sides of 8 4-inch tartlet pans. Divide all ingredients among the tartlet shells. Place on a cookie sheet and freeze until firm, about 6 hours.

Chocolate Chocolate Ice Cream Pie: Make recipe as directed, except omit marshmallow crème. Use another cup of hot fudge topping directly on the crust. Substitute 2 cups chocolate swirl, chocolate chip, or double chocolate ice cream or frozen yogurt for the vanilla ice cream.

Press Crumbs into Pan

- Mix the crumbs together with the butter until the crumbs are moistened. The mixture should stick together when pressed.

- Sprinkle the crumb mixture over the crust and press evenly onto the bottom and up the sides.

- For the most even crust, take another, slightly smaller pie pan and gently press onto the crumbs.

- Some recipes call for a baked crumb crust, but it stays more tender when it's not baked.

Layer Ingredients in Pan

- To make working with ice cream easier, let it stand at room temperature 15 minutes before scooping.

- The ingredients will get mixed together as you layer them; that's just fine. This adds texture to the pie.

- You can add more ice cream if you'd like; pile it high for a special occasion.

- Top the pie with whipped cream and more chocolate cookie crumbs to finish it off with real decadence.

DESSERTS

FRUIT TRIFLE

Homemade angel food cake is low in sodium; it's delicious in this classic trifle

It's called a trifle in England, and Tiramisu in Italy. Whatever you call it, this dessert is delicious. A light angel food cake is layered with fresh fruit and a pineapple–sour cream mixture.

The cake soaks up the juices from the fruit, and the whole thing blends together into a wonderful fresh dessert.

Use a glass bowl, preferably with a foot, to display this

beautiful dessert. Since it has to be made ahead of time, it's the perfect choice for entertaining.

Use the best-looking fruits you can find in the market. Kiwi fruits, raspberries, blueberries, and peaches can all be used in this dessert. Garnish the trifle with mint just before serving. *Yield: Serves 8*

Ingredients

1 cup low-fat sour cream

¼ cup pineapple juice

1 cup heavy whipping cream

¼ cup powdered sugar

2 teaspoons vanilla

2 cups sliced strawberries

2 cups fresh pineapple cubes

2 bananas, peeled and sliced

2 tablespoons lemon juice

1 Angel Food Cake (page 223), cut into cubes

1 tablespoon chopped fresh mint

1 cup fresh raspberries

Calories 524, **% Calories from Fat** 30%, **Fat** (g) 18, **Carbohydrates** (g) 85, **Protein** (g) 10, **Sodium** (mg) 112, **Fiber** (g) 4, **Saturated Fat** (g) 11, **Cholesterol** (mg) 53

Fruit Trifle

- In bowl mix sour cream and pineapple juice. In medium bowl, beat cream with powdered sugar and vanilla until stiff peaks form.

- Fold whipped cream mixture into sour cream mixture. Prepare all the fruit. Sprinkle bananas with lemon juice.

- Layer ⅓ cake cubes, fruit, sour cream mixture, and mint in large glass bowl.

- Top with raspberries, cover, and chill 3 to 4 hours before serving.

Angel Food Cake: Place 12 egg whites in a large bowl; add 1 tablespoon lemon juice and beat until foamy. Gradually add 1 ½ cups sugar, beating until stiff peaks form. Beat in 2 teaspoons vanilla. Sift together 1 cup each powdered sugar and flour; fold into egg whites in three batches. Place in 10-inch tube pan; run spatula briefly through batter to break large bubbles. Bake at 350°F 45 minutes; invert pan onto a funnel and cool before removing from pan.

Make Filling

Layer Ingredients

- The filling is creamy and easy to make. You can use other types of fruit juices as well.

- Peach nectar, mango nectar, or pear juice would be good substitutes for the pineapple juice.

- You can substitute low-fat or nonfat frozen whipped topping for the whipped cream and powdered sugar.

- But that may increase the sodium content of the recipe; be sure to read labels carefully.

- Make your own angel food cake for the lowest sodium recipe. A purchased cake has about 2,500 mg of sodium if the baker used 1 teaspoon salt.

- Or go to a local bakery and see if they will make a cake for you without using salt.

- Otherwise, the sodium level will increase to 347 grams per serving.

- Serve this beautiful dessert at the table so your guests can admire it before you dig in.

DESSERTS

LEMON MERINGUE PIE

A classic lemon meringue pie is naturally low in sodium

Lemon meringue pie is a traditional pie that can be tricky to make. This recipe is easy because it uses sweetened condensed milk to make the creamy, silky filling.

This pie must be made ahead of time so it can thoroughly chill in the refrigerator. The slices will cut beautifully after it has had a chance to sit in the fridge.

Because the filling is not cooked in this recipe, you really should use pasteurized eggs, especially if you are feeding elderly people, small children, a pregnant woman, or someone with chronic health conditions. The risk of problems with raw egg is low for healthy people.

Serve this pie on fancy dessert plates with fresh coffee and cream. *Yield: Serves 8*

KNACK LOW-SALT COOKING

Ingredients

16 graham crackers

$^1/_3$ cup unsalted butter, melted

$^1/_2$ cup finely chopped walnuts

1 (14-ounce) can sweetened condensed milk

$^1/_3$ cup lemon juice

3 pasteurized egg yolks

$^1/_2$ cup heavy whipping cream

2 tablespoons powdered sugar

3 egg whites

$^1/_8$ teaspoon cream of tartar

$^1/_3$ cup sugar

Calories 488, **% Calories from Fat** 52%, **Fat** (g) 28, **Carbohydrates** (g) 50, **Protein** (g) 11, **Sodium** (mg) 201, **Fiber** (g) 1, **Saturated Fat** (g) 14, **Cholesterol** (mg) 220

Lemon Meringue Pie

- Finely crush graham crackers. Add butter and nuts.

- Press crumbs into 9-inch pie pan. In bowl, mix condensed milk, lemon juice, and egg yolks.

- In another bowl, beat cream with powdered sugar; fold into lemon mixture. Pour into crust; refrigerate.

- In large bowl, beat egg whites with cream of tartar until foamy; gradually add sugar. Beat until stiff peaks form. Spoon onto pie, sealing edges. Bake at 375°F 12 to 17 minutes, until meringue is light brown. Chill 4 hours.

Lemon Meringue Tartlets: Make recipe as directed, except substitute 8 4-inch tartlet shells for the 9-inch pie pan. Divide graham cracker mixture into the shells, then divide filling onto crust. Top each with meringue, sealing to the edges. Bake at 375°F for 7 to 9 minutes, until meringue is light brown.

YELLOW ● LIGHT

If you are feeding a person with a compromised immune system, use pasteurized egg whites, too. The egg whites usually are safer than the yolks. During baking, the meringue is more exposed to heat than the filling. If you use pasteurized egg whites, the beating time will be quite long. Just don't give up!

Mix Filling

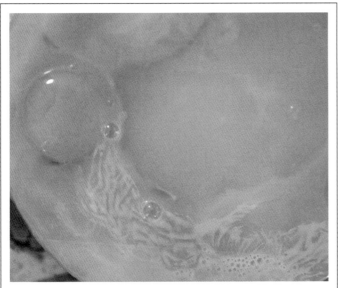

- Make sure you use sweetened condensed milk, not evaporated milk, or the pie will not set up.

- There are low-fat and non-fat sweetened condensed milks on the market, but they may not work in this recipe.

- Stir the milk and lemon juice with a wire whisk to make sure the mixture is smooth.

- The acid in the lemon juice reacts with the egg yolks and protein in the milk to thicken the filling.

Top with Meringue

- Beat the meringue until it stands in very stiff peaks and the sugar is dissolved.

- Rub a bit of the meringue between your fingers. If you feel any grains of sugar, keep beating.

- Spread the meringue on the crust and make sure it touches the crust so it doesn't shrink in the oven's heat.

- Use the back of your spoon to make peaks and swirls in the meringue for a pretty look.

DESSERTS

CARAMEL CAKE

Caramel cake is easy to make; just sprinkle with powdered sugar before serving

Homemade cake can make your house smell like heaven. There's nothing like the combination of butter, sugar, vanilla, and spices baking together and caramelizing in the heat.

Cake batters are scientific formulas, so follow the recipe to the letter. Measure carefully, and make sure you read through the recipe before you begin.

The butter should be at room temperature, and the eggs should be cool, not cold from the fridge. Let them sit out 20 minutes before you begin.

You can top this cake with caramel sauce or add a dollop of whipped cream. Some toasted chopped walnuts are the perfect finishing touch. *Yield: Serves 12*

Ingredients

- 1/2 cup unsalted butter
- 3/4 cup sugar
- 1 cup dark brown sugar
- 1/2 cup vegetable oil
- 3 eggs
- 1 tablespoon vanilla
- 1 teaspoon cinnamon
- 1/8 teaspoon cardamom
- 1/4 teaspoon salt
- 2 1/2 cups flour
- 1 teaspoon baking powder
- 1/2 teaspoon baking soda

Calories 398, **% Calories from Fat** 41%, **Fat** (g) 18, **Carbohydrates** (g) 54, **Protein** (g) 5, **Sodium** (mg) 158, **Fiber** (g) 1, **Saturated Fat** (g) 6, **Cholesterol** (mg) 73

Caramel Cake

- Melt butter in heavy pan over low heat, swirling pan occasionally, until butter is brown. Pour into bowl and chill until firm.

- Add sugar to butter; beat until creamy. Add brown sugar, oil, eggs, and vanilla; beat until smooth.

- Add cinnamon, cardamom, salt, flour, baking powder, and baking soda; beat until mixed. Pour into greased 13- x 9-inch pan.

- Bake cake at 350°F 35 to 45 minutes, until top springs back. Cool completely. Frost if desired before slicing.

Caramel Frosting: In saucepan, combine ¼ cup unsalted butter with 6 tablespoons milk and 1 cup brown sugar; bring to a boil. Boil hard 1 minute. Cool completely, then chill in fridge 2 hours. Beat 1 (8-ounce) package softened cream cheese until fluffy; add the butter mixture, then 1 cup powdered sugar and 1 teaspoon vanilla; beat until fluffy.

Caramel Cupcakes: Make recipe as directed, except line 18 muffin tins with paper liners. Make cake as directed. Divide batter among prepared muffin tins. Bake at 350°F 20 to 25 minutes, until cupcakes spring back when lightly touched in center. Remove from tins and cool on wire racks.

Mix Batter

- Watch the butter carefully when it is browning; don't let it burn. If it does burn, you must start over.

- Never measure ingredients like spices or vanilla directly over the mixing bowl; it's too easy to add too much.

- The batter has to be beaten well in order to incorporate air. Beat with a mixer 2 minutes or by hand 200 strokes.

- For best results, grease the pan by spraying with nonstick baking spray that contains flour.

Pour Batter into Pan

- When the cake is done, it will be deep golden brown and will start to pull away from the side of the pan.

- Cool the cake completely in its pan on a wire rack before frosting or cutting. You can sprinkle the cake with powdered sugar.

- For the perfect, if slightly naughty and unorthodox finish, sprinkle a few grains of good coarse sea salt on each piece before serving.

- This taps into the sweet-and-salty craze currently in vogue in the dessert world, especially if you use the caramel frosting.

DESSERTS

WEB SITES, TV SHOWS, & VIDEOS
Information for cooking low-salt foods

As the trend toward low-sodium foods increases, there is a lot of information that can help you change the way you eat.

Online message boards and forums are wonderful resources, as well. On popular boards you will get answers to your questions very quickly. Don't be afraid to ask for help!

RESOURCES

Web Sites

Low-Sodium Cooking
www.lowsodiumcooking.com
This site has lots of nutrition information and cooking tips, along with sources, recipes, and a store.

AllRecipes.com
http://allrecipes.com/HowTo/Cutting-Back-on-Salt/Detail.aspx
AllRecipes, which features reader-submitted recipes rated by members, has health articles written by experts.

American Heart Association
www.americanheart.org
This site offers lots of printable brochures on how to read food labels, a low-salt cookbook, and how to break the salt habit.

Nutrition at About.com
http://nutrition.about.com/
This time-tested site is full of information about nutrition and healthy recipes with nutrition information.

Videos

AllRecipes Videos
http://allrecipes.com/Info/Videos/Eating-Healthy/ViewAll.aspx
AllRecipes.com has a lot of excellent videos that demonstrate how to eat a healthy diet.

Expert Village
www.expertvillage.com/video/166258_what-definition-low
-sodium-diet.htm
This video teaches you all about low-sodium diets.

Food Network
www.foodnetwork.com/healthy-eating/index.html
Lots of videos that teach you how to make healthy food in a hurry.

LiveStrong.com
www.livestrong.com/video/2369-healthy-food-choices-low
-sodium/
This site has lots of information about eating well, how to eat for health conditions, and fitness tips.

ScrubTV
http://scrubtv.com/nutrition/making-sense-of-a-low-salt-diet
    -video_ccc1d7928.html
Video shows you how to cook low-sodium foods with easy ideas.

TV Cooking Shows

America's Test Kitchen
Cook's Illustrated is responsible for this show on PBS that teaches
    you how to cook.

AOL Television
H Is for Healthy Cooking
You can watch episodes of this show online at television.aol.com.

Healthy Appetite with Ellie Krieger
This show on the Food Network focuses on eating a healthy diet.

BOOKS & MAGAZINES

Hundreds of recipe books and magazines are here to help you prepare low-sodium foods

RESOURCES

Books

American Heart Association. *Low Salt Cookbook,* Third Edition, Clarkson Potter, 2007
- This book offers more than 200 recipes for low-sodium foods from Corn and Green Chile Soup to Denver Chocolate Pudding Cake.

Anderson, David C. and Thomas D. *The No-Salt Cookbook,* Adams Media, 2001
- This book includes more than 200 salt-free recipes with salt-free shopping and cooking tips.

Bagg, Elma W., Robert Ely, and Susan Bagg Todd. *Cooking Without a Grain of Salt,* Bantam, 1998
- This book has a good variety of low-sodium dishes, including advice about using lots of herbs and spices in your cooking.

Gazzaniga, Donald. *The No-Salt, Lowest Sodium Cookbook,* St. Martin's Griffin, 2002
- This cookbook has recipes for delicious no- and low-sodium recipes including Chicken in Almond Sauce.

Logue, Dick. *500 Low Sodium Recipes,* Fair Winds Press, 2007
- Delicious, simple recipes with nutritional analysis help you reduce your sodium intake.

Mostyn, Bobbie. *The No-Salt, Lowest Sodium Cookbook,* Indata Group, Inc., 2005
- Mostyn offers 300 recipes for delicious no- and low-sodium recipes that feature herbs, spices, and wine.

Magazines

Cooking Light
- Magazine has tons of healthy recipes that focus on low-fat ingredients; attention is paid to sodium content, too.

Eating Light
- Magazine from Woman's Day cuts down on fat and sodium; there is complete nutrition information.

Eating Well
- This magazine offers lots of recipes for good health, including low-fat and lower- or reduced-sodium recipes.

Heart Healthy Living

- Magazine focuses on low-cholesterol, low-fat, and low-sodium foods, along with recipes and fitness tips.

EQUIPMENT RESOURCES

Find equipment through these resources to stock your kitchen

Catalogs

Brylane Home
Catalog has lots of kitchen equipment, including specialty tools, utensils, and dishware.

Solutions
This catalog has lots of new equipment and tools to make cooking quick and easy.

Sur la Table
Catalog offers lots of kitchen equipment along with dishes, serving utensils, and flatware.

Williams-Sonoma
Catalog offers top of the line equipment, along with cookbooks and many appliances, tools, and accessories.

Web Sites

Chefsresource.com
Cutlery, flatware, gadgets, tools, knives, and brands like Cuisinart are featured at this site.

Cooking.com
Kitchen fixtures, large appliance, cutlery, cookbooks, and tools can be found at this site.

Crockpot.com
The Web site for Rival slow cookers, this site offers customer service, replacement parts, and recipes.

KitchenAid.com
This manufacturer Web site offers information on its sturdy, reliable appliances; an online store; and help finding a place to purchase equipment near you.

KitchenManualsonline.com
This Web site offers contact information for dozens of kitchen appliance manufacturers.

FIND INGREDIENTS
There are many resources for ingredients other than the grocery store

Catalogs and Online Resources

Amazon Grocery
www.agrocerydelivery.com/
Amazon.com has a grocery delivery service. Offers general foods
and hard-to-find items. Look for low-sodium foods.

The Baker's Catalog
From King Arthur's Flour, this catalog offers cooking equipment
and baking ingredients, including specialty flours and flavorings.

EatLowSodium.com
Online grocer carries may low-sodium and healthy products.

LivingLowSodium.com
An online grocery store that offers low-sodium products and a
few recipes from the Mayo Clinic.

Peapod
www.peapod.com
Online grocery store that serves some areas of the United States.

SaltWorks.us
This site offers many different types of sea and flavored salts,
which have a more intense flavor than regular table salt.

Farmers' Markets

Farmers' Markets
www.farmersmarkela.com
Los Angeles Farmers' Market Web site; the original farmers' market.

Farmers' Market Search
http://apps.ams.usda.gov/FarmersMarkets/
USDA site lets you search for a farmers' market by state, city,
county, and zip code, as well as method of payment.

National Directory of Farmers' Markets
http://farmersmarket.com/
Site has index of U.S. farmers' markets listed by state.

Seastarseasalt.com
This Web site offers lots of gray salt and sea salt, along with grind-
ers and blends.

Thebetterhealthstore.com
This grocery store, which delivers, offers lots of low-sodium
products.

HOTLINES & MANUFACTURERS

Find help with cooking problems and purchasing or maintaining equipment

Hotlines

American Dietetic Association

Eatright.org

Association of food and nutrition professionals offers lots of health and diet information, as well as news on recalls and studies.

Dairy Council of the United States

1-800-279-2643

Offers advice on dairy foods and consumption.

Dole

1-800-232-8800

Offers information about their prepared and fresh produce, including canned and frozen fruits and veggies.

Empire Kosher Poultry Hotline

1-800-367-4734

Year-round hotline answers questions about poultry.

McCormick/Schilling

1-800-632-5847

Manufacturer of spices and herb blends offers information and advice.

Mrs. Dash Sodium Hotline

1-800-622-3274

Offers advice about Mrs. Dash, a seasoning blend low in sodium, along with questions about low-sodium foods and recipes.

MyPyramid.gov

This Web site tells you all about the Food Pyramid and how to eat a healthy diet.

USDA Meat and Poultry Hotline

1-800-535-4555

Year-round line offers information about food safety and answers consumer questions about meat preparation.

Equipment Manufacturers

All-Clad

www.all-clad.com

This was one of the first manufacturers to make metal inserts for the slow cooker.

Cuisinart

www.cuisinart.com

This company can completely outfit your kitchen, from ranges to stockpots.

GE Appliances

www.geappliances.com

Outfit your entire kitchen with GE appliances. They offer online service and customer support.

Kitchenaid

www.kitchenaid.com

This manufacturer offers high-quality appliances, from refrigerators and stoves to slow cookers.

Rival

www.rivalproducts.com

This is the manufacturer of the original Crock-Pot; the site offers product information, recipes, and an online store.

METRIC CONVERSION TABLES

Approximate U.S. Metric Equivalents

Liquid Ingredients

U.S. MEASURES	METRIC	U.S. MEASURES	METRIC
¼ TSP.	1.23 ML	2 TBSP.	29.57 ML
½ TSP.	2.36 ML	3 TBSP.	44.36 ML
¾ TSP.	3.70 ML	¼ CUP	59.15 ML
1 TSP.	4.93 ML	½ CUP	118.30 ML
1¼ TSP.	6.16 ML	1 CUP	236.59 ML
1½ TSP.	7.39 ML	2 CUPS OR 1 PT.	473.18 ML
1¾ TSP.	8.63 ML	3 CUPS	709.77 ML
2 TSP.	9.86 ML	4 CUPS OR 1 QT.	946.36 ML
1 TBSP.	14.79 ML	4 QTS. OR 1 GAL.	3.79 L

Dry Ingredients

U.S. MEASURES	METRIC	U.S. MEASURES		METRIC
1/16 OZ.	2 (1.8) G	2⅘ OZ.		80 G
⅛ OZ.	3½ (3.5) G	3 OZ.		85 (84.9) G
¼ OZ.	7 (7.1) G	3½ OZ.		100 G
½ OZ.	15 (14.2) G	4 OZ.		115 (113.2) G
¾ OZ.	21 (21.3) G	4½ OZ.		125 G
⅞ OZ.	25 G	5¼ OZ.		150 G
1 OZ.	30 (28.3) G	8⅞ OZ.		250 G
1¾ OZ.	50 G	16 OZ.	1 LB.	454 G
2 OZ.	60 (56.6) G	17⅗ OZ.	1 LIVRE	500 G

GLOSSARY
Learn the language first

Al dente: Italian phrase meaning "to the tooth," which describes doneness of pasta.

Anise: Anise is a licorice-flavored plant. The seeds are used either whole or ground.

Beat: To manipulate food with a spoon, mixer, or whisk to combine.

Bread: To coat chicken with crumbs or crushed crackers before baking or frying.

Broth: Liquid extracted from meats and vegetables, used as the basis for most soups.

Brown: Cooking step that caramelizes food and adds color and flavor before cooking.

Chill: To refrigerate a soup or place it in an ice-water bath to rapidly cool.

Chop: To cut food into small pieces, using a chef's knife or a food processor.

Coat: To cover food in another ingredient, as to coat chicken breasts with bread crumbs.

Cutlet: A thin cut of meat, either pounded thin or cut very thin to cook quickly.

Deglaze: To add a liquid to a pan used to sauté meats; this removes drippings and brown bits to create a sauce.

Dice: To cut food into small, even portions, usually about ¼-inch square.

Flake: To break into small pieces; canned meats are usually flaked.

Fold: To combine two soft or liquid mixtures together, using an over-nd-under method of mixing.

Grate: A grater or microplane used to remove small pieces or shreds of skin or food.

Grill: To cook over coals or charcoal or over high heat.

Herbs: The edible leaves of certain plants that add flavor to food, including basil, marjoram, thyme, oregano, and mint.

Hypertension: Also known as high blood pressure, this is a reading higher than 120/80, or 120/70 in some cases.

Low Sodium: Any food that has 150 mg or less of sodium per serving.

Marinate: To soak meats or vegetables in a mixture of an acid and oil to add flavor and tenderize.

Melt: To turn a solid into a liquid by adding heat.

Ménière's Disease: A disease involving an abnormality of the inner ear, which usually results in vertigo, tinnitus, and hearing loss.

Pan Fry: To cook quickly in a shallow pan in a small amount of fat over relatively high heat.

Peppers: These fruits, classified as vegetables, range from sweet bell peppers to the fiery habañero and Scotch Bonnet.

Salt Substitutes: These compounds are usually made of potassium, a mineral that can be a health issue for some people.

Season: To add herbs, spices, citrus juices and zest, and peppers to food to increase flavor.

Shred: To use a grater, mandoline, or food processor to create small strips of food.

Simmer: A state of liquid cooking, in which the liquid is just below a boil.

Slow Cooker: An appliance that cooks food by surrounding it with low, steady heat.

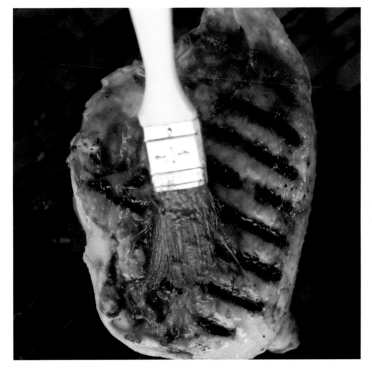

Spices: The edible dried fruits, bark, and seeds of plants, used to add flavor to food.

Toss: To combine food using two spoons or a spoon and a fork until mixed.

Whisk: Both a tool, which is made of loops of steel, and a method, which involves combining food until smooth.

INDEX

INDEX

INDEX